Lecture Notes in Computer Science 12839

More information about this subseries at http://www.springer.com/series/7409

Boris Glavic · Vanessa Braganholo ·
David Koop (Eds.)

Provenance
and Annotation of Data
and Processes

8th and 9th International Provenance
and Annotation Workshop, IPAW 2020 + IPAW 2021
Virtual Event, July 19–22, 2021
Proceedings

Editors
Boris Glavic 🆔
Illinois Institute of Technology
Chicago, IL, USA

Vanessa Braganholo 🆔
Fluminense Federal University
Niterói, Brazil

David Koop 🆔
Northern Illinois University
DeKalb, IL, USA

ISSN 0302-9743   ISSN 1611-3349 (electronic)
Lecture Notes in Computer Science
ISBN 978-3-030-80959-1   ISBN 978-3-030-80960-7 (eBook)
https://doi.org/10.1007/978-3-030-80960-7

LNCS Sublibrary: SL3 – Information Systems and Applications, incl. Internet/Web, and HCI

This Springer imprint is published by the registered company Springer Nature Switzerland AG
The registered company address is: Gewerbestrasse 11, 6330 Cham, Switzerland

Preface

This volume contains the proceedings of the 8th and 9th *International Provenance and Annotation Workshop* (IPAW), held as part of ProvenanceWeek in 2020 and 2021. Due to the COVID-19 pandemic, ProvenanceWeek 2020 was held as a 1-day virtual event with brief teaser talks on June 22, 2020. In 2021, ProvenanceWeek again co-located the biennial IPAW workshop with the annual *Workshop on the Theory and Practice of Provenance* (TaPP). Together, the two leading provenance workshops anchored a 4-day event of provenance related activities that included a shared poster and demonstration session, the first *Workshop on Provenance for Transparent Research* (T7), and the first *Workshop on Provenance and Visualization* (ProvViz). The events were held virtually during July 19–22 2021. At IPAW 2021, authors from both 2020 and 2021 presented and discussed their work.

This collection constitutes the peer reviewed papers of IPAW 2020 and 2021. These include eleven long papers which report in depth on the results of research around provenance and twelve short papers that were presented as part of the joint IPAW/TaPP poster and demonstration session. The final papers and short papers accompanied by poster presentations and demonstrations were selected from a total of 31 submissions. All full-length research papers received a minimum of three reviews.

The IPAW papers provide a glimpse into state-of-the-art research and practice around the capture, representation, querying, inference, and summarization of provenance. Papers also address applications of provenance such as security, reliability, and trustworthiness. The papers discussing provenance capture focus on templates and explore Artificial Intelligence scenarios, focusing on capturing provenance of Deep Neural Networks. Provenance representation papers include work on evidence graphs and a new JSON serialization for PROV. Several papers focus on provenance queries and inference. In particular, they explore provenance type inference, the use of provenance for query result exploration, and provenance inference of computational notebooks.

Provenance itself is meaningless if not used for a concrete purpose. The proceedings also cover papers reporting on real-world use cases of provenance. Application scenarios explored in the papers include health care and, especially, COVID-19.

We would like to thank the members of the Program Committee (PC) for their thoughtful and insightful reviews along with Dr. Thomas Moyer (local chair) and his team for their excellent organization of both IPAW and ProvenanceWeek 2020/2021. We also want to thank the authors and participants for making IPAW the stimulating and successful event that it was.

July 2021

Vanessa Braganholo
David Koop
Boris Glavic

Organization

Organizing Committee

Boris Glavic (ProvenanceWeek 2020/2021 Senior PC Chair)	Illinois Institute of Technology, USA
Vanessa Braganholo (IPAW 2020/2021 PC Chair)	Fluminense Federal University, Brazil
Thomas Pasquier (TaPP 2020 PC Chair)	University of Bristol, UK
Tanu Malik (TaPP 2021 PC Co-chair)	DePaul University, USA
Thomas Pasquier (TaPP 2021 PC Co-chair)	University of Bristol, UK
David Koop (2020/2021 Demos/Poster Chair)	Northern Illinois University, USA
Thomas Moyer (2020/2021 Local Chair)	UNC Charlotte, USA

IPAW 2020 Program Committee

Andreas Schreiber	German Aerospace Center (DLR), Germany
Barbara Lerner	Mount Holyoke College, USA
Beth Plale	Indiana University, USA
Daniel de Oliveira	Fluminense Federal University, Brazil
Daniel Garijo	University of Southern California, USA
David Corsar	Robert Gordon University, UK
Dong Huynh	King's College London, UK
Fernando Chirigati	New York University, USA
Grigoris Karvounarakis	LogicBlox, USA
Hala Skaf-Molli	Nantes University, France
Ilkay Altintas	San Diego Supercomputer Center, USA
Jacek Cala	Newcastle University, UK
James Cheney	University of Edinburgh, UK
James Frew	University of California, Santa Barbara, USA
James Myers	University of Michigan, USA
Jan Van Den Bussche	Universiteit Hasselt, Belgium
João Felipe Pimentel	Fluminense Federal University, Brazil

Luc Moreau	King's College London, UK
Luiz M. R. Gadelha Jr.	LNCC, Brazil
Paolo Missier	Newcastle University, UK
Paul Groth	University of Amsterdam, Netherlands
Pinar Alper	University of Luxembourg, Luxembourg
Shawn Bowers	Gonzaga University, USA
Seokki Lee	IIT, USA
Simon Miles	King's College London, UK
Tanu Malik	DePaul University, USA
Timothy Clark	University of Virginia, USA

IPAW 2021 Program Committee

Andreas Schreiber	German Aerospace Center (DLR), Germany
Adriane Chapman	University of Southampton, UK
Bertram Ludascher	University of Illinois at Urbana-Champaign, USA
Cláudia Bauzer Medeiros	UNICAMP, Brazil
Daniel de Oliveira	Fluminense Federal University, Brazil
Daniel Garijo	University of Southern California, USA
David Corsar	Robert Gordon University, UK
Eduardo Ogasawara	CEFET, Brazil
Grigoris Karvounarakis	LogicBlox, USA
Hala Skaf-Molli	Nantes University, France
Jacek Cala	Newcastle University, UK
James Cheney	University of Edinburgh, UK
James McCusker	Rensselaer Polytechnic Institute, USA
James Myers	University of Michigan, USA
Jan Van Den Bussche	Universiteit Hasselt, Belgium
João Felipe Pimentel	Fluminense Federal University, Brazil
Luc Moreau	King's College London, UK
Luiz M. R. Gadelha Jr.	LNCC, Brazil
Marta Mattoso	Universidade Federal do Rio de Janeiro, Brazil
Paolo Missier	Newcastle University, UK
Paul Groth	University of Amsterdam, Netherlands
Pinar Alper	University of Luxembourg, Luxembourg
Seokki Lee	University of Cincinnati, USA
Timothy Clark	University of Virginia, USA
Vasa Curcin	King's College London, UK

Contents

Provenance Capture and Representation

A Delayed Instantiation Approach to Template-Driven Provenance for Electronic Health Record Phenotyping

Elliot Fairweather[✉], Martin Chapman, and Vasa Curcin

King's College London, London, UK
`elliot.fairweather@kcl.ac.uk`

Abstract. Provenance templates are an established methodology for the capture of provenance data. Each template defines the provenance of a domain-specific action in abstract form, which may then be instantiated as required by a single call to a given service interface. This approach, whilst simplifying the process of recording provenance for the user, introduces computational and storage demands on the capture process, particularly when used by clients with write-intensive provenance requirements such as other service-based software. To address these issues, we adopt a new approach based upon delayed instantiation and present a revised, two-part paradigm for template-driven provenance, in which we separate capture and query functionality to improve the overall efficiency of the model. A dedicated capture service is first employed to record template service requests in a relational database in the form of a meta-level description detailing the construction of each document. These low-overhead records are then accessed by an independent query service to construct views of concrete provenance documents for specific time frames as and when required by the user. These views may subsequently be analysed using query templates, a new technique defined here whereby templates can also be used to search for any matching subgraphs within a document and return the respective instantiating substitutions. We evaluate the performance gains of our new system in the context of Phenoflow, an electronic health record (EHR) phenotyping platform.

Keywords: Data provenance · Health informatics · EHR phenotyping

1 Introduction

Provenance templates are an established methodology for the capture of provenance data [7]. Each template defines the provenance of a domain-specific action in abstract form, which may then be instantiated as required by a single call to a given service interface. This approach, whilst simplifying the process of recording provenance for the user, introduces computational and storage demands on the capture process, particularly when used by clients with write-intensive provenance requirements such as other service-based software.

© Springer Nature Switzerland AG 2021
B. Glavic et al. (Eds.): IPAW 2020/IPAW 2021, LNCS 12839, pp. 3–19, 2021.
https://doi.org/10.1007/978-3-030-80960-7_1

Up until now our implementation of that service interface has constructed W3C PROV [17] provenance documents in real-time, instantiating and merging those concrete provenance fragments generated upon submission. However in data provenance recording domains with write-intensive requirements, which generate a high load of requests, the computational demands placed upon the capture process by this solution can adversely impact performance. We therefore propose a new approach based upon delayed instantiation and a two-part paradigm, where for efficiency, provenance data is captured as high-level meta-provenance records of requested actions, which can then later be used to construct the provenance document in question when required for analysis. We first present a revised template model, which exhibits the properties required for such an approach, and then use this model to develop separate capture and query services. Rather than generating and storing concrete fragments, the capture service records service requests in a simple relational schema. These records are then accessed by the query service in order to construct documents upon request in an offline manner. The proposed changes to the template model also facilitate the query service in generating views of documents with respect to user-provided constraints that restrict construction to a specific time frame, which may then be queried using a new technique based upon existing template syntax.

Not only does the resulting separation of responsibilities eliminate most of the computational demands placed upon capturing provenance, it also reduces overall storage requirements, and simplifies the reproducibility of the provenance recording process itself.

One write-intensive domain that benefits from this novel approach is electronic health record (EHR) *phenotyping*, which focuses on the problem of autonomously identifying patient populations that share certain characteristics, such as one or more medical conditions (*phenotypes*), from their EHR alone [6]. Phenotyping involves the development of phenotype *definitions* – sets of rules that capture the logic for phenotype identification – that are evolved over time by different authors. These definitions are then implemented as *computable phenotypes*, which can be executed against a dataset to identify a condition cohort.

Recording this evolution of a phenotype definition is important for a number of reasons. For example, phenotype definitions have important applications in epidemiological studies, clinical trials and in clinical decision support [19]. As such, ascertaining the *validity* of a phenotype definition – that is, whether it accurately captures the disease or condition being modelled – is key, and an insight into how the definition was developed, and by whom, is an essential component of this understanding. Similarly, understanding how a definition has been developed contributes to its intelligibility and thus the accuracy with which it can be implemented across various sites and datasets (often known as *phenotype reproducibility*). While the importance of recording the evolution of a phenotype definition is clear, standard tools, such as version control, are not best suited to this task due to the richness of the data that needs to be collected, so a more comprehensive approach, such a data provenance capture, is needed. However, as authors often create or update phenotype definitions in bulk, by, for example, importing definitions into an online phenotype *library*, the domain exhibits the aforementioned write-intensive requirements.

In what follows, the revised template model is described in Sect. 2, the capture service in Sect. 3, and the query service in Sect. 4. Our prototype implementation of the system is discussed in Sect. 5 and its evaluation in Sect. 6. We survey related work in Sect. 7, and draw conclusions in Sect. 8.

2   The Revised Template Model

The proposed system requires some improvements to the existing template model as stated in [7], from which we now briefly recall the key relevant definitions.

A *template* is a document that may contain *identifier variables* (under the var namespace) in place of identifiers within the document, and *value variables* (under vvar) in place of attribute values. A template is *instantiated* using a *substitution* given as a set of bindings mapping each variable occurring within the template to a concrete value. Below, we refer to this action as a *simple* instantiation. The model also defines syntax such that templates may specify subgraphs called *zones*, which may be iterated over in series or parallel fashion by providing additional instantiating substitutions. Each instance generated is then *merged* into a concrete provenance under construction. Any identifier that already exists within the document is reused, and if not, created new.

In order to facilitate the new meta-level capture model and later construction of documents from these records, we now require instantiation actions on templates to demonstrate two key properties. Firstly, instantiations must' be *monotonic*; each instantiation must preserve all existing nodes and edges within the document. Secondly, they must be *independent*; each instantiation must not depend on information external to the instantiating substitution in order to merge the instance within the document.

The original presentation of zones breaks these requirements in several key ways. In that formulation, the instaniation of zones depends upon the context of the current template, in order to determine the generation of edges between iterations, and so requires that templates containing zones be constructed as separate *fragments* before being merged into the document. The generation of series zones in this manner also enforces an ordering on the instantiations used, and so for the both these reasons instantiations are not independent.

Further to this, when instantiating a series zone that has child nodes, edges are destroyed upon each iteration in order to insert the new subgraph instance within the fragment being constructed, with the result that the process is not monotonic. Zones with such child nodes are also of limited practical use when used in prospective fashion, because the existing service workflow for zones requires an initial simple instantiation of the template and thus values for these child nodes must be known to the user from the outset.

In order to address these issues, we propose to generalise the concept of zones, such that their semantics is the same as that for a simple instantiation, namely that, after having been generated, each *zone instantiation* will now be merged directly into the document. Zones will no longer be of series or parallel type, rather, their form will instead depend upon the identifiers in the substitution provided, as is the case when merging a simple instantiation. Nodes belonging to a zone must still be annotated with the `zone:id` attribute, but no further annotations are now required. Figures 1 and 2 illustrate these differences when defining a parallel and series zone respectively, in the context of a simple data usage scenario.

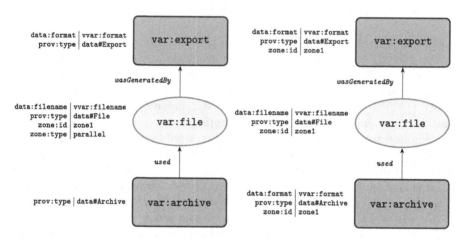

Fig. 1. Original (left) and revised (right) style parallel zones

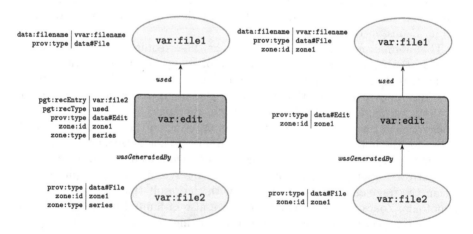

Fig. 2. Original (left) and revised (right) style series zones

Note that a zone in the revised model may need to be larger in order to represent the same functionality as one defined in the original model. This means that some zones may now in fact be templates in their own right, and this likely reflects the fact that, in our experience, many scenarios are best modelled using a larger number of smaller templates, rather than vice-versa.

We now place conditions on zone instantiations in order to model the different behaviour that was previously specified using zone types. A simple instantiation of a zone's parent template must still be made before additional instantiations of a zone are performed. This corresponds to and replaces the action of fragment *initialisation* in the original model.[1]

Call those nodes belonging to a zone for which there are incoming edges from outside the zone, *entry* nodes, and those for which there are outgoing edges to nodes outside the zone, *exit* nodes. To qualify as a parallel instantiation of a zone, each entry and exit node of the zone within the substitution for the zone must be bound to the identifier given to that node in the simple instantiation of the parent template, and every other identifier given must be *fresh*, that is, not exist in the document before merging. In the first series instantiation of a zone, each exit node must be bound to the identifier given to that node in the simple instantiation of the parent template. In each subsequent iteration, each exit node must be given the identifier for a node of the same type that was instantiated as fresh in the previous iteration. All other identifiers given must again be fresh. As mentioned above, a zone which is to be interpreted as an original series zone, may have no child nodes, and thus no entry nodes.

We also discard the notion of iteration bounds upon zone instantiations, a feature which required that fragments each undergo a check before being merged. Not only does this impact performance, but because zone instantiations are now merged immediately, their possible future invalidation is not compatible with the property of monotonicity or independence. The *finalisation* service action associated with this check in the original model, which also used to be responsible for merging fragments, is thus now redundant and so absent in the revised model.

The fact that the behaviour of zones is now decided by which identifiers already exist within a document and which are to be newly created suggests a further refinement to the model. In the existing model, when an instantiation is merged into a document and an identifier is already present and so reused, any attributes associated with that identifier in the new instance are merged with those already present. This situation can be alleviated somewhat by careful template design, but is often undesirable and occurs much more frequently under the revised presentation, and thus we propose that value variables of a template now be optional. That is, an instantiating substitution for a template or zone may omit value variable bindings. Identifier variables remain mandatory. This solution also provides additional flexibility within the template model.

---

[1] *Simultaneous* instantiations, in which an initial instantiation, together with a number of zone instantiations may be given together as one substitution, remain possible within the revised model, but are not considered here further.

3   The Capture Service

In our new two-part paradigm, provenance actions are captured as meta-provenance records. Meta-provenance in this context was first introduced by the authors in [9] as a model for capturing provenance in a fashion that can be extended to exhibit non-repudiation of origin. In that work, provenance service actions were themselves tracked in PROV documents as activities acting upon entities representing documents within the system. Each action constituting part of the service workflow was described using a separate provenance template. Instances of these templates were then appended with additional security information to allow non-repudiation of origin for each step and thus each document as a whole. We now look to use this approach to increase the flexibility and efficiency of provenance capture by recording meta-provenance using a relational schema.

The actions associated with the construction of a provenance document using the revised template model described above are illustrated in Fig. 3.

1. *new template* (one or more times) to upload templates to the server
2. (a) *new document* (once) to begin a new document
   (b) *add namespace* (zero or more times) to add a namespace to the document
   (c) *register template* (one or more times) to associate a template with the document
   (d) *instantiate* (one or more times) to use a substitution to instantiate a template, and merge it into the document
       i. *instantiate zone* (zero or more times) to use a substitution to instantiate and merge a subsequent iteration of a zone within a template

Fig. 3. How to construct a document using the capture service

Each of the above actions is associated with a corresponding method of the proposed capture service, and it is calls to these methods, which form the basis of the meta-level records stored. An interface is provided in the form of both a RESTful web service, and a message-queueing service; a summary of the details of the former are presented in Table 1. The message-queueing service is structured similarly, but with each message containing an action type, together with a dictionary of required parameters. Template data is accepted in PROV-JSON format [12]. Substitutions are written as JSON objects mapping identifier and value variable names to arrays of PROV-JSON values. For each call made to the service interface, the type and parameters of the call are recorded, together with the time the call was made, in a relational database. Call parameters containing data representations of templates or substitutions submitted for instantiations are recorded directly in JSON format, as the contents of this data may remain opaque with respect to the capture process. The schema for this relational model is given in Fig. 4.

Table 1. Summary of the web-based interface for the capture service

Method	Endpoint	Body fields	Action description
PUT	/templates/[id]	templateData	New template
PUT	/documents/[id]	defaultNamespace	New document
POST	/documents/[id]/namespaces	prefix namespace	Add namespace
POST	/documents/[id]/registrations	templateIdentifier	Register template
POST	/documents/[id]/instantiations	templateIdentifier substitutionData	Instantiate template
POST	/documents/[id]/instantiations/[zoneId]	templateIdentifier substitutionData	Instantiate zone
DELETE	/templates/[id]		Delete template
DELETE	/documents/[id]		Delete document

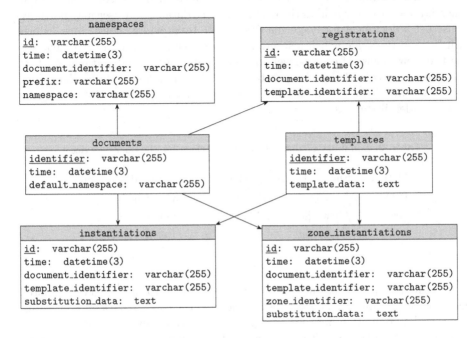

Fig. 4. Relational database schema for the capture service data model

Recording service actions in this way, rather than instantiating and merging templates in real-time, not only significantly reduces the amount of computational work needed at the time of capture, but also reduces the storage requirements needed to represent the same provenance data. The capture interface presented here could also be implemented in the form of a programming library. Together with a light-weight relational database implementation such as SQLite, this would be of particular value in a provenance capture scenario that requires a small footprint, or where data must be recorded locally for reasons of governance.

4   The Query Service

We now describe the second of our two proposed services, the query service. This service is used to manage the construction of documents from the meta-level records persisted by the capture service as presented in Sect. 3, and allows these documents to be queried using a new, intuitive template-based technique.

4.1   Document Views

A *view* of a document is a full or partial provenance document constructed from the meta-level records held in the capture service database. A user may partially construct a document for a specific time frame by providing constraints, which will be used to decide which instantiations are selected and used when generating the view. Views of object-level documents are constructed and managed by the query service and stored separately from the meta-level capture data, in a database suitable for graph-based queries. The interface presented by the query service is detailed in Table 2.

Table 2. Summary of the web-based interface for the query service

Method	Endpoint	Body fields	Action description
PUT	/views/[id]	startTime endTime	Construct view
GET	/views/[id]	templateData	Query view
DELETE	/views/[id]		Delete view

The first step in constructing a document view is to import the templates used by that document. This is done by querying the capture data and returning the template definition data for all registration actions linked to the document in question. Next the default namespace and other namespaces for the document in question are extracted from the capture data and added to a new empty document created for the view under a user-specified identifier. Instantiation actions for that document are then retrieved with respect to any time constraints provided. The substitution data recorded for the instantiation is then used together with the specified template to generate a document fragment which is immediately merged into the stored view. The instantiation of templates follows the algorithm given in [7]. Zone instantiations actions are then extracted, again with respect to any given time constraints. The required zone within the specified template is instantiated with the substitution provided within the action, and the generated fragment is merged into the view. This is executed as for a simple instantiation but restricted to those nodes and edges belonging to the zone in question.

This approach is possible due to the properties of monotonicity and independence of instantiations. Monotonicity ensures that all existing data is preserved by subsequent instantiations, and independence that each instantiation may be generated and merged without requiring implicit knowledge from any previous zone instantiation for that template.

Note however that whilst a partially constructed view will contain all nodes and edges of a document that fall within the given time frame, together with their identifiers and types, some nodes may lack all attributes. Attributes given to nodes or edges as annotations in instantiations that fall outside of the time constraints under consideration will not be included in the view document.

4.2   Query Templates

We now introduce the concept of *query templates*. Query templates are constructed using the same syntax as for standard templates. However, instead of providing a substitution with which to instantiate variables within the template, a query template is used as a pattern with which to search for matches within a given concrete document. For each match found, a substitution is returned, which maps each identifier and value variable used within the template to a concrete identifier or value respectively, within the document. All other non-variable identifiers and values within the template must be equal to those in the matching document fragment, as well as the types of the nodes and edges present in both.

For example, consider the concrete document shown in Fig. 5, which describes the provenance of some data in the context of the same simple scenario as above. Figures 6 and 7 show three possible query templates that could be used to analyse the document. The first represents a query which will identify subgraphs in the document where some data was exported to a file in CSV format, and then later archived. The format of the file is fixed by annotating the export activity with a concrete value for the data:format attribute. However, the name of the file as defined by the data:filename attribute, is given as a variable value, which will be later matched in order to extract the names of the relevant files. The output for this query with respect to the example document is shown in Listing 1.1.

```
{ "substitutions" : [
    { "var:export" : [{"$" : "export-001", "type" : "prov:QUALIFIED_NAME"}],
      "var:file" : [{"$" : "file-001", "type" : "prov:QUALIFIED_NAME"}],
      "vvar:filename" : [{"$" : "record-2020.csv", "type" : "xsd:string"}],
      "var:archive" : [{"$" : "archive-001", "type" : "prov:QUALIFIED_NAME"}]
    },
    { "var:export" : [{"$" : "export-001", "type" : "prov:QUALIFIED_NAME"}],
      "var:file" : [{"$" : "file-002", "type" : "prov:QUALIFIED_NAME"}],
      "vvar:filename" : [{"$" : "record-2021.csv", "type" : "xsd:string"}],
      "var:archive" : [{"$" : "archive-001", "type" : "prov:QUALIFIED_NAME"}]
    }
  ]
}
```

Listing 1.1. Matching substitutions from the example document for the first query template

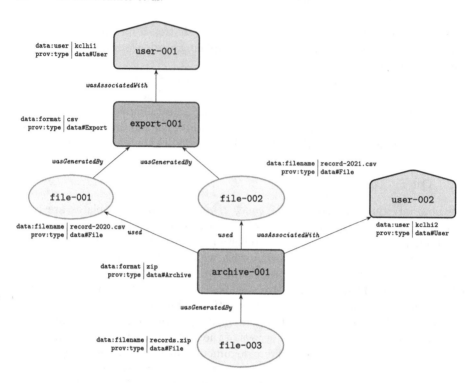

Fig. 5. Example concrete provenance document

The second query will match subgraphs corresponding to instances where a user exports data in any format to a file. For each match found the name of the user and the filename will be bound to the `vvar:user` and `filename` variables respectively. The final query matches subgraphs in which the user `kclhi2` archives a file in zip format. In this case, each substitution produced will bind the `vvar:filename` and `vvar:zipname` variables to the filenames used.

5   Implementation

We have written a prototype implementation of both the capture and query services described above. The architecture of the new system is illustrated in Fig. 8. The prototype uses MariaDB (https://mariadb.org) and Neo4j (https://neo4j.com) as storage backends for the capture service and query service respectively. We use RabbitMQ (https://www.rabbitmq.com) for the message queue, and the Spring Framework (https://spring.io) to build each service, and to provide both web interfaces and message queue integration.

The functionality of the query service is written using a revised and extended version of the core library from the original template service implementation. We realise query templates using the Neo4j Cypher query language and thus whilst

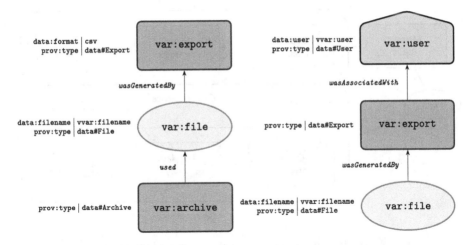

Fig. 6. Example query templates: all archived CSV files (*left*), and all files exported by any user (*right*)

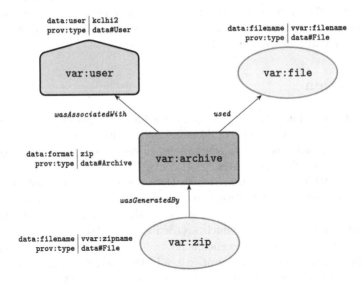

Fig. 7. Example query template: files archived in zip format by `kclhi2`

the template library supports persistence to other database types, the query service currently only supports Neo4j as a backend.

The decision to provide a message queue interface was also aimed at improving the efficiency of the system. This approach not only reduces overhead in contexts where the provenance recording service is local to the client service, but was found in practice to be more suitable in scenarios where clients generate a high request load, such as EHR phenotyping, and thus the throughput of the recording service is a priority. Note however that the use of a queue does

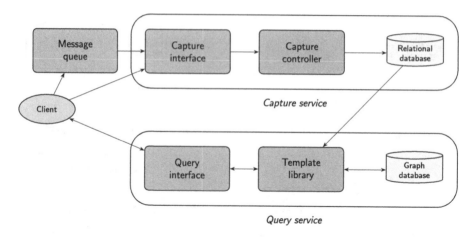

Fig. 8. Architecture of the combined capture and query services

not negate the efficiency gains introduced in the new system; the content of the queue must still be consumed efficiently by the capture service, in order to avoid memory bloat and a slowdown of the overall system.

6   Evaluation

To determine whether our new paradigm enables provenance data to be efficiently captured in write-intensive domains such as EHR phenotyping, we now evaluate the performance of the new system in relation to that of the original by analysing queue clearance rates.

We do so within *Phenoflow*, a Health Data Research UK phenotype library that represents imported definitions under a workflow-based model [3]. For each definition in a set imported by a user, the rules that comprise the definition are grouped into individual steps, which are defined by attributes such as a categorisation and description of the encapsulated logic, and each step is associated with a generated implementation unit (e.g. a Python script), allowing the definition to be downloaded as a computable phenotype. Subsequent imports by other users that contain modifications to definitions already held in the library trigger updates to the attributes of one or more steps within those definitions. In order to capture this evolving sequence of revisions to these attributes, we add calls to the provenance template client (Fig. 8) at different points within Phenoflow's import logic. An overview of the data captured is summarised by the template shown (and given from the perspective of the new system) in Fig. 9.

To generate this data, we import a set of 278 phenotype definitions into Phenoflow, which represents the typical size of an import task faced by the library. During the import, we record the exchange of messages between Phenoflow (the producer) and the new capture service (a consumer), and between Phenoflow and the service provided by the original real-time provenance document construction

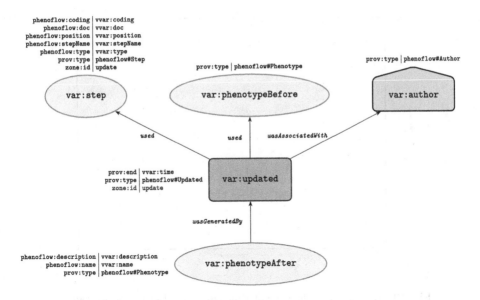

Fig. 9. Revised model template representing the import of a phenotype definition

system (a consumer), using a queue. Specifically, we monitor the length of time that elapses between a message being delivered to each consumer, and that message being acknowledged after processing. This gives us an understanding of throughput. In total, we record the exchange of 1500 deliver/acknowledgement pairs during the import of the definition set. Median acknowledgement times are shown in Fig. 10 for the three key instantiating calls to the original service: fragment initialisation (*geninit*), zone generation (*genzone*) and fragment finalisation (*genfinal*). Recall from Sect. 3 that fragment initialisation is now equivalent to a simple instantiation within the revised template model, and that a zone generation within a fragment is now represented as a zone instantiation. Fragment finalisation has no equivalent call when using the new service, and thus its acknowledgement time is not recorded.

Of immediate note is the increased throughput offered by the new system. In particular, the impact of the removal of the *genfinal* requirement is emphasised when observing the high acknowledgement times associated with the call to the original service. Across the other calls, the application of Mann-Whitney U-test, under the null hypothesis that there is no difference between the distributions, shows a significant difference in acknowledgement rates ($p < 0.05$).

The difference in throughput between the original and the new system is less marked for zone instantiation, which does show some IQR overlap. This is most likely due to the fact that in the original system, the generation of a zone already has relatively low computational requirements, and in that system, instance fragments are constructed in memory and then written directly as independent graphs within the database, a relatively lightweight I/O operation, than a call

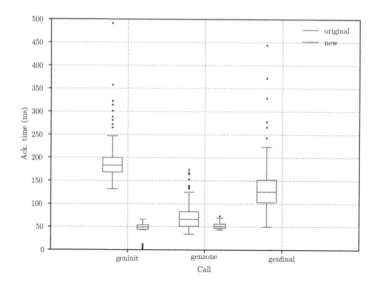

Fig. 10. System acknowledgement times for instantiating service calls

to say, *genfinal*, which must merge a completed fragment within an often much larger document at the database level.

Across different calls we also note overlap between the throughput of both the instantiation and zone instantiation calls under the new implementation, suggesting consistent performance. In contrast, a statistically significant difference is seen between the performance of the different calls to the original service. In particular, *geninit* offers the lowest throughput rate, likely because these calls require all variables within a template to be instantiated, and so are the most computationally intensive. Moreover, the range of potential acknowledgement rates is much larger under the original system. This suggests much less reliable performance, and the potential for some significant reductions in throughput.

7   Related Work

Delaying the construction of provenance graphs to reduce capture overheads has been explored in the context of provenance data recorded without the use of templates. PASSv2 uses an asynchronous user space daemon to produce post hoc graphs [18]. Similarly, SPADEv2 implements provenance collection threads to extract, filter and commit operations to a provenance log [10]. Perhaps closest to the approach employed here is Lipstick, which delays the construction until a query response is required [1].

PROV-TEMPLATES are an alternative approach to capturing and generating provenance from templates and bindings presented in [16]. In this work, bindings produced by clients are also later used to expand a predefined set of templates. Whilst the syntax of both systems is broadly similar, the works differ as to how concrete provenance is generated; the method used by PROV-TEMPLATES being more expressive yet also more complex than the process of instantiation defined in [7]. The work does not include a concept comparable to zones as presented here, and is not developed from the perspective of a service-based architecture for the third-party construction and management of provenance documents, as is the present work. Whilst the authors of PROV-TEMPLATES do suggest that templates could be of value with regard to the optimisation of queries using standard query languages, and that queries could be performed over bindings rather than concrete documents, they do not consider these issues further or present a solution based upon templates.

The authors of [11] present a rule based-system for extracting and recording provenance from structured log files in order to avoid program instrumentation. This technique is in some ways similar to that provided by template-based methodologies and also reflects the motivations of the present work with respect to its low-overhead nature.

The querying of data modelled as W3C PROV is usually carried out directly against the chosen data representation, using an appropriate query language, as seen for example in [5]. In contrast, the analysis of provenance data in general has been studied from many angles, including the development of bespoke query languages, such as ProQL [13] for tuple-based provenance, the development of new models such as TripleProv [20] that leverage the power of existing query languages, and within specific domains such as data science (VQuel) [4] and workflows (QLP) [2]. Of these, the structural relation constructs of QLP, whereby nodes may be accessed using XPath expressions describing their parent-child relationships and parameters, perhaps bear the greatest similarity to the query template technique presented here.

In terms of EHR phenotyping, several existing phenotype libraries use version control as a best-effort solution for communicating the evolution of a definition. Examples include CALIBER [8] and the Concept Library (https://conceptlibrary.saildatabank.com), both of which record iterations of their stored definitions, attributing version IDs to each. To the best of our knowledge no phenotype libraries apply formal provenance techniques to capture the interactions between users and definitions, however several tools exist to capture the provenance of workflows, upon which Phenoflow's model is based. Notable examples of such tools are CWLProv [14] and YesWorkflow [15], albeit the latter operates on an inferred workflow derived from markup placed in existing scripts. These tools tend to focus on either the implicit provenance derived from the static state of a workflow (prospective provenance), or the provenance derived from the execution of a workflow (retrospective provenance). For example, CWLProv focuses on the representation of workflow enactment (with prospective provenance considered to be a product of sharing both a workflow and its visualisation), while YesWorkflow uses prospective provenance to (further) infer enactment provenance data. The provenance requirements for phenotyping fall somewhere in between, with it being important to record the impact of different agents on the evolution of a (workflow-based) phenotype definition.

8 Conclusions and Future Work

We have presented a new approach to capturing and querying provenance using templates, based upon delayed instantiation, which is both more flexible and more efficient than our prior solution, which could suffer from performance issues when presented with a high request load. The capture of provenance data has been uncoupled from the process of querying that data, and turned into an independent service based upon the recording of meta-level records describing the construction of provenance documents. These records are then later accessed by a separate query service, which can construct views of the documents described upon request by a client. These views may be generated with reference to user-specified time frames, and then analysed using query templates, a new and intuitive way to define queries over provenance data using templates. This system is based upon a newly revised template model with regard to the instantiation of iterable zones, that exhibits properties suitable for such a methodology.

We evaluated our solution in the context of Phenoflow, a library for the development of workflow-based computable phenotypes. The results show a significant improvement in the throughput for recording the data necessary to generate and query the provenance data in question. Whilst we did not investigate the performance of the construction of provenance documents from the captured meta-level records, this is of lesser importance, because the process of querying data is orthogonal to that of capture, and does not contribute to the high request load sometimes observed. Despite that, our revised model is simpler than before, and removes a number of rate limiting steps within the construction process, and so we can safely conjecture that the process will be at least no slower than previously, and thus the overall model is indeed more efficient.

Future work will integrate our work on non-repudiation of origin for meta-level records [9] within the relational capture model presented here. We will also connect additional phenotype libraries to instances of the capture service, in order to further demonstrate the impact of our approach on EHR phenotyping. The techniques presented here are a good match for challenges of capturing provenance of Trusted Research Environments (TREs), which also require efficient and scalable solutions, and we shall explore the exact improvements in time and space usage for generic TRE use cases. Other future work will focus on the query service, improving the expressivity of the query template model, and optimising the representation of constructed documents for such queries.

References

1. Amsterdamer, Y., Davidson, S.B., Deutch, D., Milo, T., Stoyanovich, J., Tannen, V.: Putting lipstick on pig: enabling database-style workflow provenance. In: Proceedings of the VLDB Endowment, pp. 346–357. Association for Computing Machinery, December 2011
2. Anand, M.K., Bowers, S., Ludäscher, B.: Techniques for efficiently querying scientific workflow provenance graphs. In: Proceedings of the 13th International Conference on Extending Database Technology, pp. 287–298. Association for Computing Machinery (2010)

3. Chapman, M., Rasmussen, L., Pacheco, J., Curcin, V.: Phenoflow: a microservice architecture for portable workflow-based phenotype definitions. In: AMIA Summits on Translational Science, pp. 142–151 (2021)
4. Chavan, A., Huang, S., Deshpande, A., Elmore, A., Madden, S., Parameswaran, A.: Towards a unified query language for provenance and versioning. In: 7th USENIX Workshop on the Theory and Practice of Provenance (TaPP 15), July 2015
5. Closa, G., Masó, J., Proß, B., Pons, X.: W3C PROV to describe provenance at the dataset, feature and attribute levels in a distributed environment. Comput. Environ. Urban Syst. **64**, 103–117 (2017)
6. Curcin, V.: Why does human phenomics matter today? Learn. Health Syst. **4**(4) (2020)
7. Curcin, V., Fairweather, E., Danger, R., Corrigan, D.: Templates as a method for implementing data provenance in decision support systems. J. Biomed. Inform. **65**, 1–21 (2017)
8. Denaxas, S., et al.: UK phenomics platform for developing and validating electronic health record phenotypes: CALIBER. J. Am. Med. Inform. Assoc. **26**(12), 1545–1559 (2019)
9. Fairweather, E., Wittner, R., Chapman, M., Holub, P., Curcin, V.: Non-repudiable provenance for clinical decision support systems. In: Proceedings of IPAW 2020 (2020)
10. Gehani, A., Tariq, D.: SPADE: support for provenance auditing in distributed environments. In: Narasimhan, P., Triantafillou, P. (eds.) Middleware 2012. LNCS, vol. 7662, pp. 101–120. Springer, Heidelberg (2012). https://doi.org/10.1007/978-3-642-35170-9_6
11. Ghoshal, D., Plale, B.: Provenance from log files: a BigData problem. In: Proceedings of the Joint EDBT/ICDT 2013 Workshops, pp. 290–297. Association for Computing Machinery (2013)
12. Huynh, T.D., Jewell, M.O., Keshavarz, A.S., Michaelides, D.T., Yang, H., Moreau, L.: The PROV-JSON serialization. Technical report, World Wide Web Consortium, April 2013
13. Karvounarakis, G., Ives, Z., Tannen, V.: Querying data provenance. In: Proceedings of the ACM SIGMOD International Conference on Management of Data, SIGMOD 2010, pp. 951–962 (2010)
14. Khan, F.Z., Soiland-Reyes, S., Sinnott, R.O., Lonie, A., Goble, C., Crusoe, M.R.: Sharing interoperable workflow provenance: a review of best practices and their practical application in CWLProv. GigaScience **8**(11), 1–27 (2019)
15. McPhillips, T., Bowers, S., Belhajjame, K., Ludäscher, B.: Retrospective provenance without a runtime provenance recorder. In: 7th USENIX Workshop on the Theory and Practice of Provenance, TaPP 2015 (2015)
16. Moreau, L., Batlajery, B., Huynh, T., Michaelides, D., Packer, H.: A templating system to generate provenance. IEEE Trans. Software Eng. **44**(2), 103–121 (2018)
17. Moreau, L., et al.: PROV-DM: the PROV data model. Technical report, World Wide Web Consortium (2013)
18. Muniswamy-Reddy, K.K., et al.: Layering in provenance systems. In: Proceedings of the 2009 USENIX Annual Technical Conference, USENIX 2009 (2009)
19. Richesson, R.L., et al.: Electronic health records based phenotyping in next-generation clinical trials: a perspective from the NIH health care systems collaboratory. J. Am. Med. Inf. Assoc. **20**(E2)(2013)
20. Wylot, M., Cudre-Mauroux, P., Groth, P.: TripleProv: efficient processing of lineage queries in a native RDF store. In: Proceedings of the 23rd International Conference on World Wide Web, WWW 2014, pp. 455–466, April 2014

Provenance Supporting Hyperparameter Analysis in Deep Neural Networks

Débora Pina[1(✉)], Liliane Kunstmann[1], Daniel de Oliveira[2], Patrick Valduriez[3], and Marta Mattoso[1]

[1] Federal University of Rio de Janeiro, Rio de Janeiro, Brazil
{dbpina,lneves,marta}@cos.ufrj.br
[2] Fluminense Federal University, Niterói, Rio de Janeiro, Brazil
danielcmo@ic.uff.br
[3] Inria, University of Montpellier, CNRS, LIRMM, Montpellier, France
Patrick.Valduriez@inria.fr

Abstract. The duration of the life cycle in deep neural networks (DNN) depends on the data configuration decisions that lead to success in obtaining models. Analyzing hyperparameters along the evolution of the network's execution allows for adapting the data. Provenance data derivation traces help the parameter fine-tuning by providing a global data picture with clear dependencies. Provenance can also contribute to the interpretation of models resulting from the DNN life cycle. However, there are challenges in collecting hyperparameters and in modeling the relationships between the data involved in the DNN life cycle to build a provenance database. Current approaches adopt different notions of provenance in their representation and require the execution of the DNN under a specific software framework, which limits interoperability and flexibility when choosing the DNN execution environment. This work presents a provenance data-based approach to address these challenges, proposing a collection mechanism with flexibility in the choice and representation of data to be analyzed. Experiments of the approach, using a convolutional neural network focused on image recognition, provide evidence of the flexibility, the efficiency of data collection, the analysis and the validation of network data.

Keywords: Provenance · Deep Learning · Workflow steering

1 Introduction

Provenance data [9,17,26] constitute a natural solution to assist users in the registration of algorithms, the data derivation path, metadata and parameters relevant to the data transformation steps [18]. Provenance data have already

This work is funded by CNPq, FAPERJ, and Inria (HPDaSc associated team). D. Pina and L. Kunstmann are supported by the Coordenação de Aperfeiçoamento de Pessoal de Nível Superior - Brasil (CAPES) - Finance Code 001.

B. Glavic et al. (Eds.): IPAW 2020/IPAW 2021, LNCS 12839, pp. 20–38, 2021.
https://doi.org/10.1007/978-3-030-80960-7_2

been successfully used in many scenarios and domains over the last decade (*e.g.*, bioinformatics [3,29], health [5,7], visualization [8], etc.). Recently, its usage in the Machine Learning (ML) life cycle has gained importance. Among the ML methods, Deep Learning (DL) and Deep Neural Network (DNN) models have gained much attention. Similar to large-scale scientific workflows, ML models are also a result of an iterative process [44]. ML workflows commonly involve several data transformations, users, algorithms, datasets, parameters, and add the challenge of feedback loops [37]. According to Silva *et al.* [37] there is a lack of capabilities for enabling ML workflow steering and dynamic workflow execution. Associating provenance data with the results of an ML workflow can support user steering to improve fine-tuning of parameters (or hyperparameters), at runtime, which is desired by several users [18,45,46].

The ML life cycle can be seen as a data centric workflow, as it produces an ML model based on input raw data through a data transformation flow. Figure 1 presents the data transformation flow in the ML life cycle using DNNs (steps ❶ to ❼). The process starts with the data preparation (step ❶), where outliers can be analyzed, missing values can be imputed and feature engineering may be performed. Once the dataset is prepared, it is split into three subsets (step ❷): training set, test set, and validation set. The first two sets are used to generate an ML model (step ❸), *e.g.*, multi-class classification, regression, etc. These models can be tuned (step ❹), *i.e.*, to set the values of the hyperparameters that produce the most accurate model. ML models are sensitive to hyperparameters [31], adjusting them in DNNs may be costly. Finally, the generated model is evaluated using the validation set (step ❺). There are several evaluation loops where the user may fine-tune parameters. To fine-tune, the user needs to have access to cause and effect data, like what filter was applied to the current model when the dropout value was below a specific threshold. By analyzing the evaluation (step ❻), the user may decide to accept the generated model or to select a new configuration (step ❼) and retrain the model. In this paper, we focus on the training phase where fine-tuning happens based on provenance data analysis at runtime (dotted red rectangle in Fig. 1).

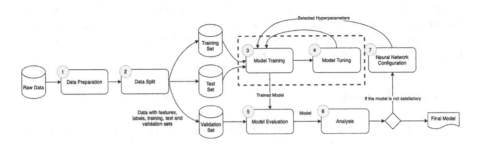

Fig. 1. Data transformation flow in the ML life cycle using DNNs (Color figure online)

The advantages of capturing provenance data are well-known [9,17,18,21,26], such as data quality, data interpretation, and reproducibility of the results. According to Cheney *et al.* [4] it is important to consider the use and needs of provenance at an early stage, before adopting a provenance capture approach. Specifically, in DL-based workflows [15], provenance data have a lot to contribute to data analysis at runtime for user steering. Provenance data along with metadata, when available during execution (*i.e.*, at runtime), have great potential to support the analysis made by humans regarding hyperparameter configurations or even training data. The evaluation of the several hyperparameters requires that the user is aware of the relationship between many types of metadata, *e.g.*, the chosen hyperparameter values, performance data, environment configuration, etc. This data analysis during the training process can support the user in fine-tuning decisions, complementing auto-tuning solutions [43].

Adding provenance data to ML workflows is challenging. Despite the provenance support of several workflow systems, using these systems to invoke popular ML libraries or platforms can result in several execution conflicts, particularly in high-performance computing environments [37]. Basically, there are two approaches to make ML workflows provenance aware. The first is provenance provided for a specific ML platform [2,20,24,30,35,36,40,46] and the second is the provenance systems that are independent of the domain [32]. In the first approach, each ML platform provides provenance using its proprietary representation, which is difficult to interpret and compare with execution between different platforms. The provenance systems approach is often tightly coupled to a script programming language, limiting the use of well-known ML platforms or it is too generic requiring a lot of data modeling and instrumenting the workflows.

In this paper, we present DNNProv and Keras-Prov, two provenance service management approaches that are designed for supporting hyperparameter analysis in DNNs. DNNProv and Keras-Prov integrate both traditional retrospective provenance data (r-prov) with domain-specific DL data. Both solutions provide an API that allows for users to develop their ML-based workflows using different DL frameworks (*e.g.*, Tensorflow, Theano) while being able to share and analyze captured provenance data using W3C PROV. The remainder of this paper is structured as follows. Section 2 discusses related work, Sect. 3 details the proposed approach. Section 4 presents the experimental evaluation and discussion of results. Finally, Sect. 5 concludes the paper.

2   Related Work

With the recent interest in DL methods, several works propose provenance management approaches for data analysis during DNN training [11]. There are several challenges in making ML workflows provenance aware like taking into account the execution framework that may involve CPUs, GPUs, TPUs, and distributed environments such as clusters and clouds as discussed in [14,36,42]. In this section, we discuss related work for provenance data management, considering the intention of using provenance for runtime data analysis. We group these works in sections, with approaches that are either focused on the ML domain or that provide domain-agnostic provenance systems. Our provenance services also provide data capture modeled for DL characteristics and analyses, but unlike the approaches that are focused on the DL domain, adopt best practices of provenance systems that follow W3C PROV recommendations. Having preset classes that already represent typical entities and activities from the DL domain improves provenance data preparation for runtime analyses. The result is flexibility in defining new domain data to the DL workflow and being able to execute with different ML platforms with distributed environments having CPUs and GPUs.

2.1   Machine- and Deep Learning-Specific Approaches

The approaches in this category manage provenance for several purposes in ML platforms [2,12,24,30,35,36,40,41,46]. They are all based on a proprietary representation of provenance data, i.e., that does not follow recommendations like W3C PROV. These proprietary representations of provenance data can make interoperability and analysis difficult. If one user needs to compare the results of multiple training processes performed in different frameworks, additional implementations will be required. Next, we discuss the approaches that are focused on the use of provenance to interpret and tune hyperparameters and that are closer to our solution. ModelDB [41] is a system that aims at addressing model management. Its goal is to automatically track ML models in their native environment, storing trained models and their results to allow for visual exploration (or using SQL). Currently, ModelDB is customized for models generated using scikit-learn and SparkML, and uses visualization only as a way to perform *postmortem* analysis of the ML pipeline, i.e., it does not support runtime provenance analysis. Another solution focused on ML experiments is Runway [40]. Runway manages ML and DL artifacts, such as models, data, or experiments, as well as their provenance. In this sense, Runway allows for tracking the model and data, easing reproducibility. However, in addition to being a proprietary solution, which means that the solution does not follow W3C PROV standard to represent provenance data, Runway is restricted to the Python 3 programming language.

ModelKB (Model Knowledge Base) [12] aims at automating the life cycle management process for DL models with minimal user intervention. The contributions of ModelKB are to automatically extract and store model metadata and artifacts, in addition to viewing, consulting, comparing experiments, and reproducing models. ModelKB itself is not a modeling tool, but a complementary system that can automatically manage experiments in their native frameworks, such as TensorFlow [1]. However, ModelKB does not make the captured data available for analysis at runtime. Schelter *et al.* [35] provide an automated tool to extract metadata from the model with an interactive view to query and compare experiments. A declarative language is proposed for users to specify their queries. Thus, this solution focuses on tracking metadata and the provenance of ML experiment data. However, this approach does not use the W3C PROV standard, being an obstacle to foster interoperability.

2.2 Domain-Agnostic Approaches

There are several approaches for capturing provenance data [32] that can be applied (with specializations) to the ML domain. Approaches for automatic capturing provide very fine granularity, generating a significant execution overhead in the process. Systems like noWorkflow [27], capture and store provenance data from Python scripts in an automatic way. noWorkflow allows provenance data capture without requiring any modifications in the original Python script. However, it is coupled to the Python language and does not execute in distributed and parallel environments, which limits the use of parallelism of popular ML libraries. Similar to noWorkflow, SPADE [10] automatically collects provenance from a workflow script including distributed and parallel environments, but this script has to be compiled using an LLVM compiler. In the automatic capture, the user does not spend time defining what provenance data to capture. However, when it comes to analyzing this provenance, significant time and effort are required to understand what and how data was modeled. In addition, due to the fine granularity, the user has to filter and aggregate data before starting the analysis. Having to do this during the training cycle may not be an option.

Different from the approaches based on automatic provenance capturing, the approaches based on the participation of the user allow to pre-select relevant data for analysis, having less impact on the execution and analysis time. When the user identifies attributes and parameters in W3C PROV entities, activities with their relationships, these chosen names become familiar for runtime analysis. One of these tools is DfAnalyzer [39], which is a tool that allows users to set the relevant data to be captured for runtime analysis in high-performance execution environments. One advantage of DfAnalyzer is that it captures provenance throughout the training of a DNN, and does not interfere in the performance of the training. Although DfAnalyzer is W3C PROV compliant and has been used in different domains, it is not designed for supporting provenance capturing during the ML life cycle. Therefore, repetitive work on designing and instrumenting has to be done. Sumatra [6] captures provenance from the script execution based on a series of annotations in the script. However, Sumatra only supports *post-mortem* analysis, *i.e.*, only after the ML model is generated. YesWorkflow [22] is another example of a tool capable of analyzing provenance data. YesWorkflow does not depend on a programming language, adopting a strategy of adding annotations to the scripts to identify provenance data. However, its queries are based on URIs and hyperparameter runtime analyses are not URI-based. Similar to YesWorkflow, in [13] there is no runtime provenance capture. Instead, they take advantage of applications that provide log files to extract provenance from them. This could be adopted by systems like TensorFlow and Keras, which provide provenance logs. However, the queries are limited to the logged data and it is a *post-mortem* analysis approach.

UML2PROV [34] aims at making UML (Unified Modeling Language) based applications provenance aware automatically. It is an approach that provides a mapping strategy from UML class, State Machine, and Sequence diagrams to define an automatic code generation technique that deploys artifacts for provenance generation in an application. UML2PROV assumes the existence of these diagrams or requires that they be designed or generated through reverse engineering, which limits its use in most ML environments.

Therefore, capturing provenance for runtime analysis in DL domains using domain-agnostic approaches may be complicated due to several reasons: (i) programming language and compiler dependencies, (ii) lack of support for provenance capturing in HPC and distributed environments, and (iii) lack of support for runtime provenance analysis. The next section describes how DNNProv and Keras-Prov address these limitations.

3   DNNProv and Keras-Prov

Due to the continuous increase in the use of ML and DL methods for developing workflows in different domains, the use of provenance data to support analysis has been gaining importance. The analytical potential of provenance data contributes to the analysis of hyperparameter configurations (and their impact on the accuracy of the generated model) and, consequently, supports the fine-tuning [12,23,35]. As the training of DNNs can last for several hours or even days (depending on the computational environment), and a large amount of data is consumed and produced, the user needs to be able to evaluate the training to make adjustments to hyperparameters. Therefore, hyperparameter analysis tools should work during the training of the DNN and quickly provide the required data and entity attributes for analysis without competing for computational resources with the training process.

To capture, store and analyze provenance data from DNNs in an efficient way, we propose two provenance service management approaches, one independent from the DNN framework (named DNNProv) and the other coupled to a DNN framework (named Keras-Prov). DNNProv and Keras-Prov extend DfAnalyzer [38,39], which allows monitoring, debugging, and analyzing provenance during the execution of scientific workflows. One advantage of DfAnalyzer is that it explores *in-situ* or asynchronous provenance data management, without interfering with ML and DL workflow performance even in HPC environments. Since DfAnalyzer is domain-agnostic, it is not designed for ML and DL domains and targets mainly binary scientific data, this section presents the extensions to DfAnalyzer for ML and DL domains.

DNNProv and Keras-Prov data representation follows the data model based on the recommendations of the PROV-DM of the W3C PROV [26] which is an initiative for the representation of different types of provenance data without being specific to a domain. W3C PROV is based on *Agent*, *Activity* and *Entity* concepts. An agent is something that bears some form of responsibility for an activity, an entity, or for another agent's activity. An activity is something that occurs over a period of time upon or with entities and an entity is a thing with some fixed aspects. The diagram in Fig. 2, generated by Prov Python[1] and Graphviz[2], represents some activities of the neural network training process with DNNProv and Keras-Prov, following the notation from [25]. The orange pentagon represents the Agent concept, yellow ovals represent Entity and blue rectangles represent Activity. The diagram shows what was used directly from PROV-Df (with the tag dfanalyzer) and what was extended on our approach (with the tag dnnprov).

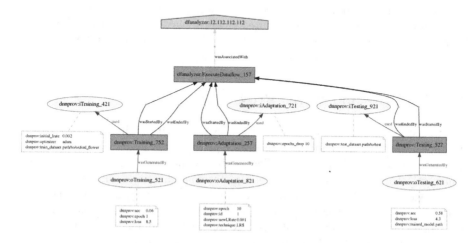

Fig. 2. W3C PROV graph fragment of DNNProv and Keras-Prov

3.1   Provenance Model

The association of provenance data with domain data can assist DNN users to perform rich analyses at runtime and allows the monitoring of the training process. Thereby, in this paper, we present a solution capable of tracking activities that occur in the DL life cycle, providing efficient provenance data capturing and analysis. The proposed approach considers the steps of the DL life cycle as a dataflow. To represent specific data from the DL training process, a specialization of the PROV-Df [39] model, named DNNProv-Df, is proposed in this subsection. Based on this new model, the user is able to (i) track epochs, learning rate, accuracy, loss function, execution time, etc., (ii) discover which pre-processing methods were used before training the model, (iii) monitor the training process and perform fine-tuning, (iv) discover which files were generated in different execution steps, and (v) interpret the generated results.

Figure 3 presents the DNNProv-Df model represented as a UML class diagram. The classes inside the dotted red area are classes related to the steps of the

---

[1] https://prov.readthedocs.io/en/latest/prov.html.
[2] http://www.graphviz.org/.

DL life cycle considered in this paper, with attributes that represent the data related to training metrics and hyperparameters. In the DL life cycle, several different hyperparameters have to be set, *e.g.*, learning rate, batch size, number of epochs, momentum and dropout. Choosing the best hyperparameter values is far from trivial and many combinations are commonly explored. This process is compute-intensive, usually performed in HPC environments, and, several models are generated. Only one of these models is chosen as the best one and this choice must be registered for *a posteriori* analysis. In addition, as the training process takes a long time, it is necessary to steer it, *e.g.*, by inspecting how the evaluation metrics are evolving during the training so that one can change parameters and start training again if needed.

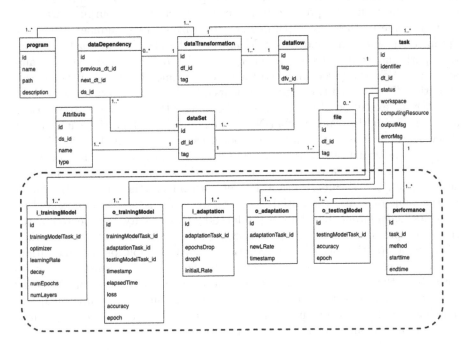

Fig. 3. DNNProv-Df model

The classes related to the dataflow specification are inherited from the PROV-Df model, which are *dataflow, dataTransformation, dataset, dataDependency, program* and *attribute*. These classes represent prospective provenance (p-prov). The class *dataflow* is responsible for representing the different dataflows whose content has been stored in the provenance database. This class contains a name for each dataflow. The class *dataTransformation* represents the multiple activities associated with a given dataflow. An activity is associated with a *program* or a script that is executed. To represent retrospective provenance (r-prov), DNNProv-Df contains the classes *task* and *file*. The class *task* represents the instances of activities that are executed, and the class *file* represents the entity attributes that were eventually used and generated at runtime.

As described in [23], the hyperparameters are adjusted after or during each iteration. To make decisions regarding the fine-tuning of these hyperparameter values, the user needs to evaluate several data associated with the behavior of the DNN with the hyperparameter configuration used in that iteration, *e.g.*, the training time for each epoch, and the loss associated with each epoch. Thus DNNProv-Df contains the following classes to represent domain-specific data regarding the DNN training process: *i_trainingModel*, *o_trainingModel*, *i_adaptation*, *o_adaptation* and *o_testingModel*.

The class *i_trainingModel* contains the hyperparameters that have to be set in the DNN before the training process (the prefix *i* refers to the input parameters of a task and the prefix *o* in the classes refers to the output parameter values). Some of these hyperparameters are learning rate, number of epochs, optimizer, momentum, and decay. Meanwhile, the class *o_trainingModel* contains performance metrics for the generated model by epoch. This class contains attributes such as elapsed time and the date and time of the end of the epoch's execution. The elapsed time attribute defined in this class allows users to check whether the execution of an epoch is taking longer than expected. Adaptations are made during the training of a DNN. For example, an adaptation can generate a new learning rate at the end of an epoch, using a function that significantly decreases the value of the learning rate every n times by a m factor. Thus, the activity *Adaptation* receives as input data the set produced by the previous activity (activity *Training*) and a dataset with information such as the factor m, the value of n and the initial learning rate. This dataset is represented by the class *i_adaptation*. The dataset produced by this activity, represented by the class *o_adaptation*, contains the new learning rate, epoch and the date and time when the adaptation occurred, in addition to identification for the adaptation. Finally, the class *o_testingModel* is related to the activity *Testing* and provides data about the evaluation of the model. Thus, similarly to the *o_trainingModel* class, *o_testingModel* contains performance metrics, such as accuracy and loss function values. It is worth mentioning that this model can be extended as new hyperparameters and metrics are needed.

3.2 Architecture of DNNProv and Keras-Prov

We present two provenance service management solutions for hyperparameters analysis. The architectures of DNNProv and Keras-Prov are presented in Fig. 4. The main difference between DNNProv and Keras-Prov is where the *Provenance Extractor* component is deployed. The architecture of both services is composed of three layers, according to Fig. 4, which are: (i) Training Layer, (ii) Data Layer, and (iii) Analysis Layer. The *Training Layer* is where the training library executes and interacts with the *Provenance Extractor*, which accesses the hyperparameter values at runtime and gets their values.

For DNNProv, the *Provenance Extractor* is implemented and deployed outside the DNN library. This way, the user can choose any DNN library or framework, and then instrument the code (adding calls to the provenance extractor component) to define which data to capture. Using DNNProv we assume that the programs in the DL life cycle are gray boxes, *i.e.*, part of their source code can be adapted, while the other part can invoke a private source code (black box). In DNNProv, the user defines which domain data and hyperparameters values will be captured and where they should be captured (step **1a**). With this instrumentation, the *Provenance Extractor* can access the data during training (step **2**).

In the case of Keras-Prov, the *Provenance Extractor* is already implemented within the Keras library, so the user does not need to instrument the code. The user chooses, among the predefined provenance choices, domain data and hyperparameters to be captured (step **1b**). The *Provenance Extractor* automatically extracts the values of the hyperparameters used in each training (step **2**). In both Keras-Prov and DNN-Prov, once captured, the provenance data is managed asynchronously with the DL execution. After, the *Provenance Extractor* interacts with the *Data Layer* to get the JSON file paths describing the DNN (step **3**). These file paths, with hyperparameters values, metrics and, etc., are sent to the provenance database (step **4**). Then, the *Provenance Exporter* queries the provenance database (step **5**) and sends query results to the *Provenance Viewer* (step **6**), which generates a visual representation of the provenance graph as an alternative to the user runtime analysis.

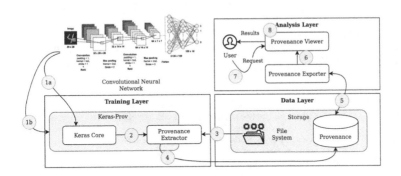

Fig. 4. Architecture of DNNProv and Keras-Prov

3.3 Using DNNProv and Keras-Prov

If the user chooses to use DNNProv, one important step is the code instrumentation. In this step, the user defines which data to capture. The first step is to define the dataflow structure in the source code of the DNN workflow (p-prov). Let us assume that a user needs to capture the data defined in Fig. 3, thus one

has to include in the source code the fragment shown in Fig. 5. In this fragment, the user specifies an identifier for the dataflow (dataflow_tag = "alexnet")
and sets the automatic definition of activities to *True*. By setting the automatic
definition of p-prov, the DNNProv queries the provenance database and identifies the registered activities. If the user chooses to set the automatic definition
of p-prov to *False*, one has to define which activities are part of this dataflow
manually.

Once the dataflow and its transformations are defined, the user needs to set
in the source code where a task starts (and finishes) and where DNNProv can
extract (at runtime) the values of the hyperparameters. Note that the dataflow
and data transformations specifications are p-prov, while the definition of tasks
is r-prov. When the user is defining a task in the source code, one can also define
the data dependencies among tasks, *i.e.*, the user specifies in the source code
which tasks are responsible for the production and consumption of data in a
given dataflow. This step is also shown in Fig. 5 (*dependency=t1* - this means
that task *t2* only starts after task *t1* produces data). Multiple dependencies are
modeled with binary relationships and queried with join predicates. Once set,
this provenance schema can be reused for further DNN analyses.

```
#Prospective provenance
df = Dataflow("alexnet", True)
df.save()

#Retrospective provenance
...
t2 = Task(2, "alexnet", "Adaptation", dependency=t1)
initial_lrate = 0.002
drop = 0.5
epochs_drop = 10.0
t2_input = DataSet("iAdaptation", [Element([epochs_drop,
drop, initial_lrate])])
t2.add_dataset(t2_input)
t2.begin()
...
def on_epoch_begin(self, epoch, logs=None):
    lr = K.get_value(self.model.optimizer.lr)
    temp_lr= schedule(self.epoch)
    K.set_value(self.model.optimizer.lr, lr)
    t2_output = DataSet("oAdaptation", [Element([lr,
    datetime.now(), epoch, adaptation_id])])
    t2.add_dataset(t2_output)
    t2.save()
```

Fig. 5. A fragment of the source code instrumented for DNNProv

This instrumentation of the source code to capture the provenance data can
be a barrier to the adoption of provenance tools by many scientists that are not
computer science experts, given the effort that may be required from the user.
With this in mind, we proposed Keras-Prov, which is the second provenance service management approach proposed in this paper. Keras-Prov is an extension

of the DNN library Keras[3] and its goal is to reduce the effort to adapt the code to capture provenance data during the DNN training process by reducing the need for instrumentation. In the implementation of Keras-Prov, modifications were performed to the source code of Keras[4] to embed the *Provenance Extractor* component, since Keras does not capture provenance data natively. A class *Provenance* was created containing methods to deal with the creation of the activities that follow the DL life cycle, following the representation presented in Fig. 3. In addition to this data, Keras-Prov captures and stores information about the layers of the DNN, that is, the name that identifies the layer (*e.g.*, activation_1, dropout_1), the type of layer (*e.g.*, activation, dropout) and the value of this layer (*e.g.*, for activation the value is *relu*, the value for dropout is 0.4). Although Keras-Prov captures several hyperparameter values automatically, it is worth noticing that the user can define new data to be captured. For more information about defining new data to be captured using Keras-Prov please visit https://github.com/dbpina/keras-prov.

In the *Model* class of Keras, a *provenance* method was created to capture provenance data. This method receives a *tag* to identify the dataflow, if there is an adaptation of the hyperparameters during training (e.g., an update of the learning rate), that is, the use of methods such as *LearningRateScheduler* offered by Keras, and the list of hyperparameters to be captured. The data received by the *provenance* method are defined by the user in the source code of the DL workflow following the example presented in Fig. 6. Different from DNNProv, when using Keras-Prov the user needs only to set which hyperparameters to capture, and no additional instrumentation is required. After setting *True* to the hyperparameters of interest, the user adds a call to the method *provenance*.

```
hyps = {"OPTIMIZER_NAME": True,        model.provenance(
    "LEARNING_RATE": True,                 dataflow_tag= "alexnet",
    "DECAY": True,                         adaptation=False,
    "MOMENTUM": True,                      hyps = hyps)
    "NUM_EPOCHS": True,
    "BATCH_SIZE": True,
    "NUM_LAYERS": True}
```

Fig. 6. Setting the hyperparameters of interest in Keras-Prov

Considering that ML workflows follow the life cycle of Fig. 1, the inclusion of DNNProv in popular ML systems like Keras, requires the identification, in the source code, of the points at which such activities (network configuration, training, and testing) are performed and how the neural network data, hyperparameters, and metrics (from the training and testing steps) are being manipulated. This step allows to define PROV relationships between them and establishes data extraction into the database for automatic provenance design and capture in those systems.

---

[3] https://keras.io/.

[4] https://github.com/keras-team/keras.

4 Evaluation

In this section, we evaluate DNNProv and Keras-Prov. We discuss the results obtained using both approaches for the analysis of hyperparameter configurations during the training of DNNs using provenance data. In the experiments presented in this section, we trained AlexNet [19] in both DNNProv and Keras-Prov in the cluster Lobo Carneiro (SGI cluster with 504 CPUs Intel Xeon E5-2670v3 (Haswell) - total of 6.048 processors) at COPPE/UFRJ using the Oxford Flower [28] dataset, which consists of 17 species of flowers with 80 images for each class. The flower categories in this dataset are deliberately chosen to have some ambiguity in each aspect. For example, some classes cannot be distinguished only in colors, such as dandelions and buttercups, others cannot be distinguished only in shapes, such as daffodils and wild windflowers. The images of the flowers were retrieved from different websites and some images from the authors' own photographs [28].

The Alexnet dataflow is composed of the following activities: (i) *Training*, (ii) *Adaptation*, and (iii) *Testing*. *Training* consumes (*used*) the following hyperparameters: the name of the optimizer, the learning rate, number of epochs, and number of layers in the network, and produces (*wasGeneratedBy*) a set of metrics that helps in the evaluation of results obtained during training, *e.g.*, accuracy, the value of the loss function, the elapsed time and the date and time of the end of the execution of each epoch. *Adaptation* consumes (*used*) the dataset produced by the previous activity (*Training*), a dataset with information for the adaptation that has taken place and the output contains the values for the new learning rate, the value of the epoch and the date and time when the adaptation occurred, in addition to identification for the adaptation. *Testing* provides data on the evaluation of the model according to the training dataset and outputs the accuracy and loss function values.

Several training runs were performed for AlexNet, with variations in hyperparameters values, *e.g.*, learning rate (0.0005, 0.001, 0.002), optimizer (Adam, SGD) and dropout (0.4, 0.7). After a few training executions, the user decided to apply a filter to convert the images (input dataset) to a gray-scale. Because of that, the user needed to add a new activity called *Filters*, also wanting this activity to be registered at the provenance database. Due to DNNProv's flexibility, a modification was made to the p-prov and this activity was included, which means that in the next training executions, the data defined by the user for this activity started to be captured. Likewise, other extensions can be done to the relational schema showing the flexibility of the approaches.

Table 1 defines provenance queries based on the most frequent queries from [12, 24, 35, 40, 41]. We categorize the set of possible provenance queries as illustrated in Table 2. Queries are classified according to the provenance data processing needed to answer them. For instance, queries in class C1 get entity attributes from a single provenance graph, while queries in class C2 access multiple provenance graphs. Queries in class C3 require relating entity attributes and data derivation path on one graph, while C4 queries multiple provenance graphs. ML frameworks like Tensorflow or Keras mention their provenance support through logs. Despite the possibility of extracting provenance from logs [13], it is far from trivial. It requires repetitive log post-processing for every trial, with no flexibility on defining what to capture. Running aggregation queries through epoch iterations from logs, like Q6 and Q8, is also time-consuming and demands a significant effort from the user.

Table 1. Example of provenance queries.

#	Queries	Class
Q1	What is the loss value of epoch 10 of a specific training t' of a specific model m'?	C1
Q2	What are the layers of model m'?	C1
Q3	Retrieve the time consumed and loss by each epoch in the training t' of model m'	C1
Q4	What is the initial value of the learning rate when the training for model m' was more accurate?	C2
Q5	Retrieve the combinations of hyperparameters where was obtained the 3 best accuracy values in previous training for model m'?	C2
Q6	Was there an adaptation of the learning rate in the training of the model m' that obtained the best accuracy? If so, at what epoch did it occur and what technique was used for this adaptation? And what is the new value?	C3
Q7	What filter was applied to model m' when the dropout value was 0.4?	C4
Q8	Which filter was applied in the training executions that showed the best and the worst accuracy for model m'? What was the number of epochs in these executions?	C4

Table 2. Classification of queries.

Class	Entity attributes	Derivation path	Single graph	Multiple graphs
C1	Yes	No	Yes	No
C2	Yes	No	No	Yes
C3	Yes	Yes	Yes	No
C4	Yes	Yes	No	Yes

Using the queries presented in Table 1, during the training of the DNN, the user is able to monitor metrics by epoch and steer the training at runtime. If, for instance, the loss value is not meeting the criteria defined by the user, one may decide to stop training or modify the learning rate. In this case, these adaptations are also saved (time and date when it happened) since they are important for *a posteriori* analysis, even at the end of the training process. The user may want to discover if the training with adaptation at runtime produced better results than the training that used the same value for the learning rate without modifications at runtime. It is worth noticing that DNNProv and Keras-Prov can also be connected to data visualization tools, as a setup option, such as Kibana[5], to create dashboards and other resources to support the user's analysis.

To evaluate the potential of DNNProv and Keras-Prov, queries Q3, Q6, and Q8 were submitted to the provenance database that was populated with the different training data of AlexNet (from multiple training runs). The results consider the number of epochs, if a gray-scale filter was applied to the input dataset and the use of LearningRateScheduler (LRS) for adaptations in the learning rate during training. These results are presented in Tables 3, 4 and 5.

From the result of Q3 (Table 3), it is possible to investigate, for example, if any epoch is taking longer than usual. In addition, if the loss value attribute is selected along with the identification of the epoch, the specialist can verify whether the increase in the number of epochs no longer contributes to better accuracy after a certain epoch. The result of Q6 (Table 4) shows the impact of learning rate adaptations in model convergence. Though decreasing the learning rate is a known technique, the registered values help the user trace the cause of changes when analyzing different models. These data are also important if the user is evaluating the impact of different learning rate adaptation techniques or different parameters for decreasing learning rate functions, such as Step Decay. From the result of Q8 (Table 5), we observed that the application of the filter that converts the images to a gray-scale presented a worse accuracy in the test set, 0.37, than the training without this filter, which presented an accuracy of 0.59.

Table 3. Results for the Query Q3

Epoch	Time (seconds)	Loss value
1	22.075	3.484
2	20.560	2.870
3	19.996	2.542
4	20.478	2.188
5	20.378	2.015
6	20.006	1.784
7	20.486	1.600
8	20.238	1.466
9	20.395	1.246
10	20.318	0.977

It is worth mentioning that for the results presented in this paper, AlexNet was trained with a maximum of 100 epochs. AlexNet was also trained a few times

---

[5] https://www.elastic.co/kibana.

Table 4. Results for the Query Q6   **Table 5.** Results for the Query Q8

Epoch	Learning rate	Technique
10	0.001	LRS
30	0.00025	LRS

Filter	Accuracy	Epochs
None	0.59	100
Gray-scale	0.37	100

with a larger number of epochs, such as 500 and 1000, which took about three and six hours, respectively. Due to this training time, we chose to train with fewer epochs to show provenance helping in evaluating different variations of hyperparameters. Furthermore, provenance queries like Q6 show that the highest accuracy reached by AlexNet with 500 epochs was around 65%, which is consistent with the top accuracy of 68.68% presented for AlexNet in flower categorization [16].

Moreover, we observed the overhead introduced by the proposed approach. The purpose of this measurement was to assess the impact of capturing provenance on training time. We observed that the time overhead corresponds to an increase of 2% in the worst case over the total workflow time. This overhead can be considered negligible, especially in longer executions, considering that the user will have the benefit of queries and visualizations to the captured provenance data. In addition, the size of the provenance database was 5MB and with such a size it is already possible to answer relevant questions.

5   Conclusions

The approach presented in this paper aims at supporting the analysis of hyperparameter configurations and adaptations in the training of DNNs by capturing relevant provenance data. We present a provenance-based user steering approach that allows for capturing and storing data to query during and after the training. This approach is implemented in two modes, independent and dependent of the DNN library or framework. By adopting the W3C PROV recommendation, both modes aim at reducing the diversity of data representation and the effort in modeling and querying DL training data related to PROV. The first, DNNProv, is not specific to programming languages or libraries, and does not require the use of a particular ML execution environment. However, DNNProv requires the user to instrument the script code of the DNN workflow, which may require some effort. To provide a solution that does not require instrumentation, Keras-Prov adds DNNProv components into Keras to capture the provenance data automatically. In addition, the approach is flexible since it allows for the inclusion of new types of data to be captured, like the DL domain application data. Experiments show the adequacy of the use of provenance in the analysis throughout the training of DNNs, including extensions for capturing data related to pre-processing. As future work, we plan to extend the approach to the domain of Physics Informed Neural Networks (PINN) [33]. PINNs define the neural network loss function based on partial differential equations that inform physics. Analyzing loss function data in PINNs increases the complexity of provenance data management.

References

1. Abadi, M., et al.: Tensorflow: large-scale machine learning on heterogeneous distributed systems. arXiv preprint arXiv:1603.04467 (2016)
2. Agrawal, P., et al.: Data platform for machine learning. In: Proceedings of the 2019 International Conference on Management of Data, pp. 1803–1816 (2019)
3. Almeida, R.F., et al.: Managing data provenance for bioinformatics workflows using AProvBio. Int. J. Comput. Biol. Drug Des. **12**(2), 153–170 (2019). https://doi.org/10.1504/IJCBDD.2019.099761
4. Cheney, J., Chapman, A., Davidson, J., Forbes, A.: Data provenance, curation and quality in metrology. arXiv preprint arXiv:2102.08228 (2021)
5. Corrigan, D., Curcin, V., Ethier, J., Flynn, A.J., Sottara, D.: Challenges of deploying computable biomedical knowledge in real-world applications. In: AMIA 2019, American Medical Informatics Association Annual Symposium, Washington, DC, USA, 16–20 November 2019. AMIA (2019), http://knowledge.amia.org/69862-amia-1.4570936/t002-1.4575206/t002-1.4575207/3201770-1.4575319/3203261-1.4575316
6. Davison, A.: Automated capture of experiment context for easier reproducibility in computational research. Comput. Sci. Eng. **14**(4), 48–56 (2012)
7. Fairweather, E., Wittner, R., Chapman, M., Holub, P., Curcin, V.: Non-repudiable provenance for clinical decision support systems. CoRR abs/2006.11233 (2020). https://arxiv.org/abs/2006.11233
8. Fekete, J., Freire, J., Rhyne, T.: Exploring reproducibility in visualization. IEEE Comput. Graph. Appl. **40**(5), 108–119 (2020). https://doi.org/10.1109/MCG.2020.3006412
9. Freire, J., Koop, D., Santos, E., Silva, C.T.: Provenance for computational tasks: a survey. Comput. Sci. Eng. **10**(3), 11–21 (2008)
10. Gehani, A., Tariq, D.: SPADE: support for provenance auditing in distributed environments. In: Narasimhan, P., Triantafillou, P. (eds.) Middleware 2012. LNCS, vol. 7662, pp. 101–120. Springer, Heidelberg (2012). https://doi.org/10.1007/978-3-642-35170-9_6
11. Gharibi, G., Walunj, V., Alanazi, R., Rella, S., Lee, Y.: Automated management of deep learning experiments. In: Proceedings of the 3rd International Workshop on Data Management for End-to-End Machine Learning, p. 8. ACM (2019)
12. Gharibi, G., Walunj, V., Rella, S., Lee, Y.: ModelKB: towards automated management of the modeling lifecycle in deep learning. In: Proceedings of the 7th International Workshop on Realizing Artificial Intelligence Synergies in Software Engineering, pp. 28–34. IEEE Press (2019)
13. Ghoshal, D., Plale, B.: Provenance from log files: a bigdata problem. In: Proceedings of the Joint EDBT/ICDT 2013 Workshops, pp. 290–297 (2013)
14. Gil, Y., et al.: Artificial intelligence for modeling complex systems: taming the complexity of expert models to improve decision making. ACM Trans. Interact. Intell. Syst. (2021)

15. Goodfellow, I., Bengio, Y., Courville, A., Bengio, Y.: Deep Learning, vol. 1. MIT press Cambridge (2016)
16. Gurnani, A., Mavani, V., Gajjar, V., Khandhediya, Y.: Flower categorization using deep convolutional neural networks. arXiv preprint arXiv:1708.03763 (2017)
17. Herschel, M., Diestelkämper, R., Lahmar, H.B.: A survey on provenance: what for? what form? what from? VLDB J. **26**(6), 881–906 (2017)
18. Huynh, T.D., Stalla, S., Moreau, L.: Provenance-based explanations for automated decisions: final IAA project report (2019)
19. Krizhevsky, A., Sutskever, I., Hinton, G.E.: ImageNet classification with deep convolutional neural networks. In: Advances in Neural Information Processing Systems, pp. 1097–1105 (2012)
20. Lourenço, R., Freire, J., Shasha, D.: Debugging machine learning pipelines. In: Proceedings of the 3rd International Workshop on Data Management for End-to-End Machine Learning, pp. 1–10 (2019)
21. Mattoso, M., et al.: Dynamic steering of HPC scientific workflows: a survey. Future Gener. Comput. Syst. **46**, 100–113 (2015)
22. McPhillips, T., Bowers, S., Belhajjame, K., Ludäscher, B.: Retrospective provenance without a runtime provenance recorder. In: 7th USENIX Workshop on the Theory and Practice of Provenance (TaPP 2015) (2015)
23. Miao, H., Li, A., Davis, L.S., Deshpande, A.: ModelHUB: lifecycle management for deep learning. Univ. of Maryland (2015)
24. Miao, H., Li, A., Davis, L.S., Deshpande, A.: Towards unified data and lifecycle management for deep learning. In: 2017 IEEE 33rd International Conference on Data Engineering (ICDE), pp. 571–582. IEEE (2017)
25. Missier, P., Belhajjame, K., Cheney, J.: The W3C PROV family of specifications for modelling provenance metadata. In: Proceedings of the 16th International Conference on Extending Database Technology, pp. 773–776 (2013)
26. Moreau, L., Groth, P.: Provenance: an introduction to PROV. Synthesis Lect. Semant. Web Theory Technol. **3**(4), 1–129 (2013)
27. Murta, L., Braganholo, V., Chirigati, F., Koop, D., Freire, J.: noWorkflow: capturing and analyzing provenance of scripts. In: Ludäscher, B., Plale, B. (eds.) IPAW 2014. LNCS, vol. 8628, pp. 71–83. Springer, Cham (2015). https://doi.org/10.1007/978-3-319-16462-5_6
28. Nilsback, M.E., Zisserman, A.: A visual vocabulary for flower classification. In: 2006 IEEE Computer Society Conference on Computer Vision and Pattern Recognition (CVPR 2006), vol. 2, pp. 1447–1454. IEEE (2006)
29. Ocaña, K.A.C.S., Silva, V., de Oliveira, D., Mattoso, M.: Data analytics in bioinformatics: data science in practice for genomics analysis workflows. In: 11th IEEE International Conference on e-Science, e-Science 2015, Munich, Germany, 31 August–4 September 2015. pp. 322–331. IEEE Computer Society (2015). https://doi.org/10.1109/eScience.2015.50
30. Ormenisan, A.A., Ismail, M., Haridi, S., Dowling, J.: Implicit provenance for machine learning artifacts. Proc. MLSys **20** (2020)
31. Orr, G.B., Müller, K.R.: Neural Networks: Tricks of the Trade. Springer (2003)
32. Pimentel, J.F., Freire, J., Murta, L., Braganholo, V.: A survey on collecting, managing, and analyzing provenance from scripts. ACM Comput. Surv. **52**(3), 47:1–47:38 (2019). https://doi.org/10.1145/3311955
33. Raissi, M., Perdikaris, P., Karniadakis, G.E.: Physics informed deep learning (part I): data-driven solutions of nonlinear partial differential equations. arXiv preprint arXiv:1711.10561 (2017)

34. Sáenz-Adán, C., Moreau, L., Pérez, B., Miles, S., García-Izquierdo, F.J.: Automating provenance capture in software engineering with UML2PROV. In: Belhajjame, K., Gehani, A., Alper, P. (eds.) IPAW 2018. LNCS, vol. 11017, pp. 58–70. Springer, Cham (2018). https://doi.org/10.1007/978-3-319-98379-0_5

35. Schelter, S., Böse, J.H., Kirschnick, J., Klein, T., Seufert, S.: Automatically tracking metadata and provenance of machine learning experiments. In: Machine Learning Systems workshop at NIPS (2017)

36. Scherzinger, S., Seifert, C., Wiese, L.: The best of both worlds: challenges in linking provenance and explainability in distributed machine learning. In: 2019 IEEE 39th International Conference on Distributed Computing Systems (ICDCS), pp. 1620–1629. IEEE (2019)

37. Ferreira da Silva, R., et al.: Workflows community summit: Bringing the scientific workflows research community together, March 2021

38. Silva, V., et al.: Dfanalyzer: runtime dataflow analysis tool for computational science and engineering applications. SoftwareX **12**, 100592 (2020)

39. Silva, V., de Oliveira, D., Valduriez, P., Mattoso, M.: DfAnalyzer: runtime dataflow analysis of scientific applications using provenance. Proc. VLDB Endow. **11**(12), 2082–2085 (2018)

40. Tsay, J., Mummert, T., Bobroff, N., Braz, A., Westerink, P., Hirzel, M.: Runway: machine learning model experiment management tool (2018)

41. Vartak, M., et al.: Model DB: a system for machine learning model management. In: Proceedings of the Workshop on Human-in-the-Loop Data Analytics, p. 14. ACM (2016)

42. Wang, D., et al.: From human-human collaboration to human-AI collaboration: designing AI systems that can work together with people. In: Extended Abstracts of the 2020 CHI Conference on Human Factors in Computing Systems, pp. 1–6 (2020)

43. Wang, D., et al.: Human-AI collaboration in data science: exploring data scientists' perceptions of automated AI. Proc. ACM Hum. Comput. Interact. **3**(CSCW), 1–24 (2019)

44. Warnke, T., Helms, T., Uhrmacher, A.M.: Reproducible and flexible simulation experiments with ml-rules and SESSL. Bioinformatics **34**(8), 1424–1427 (2018). https://doi.org/10.1093/bioinformatics/btx741

45. Xin, D., Ma, L., Liu, J., Macke, S., Song, S., Parameswaran, A.: Accelerating human-in-the-loop machine learning: challenges and opportunities. In: Proceedings of the Second Workshop on Data Management for End-to-End Machine Learning, pp. 1–4 (2018)

46. Zhang, Z., Sparks, E.R., Franklin, M.J.: Diagnosing machine learning pipelines with fine-grained lineage. In: Proceedings of the 26th International Symposium on High-Performance Parallel and Distributed Computing, pp. 143–153 (2017)

Evidence Graphs: Supporting Transparent and FAIR Computation, with Defeasible Reasoning on Data, Methods, and Results

Sadnan Al Manir[1] , Justin Niestroy[1] , Maxwell Adam Levinson[1] ,
and Timothy Clark[1,2(✉)]

[1] Department of Public Health Sciences, University of Virginia, Charlottesville, VA, USA
twclark@virginia.edu
[2] School of Data Science, University of Virginia, Charlottesville, VA, USA

Abstract. *Introduction*: Transparency of computation is a requirement for assessing the validity of computed results and research claims based upon them; and it is essential for access to, assessment, and reuse of computational components. These components may be subject to methodological or other challenges over time. While reference to archived software and/or data is increasingly common in publications, a single machine-interpretable, integrative representation of how results were derived, that supports defeasible reasoning, has been absent.

Methods: We developed the Evidence Graph Ontology, EVI, in OWL 2, with a set of inference rules, to provide deep representations of supporting and challenging evidence for computations, services, software, data, and results, across arbitrarily deep networks of computations, in connected or fully distinct processes.

EVI integrates FAIR practices on data and software, with important concepts from provenance models, and argumentation theory. It extends PROV for additional expressiveness, with support for defeasible reasoning. EVI treats any computational result or component of evidence as a defeasible assertion, supported by a DAG of the computations, software, data, and agents that produced it.

Results: We have successfully deployed EVI for large-scale predictive analytics on clinical time-series data. Every result may reference its evidence graph as metadata, which can be extended when subsequent computations are executed.

Discussion: Evidence graphs support transparency and defeasible reasoning on results. They are first-class computational objects and reference the datasets and software from which they are derived. They support fully transparent computation, with challenge and support propagation. The EVI approach may be extended to include instruments, animal models, and critical experimental reagents.

Keywords: Provenance · Evidence graphs · Computation · FAIR

1 Introduction

1.1 Motivation

It is now increasingly understood that dramatically enhanced capabilities for generating and analyzing very large datasets, with increasingly sophisticated methods, require

© Springer Nature Switzerland AG 2021
B. Glavic et al. (Eds.): IPAW 2020/IPAW 2021, LNCS 12839, pp. 39–50, 2021.
https://doi.org/10.1007/978-3-030-80960-7_3

systematic referencing of archived datasets and software as persistent first-class objects, with some machine-readable record of their provenance. There is now beginning to be an additional, and necessary, focus on software citation, and provenance. Principles and methods for achieving these goals have been defined and are in various stages of transition to practice in the scientific communications ecosystem [1–11].

Incorporating these practices has been advocated to improve verifiability, replicability, reproducibility, and reusability of computational results. The goal, which was established as a requirement at the dawn of modern science [12–15], is to make the process by which results and the claims they support are arrived at, transparent, and to allow the methods involved to be inspected—at least virtually—for adequacy, and if possible, reused, and improved upon in various applications.

We would like to do this for computations, using a clean, formal, and integrated approach, that does not require "boiling the ocean"; and in which artifacts such as provenance records, which may benefit a broad community of research, are generated principally as side-effects of normal computational work. We do not want to place unwanted burdens or requirements on researchers, with which they cannot realistically be expected to comply. Any system or method that generates such artifacts ought to have other attributes of significant value to researchers. In particular, we would like an ontology providing these features to provide useful functionality in a *digital commons* environment, where asynchronous reuse of results by various researchers occurs, and not necessarily as coherent workflows.

Of course, all published scientific results (including mathematical proofs) [16–19], are provisional. Results, methods, reasoning, computations, and interpretations may be challenged by others in the community, and frequently are [20, 21]. A major reason for methodological transparency is to support such reviews and challenges. Results in science are reviewed "by a jury of peers", similarly to adversarial proceedings in law: a case is made, which may be argued for and against, based on evidence. Published "findings" or claims, and indeed computational results, are not facts. They are *defeasible assertions* [22], which rely upon a chain of evidence as warrants for belief. That makes them part of a chain of argumentation. We, therefore, treat computations and their provenance as defeasible arguments for provisional results.

1.2 Related Work

We previously undertook an analysis of the scientific communications life cycle to develop the Micropublications Ontology (MP) [23], which introduced a focus on chains of evidence and defeasible reasoning, and an emphasis on the nature of scientific claims as embedded in arguments. This approach was inspired by argumentation theory and by Greenberg's detailed model of citation distortion [24, 25], which highlights empirical issues with citation chains in the scientific literature. It was also motivated by a perceived tendency amongst some computer scientists to take claims in the biomedical literature as "facts", without subjecting them to further scrutiny.

Argumentation frameworks [26–34] and abstract dialectical frameworks [35, 36] are important sets of tools and concepts developed in the broader AI community, with an extensive literature. Bipolar Argumentation Frameworks (BAFs) as developed by Cayrol and others [31, 37, 38], allow both supporting and challenging arguments to be asserted and reasoned over in formal models. We discuss the relationship of our work to formal argumentation frameworks further in the Methods section.

The W3C PROV model [39–41] provides a well-thought-out and extensively tested set of core classes and properties, which may be used to document almost any computational provenance, in arbitrarily fine detail, and can serve as the basis for useful extensions. While PROV deals comprehensively and rigorously with core internal aspects of provenance, it does not engage explicitly with the role that provenance may play as evidence for computational results and interpretive claims. Nor does it conceptualize provenance as part of an argument for the validity of results, which may be countered, for example by later researchers finding bugs in code [42–45], flaws in datasets [46, 47], statistical errors [20], or fallacies in mathematical arguments [18].

Ontologies or schemas directly engaging the topic of experiments and experimental results include the Evidence and Claims Ontology (ECO) [48]; the Investigation, Study, Assay (ISA) model [49]; and the Ontology of Biomedical Investigations (OBI) [50]. All of these works are capable of representing machine-interpretable instances of scientific experiments within their proposed models and of offering limited provenance information. However, their focus is on characterizing individual experiments—principally in the wet lab—sometimes in exquisite detail, with over 4000 classes in OBI, which make it best suited to use by highly trained specialist annotators. None of these models directly treat computational results, and none treat results as components of argumentation.

The ambitious Nanopublications model [51–54], was developed to standardize the form of research claims by recasting them as RDF triples, and aggregating holotypic claims with their paratypes, thus making the claims computable in some sense. What the nanopublications model currently lacks, is the ability to show evidential support in argumentation for the results it models.

Finally, there are related works that deal with computational results by packaging them up with their provenance records and other materials for citation or reference in metadata. These would include the Research Objects (RO) model [55–57] and its companion, RO-Crate [58]. The initial RO publication states as an explicit goal, replacing the "static PDF" form of scientific publication, and as such RO provides an integration framework across many related models involved in scientific specification, description, and communication. RO-Crate is a lightweight packaging initiative, or implementation realization, for RO and related material.

2   Methods

Cayrol and Lagasquie-Schiex's work on BAFs supplied inspiration for our approach; which has, however, somewhat different semantics from their model, regarding the support relation, and the meaning of an argument.

In BAFs, arguments are opaque, and without internal structure. This extremely abstract treatment derives from Dung's original presentation [33], enhanced to provide explicit bipolarity. In BAFs, if an argument A supports B, it agrees with B, similar to having an ally in a dispute. Therefore, an attack of C upon A also attacks B.

Our model, in contrast, treats support as it occurs in the scientific literature, as supporting evidence cited by the author of an argument. If C challenges A, a challenge by C on the supporting evidence for A cannot be inferred. However, as in Toulmin argumentation, and the work of Verheij [59–61], a challenge to A's supporting evidence undercuts A—it reduces the *warrant for belief* in A.

Evidence graphs in our approach may be represented abstractly as:

$$EG = \langle A, R+, R- \rangle, \text{ where:} \tag{1}$$

A is a set of representations;
$R+ \in A \times A$ is the set of *support* relations;
$R- \in A \times A$ is the set of *challenge* relations; and
$R+ \cap R- = \emptyset$

In our treatment, Representations are generalized forms of the various types of assertions and evidence found in the scientific literature. All Representations have provenance, if only to the extent that they have authorship. A Representation may be a statement, or a set of assertions, claims, or declarations, with provenance as its support.

The simplest form of provenance is the attribution of an assertion to an *Agent*. A declarative sentence is an argument of this simple form, where a statement's attribution is its simplest supporting evidence. This corresponds to Aristotle's view of argument as having a significant measure of support from ήθος (ethos), the character of the speaker [62]; and relates to our common experience of tending to give more credence to statements from trusted, highly reputed sources. This notion can be extended to results produced by computational agents whose operations are well-validated and transparent.

A *Method* or *Material* representation in a publication, provided as provenance, constitutes a set of assertions about what was done to get a result. Software source code is a set of assertions of this form when used in a provenance description for a computation.

Source code has a dual nature, in that as a set of instructions, it is a collection of performatives [63], not evaluable as strictly true or false. We distinguish here between software as a set of instructions to a computer, which does something; and software provided as a description of what was done by the computer, i.e. "it ran this code".

We have adapted these notions to computational provenance representation. We base our model on the following key ideas:

- All data, methods descriptions, and results are sets of defeasible assertions.
- The evidence for the correctness of any result is the record of its provenance.
- Subsequent research or discussion may challenge results, datasets, or methods.

The EVI ontology is a formal representation of the evidence for any result or claim as an EvidenceGraph, which unifies existing models for both software and data citation and supports machine-based defeasible reasoning.

We first introduced several of the concepts used in EVI in our previous work on Micropublications. EVI simplifies, revises, and adapts many features of the micropublications model to a purely computational digital commons environment, where evidence graphs may be generated by a computation service. The computation service we developed, described elsewhere [64], provides affordances to the user by greatly simplifying access to very large-scale data and underlying parallel computation and workflow services. At the same time, it produces and extends evidence graphs transparently, as a side effect.

3 Results

EVI is an extension of W3C PROV, based on argumentation theory, which enables defeasible reasoning about computations, their results, data, and software. It can be extended to incorporate non-computational evidence important to the results of a computation, for example, the specific instrument (manufacturer and catalog number) used to obtain a dataset or the reagent used in a binding assay.

Evidence Graphs are directed acyclic graphs, DAGs, produced by a service when a computation is run. They are first-class digital objects and may have their own persistent identifiers and be referenced as part of the metadata of any result. They may be arbitrarily deep. We model these using an OWL 2 vocabulary and set of rules [65, 66] which provide for propagation of support and challenge relations, with direct supports/challenges distinguished from indirect. A diagram of the classes and relations is provided in Fig. 1.

The classes within the dotted-line box in the figure are basic PROV classes: *Entity*, *Agent*, and *Activity*. All relations in the box are subproperties of PROV relations.

The argumentation relations *supports* and *challenges* are introduced on the new class, *Representation*, a subclass of *prov:Entity*. A *Representation* is a *prov:Entity* that *represents* another *Entity*. All digital objects in EVI are considered to be *Representations*, which may contain other *Representations*.

Supports and *challenges* are superproperties of *directlySupports* and *directlyChallenges* (not shown in the Figure). *Supports* is transitive, *directlySupports* is not. *DirectlySupports* is a superproperty of the relation *usedBy* (inverse of *prov:used*), and of the property *generates* (inverse of generatedBy) so that if a recorded *Activity* D used a particular *Representation* C as input, and *generates* E as output, then C *directlySupports* D and D *directlySupports* E.

This is shown in Example 1 below, illustrating how the property chain rule evaluates distant support in the graph, where <s> stands for the *supports* property, and <dS> stands for *directlySupports*.

$$(D \langle used \rangle\ C \wedge D \langle generates \rangle\ E) \Rightarrow \qquad (2)$$

$$(C \langle dS \rangle\ D \wedge D \langle dS \rangle\ E) \Rightarrow$$

$$(C \langle s \rangle\ D \wedge D \langle s \rangle\ E) \Rightarrow C \langle s \rangle\ E$$

Supports and *directlySupports* properties are distinguished in this way because they serve different purposes in the model. The *directlySupports* property gives us our DAG, connecting the various Representations to form an evidence graph. It is simply a generalization over several PROV properties. The *supports* property is transitive and allows us to infer distant support relations. By analogy with genealogical trees, *directlySupports* equates roughly to *hasParent* relations; *supports* equates roughly to *has-Ancestor* relations.

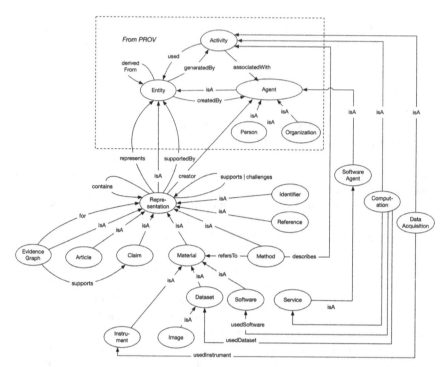

Fig. 1. Classes and relations in the Evidence Graph Ontology, EVI. https://w3id.org/EVI

Articles, *Claims*, *Material* (as used in a typical "Materials and Methods" section), *Methods* (likewise), and *EvidenceGraphs* themselves, are *Representations*. A *Method* describes an *Activity* that may *referTo* a *Material*. The class *Material* is iteratively subclassed into *Instrument, Dataset, Image, Software*, and *Downloads*. *Downloads* are particular distributions of a *Dataset* or *Software*, representing e.g. different formats of a *Dataset*, in the same manner, this approach is used in the schema.org class *DataDownload*. An *Agent* in EVI may be a *SoftwareAgent, Person*, or *Organization*. A *Service* *usedBy* a *Computation* is a kind of *SoftwareAgent*. An *Activity* may be a *DataAcquisition* or a *Computation*.

Detailed formal definitions of all these terms, and equivalent schema.org [67] terms where they exist, are provided in the ontology description page at https://w3id.org, which has the latest updates. The OWL 2 vocabulary and its version history are on GitHub, here: https://github.com/EvidenceGraph/EVI/blob/master/Ontology/versions/v0.2/evi.owl, and the version we used for this article, is archived on Zenodo [68].

The diagram in Fig. 1 omits detail relevant to rules and supports/challenges propagation, for pictorial clarity. The *supports* and *challenges* properties have subproperties *directlySupports, indirectlySupports, directlyChallenges*, and *indirectlyChallenges*, not shown in the figure. The *supports* property is propagated through the evidence graph via transitivity on *supports*.

$$(A\ directlySupports\ B \wedge B\ directlySupports\ C) \Rightarrow A\ supports\ C \qquad (3)$$

Challenges are propagated through a property chain on *challenges* and *supports*.

$$(A \; supports \; B \; \wedge \; X \; challenges \; A) \Rightarrow X \; challenges \; B \tag{4}$$

4 Discussion

In developing and validating our approach, we performed a very large-scale time series analysis of 10 years of vital signs time series data from the Neonatal Intensive Care Unit (NICU) at the University of Virginia Hospital, collected on 5957 infants. This extended proof-of-concept was a significant research study in its own right, in which NICU time series were analyzed using 80 different algorithms in 11 mathematical families from diverse domains [69]. Computations were performed over a period of 15 months, in various stages, using the FAIRSCAPE microservices framework [64], producing an evidence graph of 17,996 nodes [70]. This evidence graph is queryable from a Stardog™ quad store via one of the microservices and is also deposited in the University of Virginia's Dataverse with a *prov:wasDerivedFrom* property associating it with the underlying dataset, which is also in Dataverse [71].

Whether using our FAIRSCAPE framework or some other approach, EVI statements are intended to be transparently generated by a *computation service*, similar to how ordinary PROV statements are generated by workflow engines. Thus, evidence graphs become side effects of doing useful computations. In our case, these computations are run within a FAIR digital commons environment.

Figure 2 illustrates a section of this graph for one of the 5957 subjects in the NICU analysis. In our microservices framework the EvidenceGraph service stores and retrieves the graphs in a Stardog™ RDF quad store, which also performs the inferencing. The PATH query, an extension to SPARQL, generates an *EvidenceGraph* DAG from the root object, using the *directlySupportedBy* abstraction (not shown here) to structure the graph and the *supports* superproperty of its transitive inverse, *supportedBy*, to infer distant evidential support.

As can be seen in the example, every node in the graph has a persistent identifier, based on the ARK system [72] in our implementation. This approach provides the important unification of all available digital evidence for (and potentially, against) a result, by supporting persistent resolution to the cited objects.

One could ask, in a practical sense, if a challenge is made to some leaf node deep in the graph, should it always invalidate the root assertion? The answer to this is that challenges do not invalidate, they present an opposing view. They ultimately require human judgment as to their validity and strength. We do, however, wish to know about them. This becomes important in digital commons environments, and in, for example, meta-analyses reusing prior results. It can have a further impact if computational results are properly referenced and tied to textual claims in citation networks, such as those explored by Greenberg [24] and others.

We believe that EVI provides an important generalization of provenance as evidence for correctness, which can be further extended beyond computation to include the other types of evidence presented in scientific publications, for example by including identifiers such as RRIDs [73] of important experimental reagents and animal models in the protocols from which the data was derived. Our end goal is to be able to provide, with the metadata of any datasets we store in an archive, a link to the corresponding evidence graph. With this practice, any result presented in a publication, with appropriate data citation, ought to be resolvable to its entire evidence graph, and transitively closed to its components. Future research directions include extended support for packaging evidence graphs; support for extended descriptive metadata; service integration with data and software archives; and continued alignment with other initiatives in this space. As a component of the FAIRSCAPE digital commons framework, we plan for EVI to continue its evolution with direct input from computational users.

```
{'@context': {'@vocab': 'http://schema.org/', 'evi': 'http://w3id.org/EVI#'},
 '@id': 'ark:59853/4d38f7c2-4f19-409e-a864-fa3734fe7f2a',
 '@type': 'Dataset',
 'evi:generatedBy': {'@id': 'ark:59853/f581d2cc-8709-4110-8f1c-eac767065e72',
 '@type': 'evi:Computation',
 'evi:usedDataset': {'@id': 'ark:59853/7fe5f0a8-a65c-458d-a8dc-448a72a36da7',
  '@type': 'Dataset',
  'evi:generatedBy': {'@id': 'ark:59853/de0e548c-2471-47da-8732-eac617c63b54',
   '@type': 'evi:Computation',
   'evi:usedDataset': {'@id': 'ark:59853/b845a90e-b126-4676-bc17-3db5b2677fb1',
    '@type': 'Dataset',
    'author': {'@id': 'https://orcid.org/0000-0002-1103-3882',
     '@type': 'Person',
     'name': 'Justin Niestroy'},
    'name': 'Raw Time Series Feature Set'},
   'evi:usedSoftware': {'@id': 'ark:59853/4fedddb5-7674-4ece-8a64-c595c50f5685',
    '@type': 'SoftwareSourceCode',
    'author': {'@id': 'https://orcid.org/0000-0002-1103-3882',
     '@type': 'Person',
     'name': 'Justin Niestroy'},
    'name': 'Raw Data Analysis Script'},
   'name': 'Computation'},
  'name': 'part-00000-ed4b79c0-43f8-437d-9959-a98c9d63be39-c000.csv'},
 'evi:usedSoftware': {'@id': 'ark:59853/789b5f8e-2277-4e64-847e-86b201b4660a',
  '@type': 'SoftwareSourceCode',
  'author': {'@id': 'https://orcid.org/0000-0002-1103-3882',
   '@type': 'Person',
   'name': 'Justin Niestroy'},
  'name': 'HCTSA Cluster Script'},
 'name': 'Computation'},
 'name': 'HCTSA Heatmap.png'}
```

Fig. 2. JSON-LD of a portion of the evidence graph for one of the 5997 infant subjects from clustering step in comparative time-series analysis, adapted from [64].

Information Sharing Statement

- The EVI ontology OWL2 vocabulary is available at https://w3id.org/EVI# under MIT license.

Acknowledgements. We thank Chris Baker (University of New Brunswick), Carole Goble (University of Manchester), and John Kunze (California Digital Library) for helpful discussions. This work was supported in part by the U.S. National Institutes of Health, grant NIH 1U01HG009452; and by a grant from the Coulter Foundation.

References

1. Cousijn, H., et al.: A data citation roadmap for scientific publishers. Sci. Data **5**, 180259 (2018). https://doi.org/10.1038/sdata.2018.259
2. Data Citation Synthesis Group: Joint declaration of data citation principles. In: Future of Research Communication and e-Scholarship (FORCE11), San Diego (2014)
3. Fenner, M., et al.: A data citation roadmap for scholarly data repositories. Sci. Data **6**, 28 (2019). https://doi.org/10.1038/s41597-019-0031-8
4. Groth, P., Cousijn, H., Clark, T., Goble, C.: FAIR data reuse—the path through data citation. Data Intell. **2**, 78–86 (2020). https://doi.org/10.1162/dint_a_00030
5. Juty, N., Wimalaratne, S.M., Soiland-Reyes, S., Kunze, J., Goble, C.A., Clark, T.: Unique, persistent, resolvable: identifiers as the foundation of FAIR. Data Intell. **2**, 30–39 (2020). https://doi.org/10.5281/zenodo.3267434
6. Katz, D.S., et al.: Recognizing the value of software: a software citation guide. F1000Research **9**, 1257 (2021). https://doi.org/10.12688/f1000research.26932.2
7. Katz, D.S., Gruenpeter, M., Honeyman, T.: Taking a fresh look at FAIR for research software. Patterns **2**(3), 100222 (2021). https://doi.org/10.1016/j.patter.2021.100222
8. Smith, A.M., Katz, D.S., Niemeyer, K.E.: FORCE11 Software Citation Working Group: software citation principles. PeerJ Comput. Sci. **2**, e86 (2016). https://doi.org/10.7717/peerj-cs.86
9. Starr, J., et al.: Achieving human and machine accessibility of cited data in scholarly publications. PeerJ Comput. Sci. **1**, e1 (2015). https://doi.org/10.7717/peerj-cs.1
10. Wilkinson, M.D., et al.: The FAIR Guiding Principles for scientific data management and stewardship. Sci. Data **3**, 160018 (2016)
11. Wimalaratne, S.M., et al.: Uniform resolution of compact identifiers for biomedical data. Sci. Data **5**, 180029 (2018). https://doi.org/10.1038/sdata.2018.29
12. Dear, P.: Revolutionizing the Sciences: European Knowledge and Its Ambitions, 1500–1700. Princeton University Press, Princeton and Oxford (2009)
13. Holmes, F.L.: Argument and narrative in scientific writing. In: Dear, P. (ed.) The Literary Structure of Scientific Argument: Historical Studies, p. 224. University of Pennsylvania Press, Philadelphia (1991)
14. Rossi, P.: Philosophy, Technology, and the Arts in the Early Modern Era. Harper & Row, New York (1970)
15. Shapin, S.: Pump and circumstance: Robert Boyle's literary technology. In: Hellyer, M. (ed.) The Scientific Revolution. Blackwell, Oxford (2003)
16. Committee on Science: Engineering, and Public Policy of the National Academies: On Being a Scientist: Responsible Conduct in Research. National Academies Press, Washington (1995)
17. Lakatos, I.: Proofs and Refutations. Cambridge University Press, Cambridge (1976)
18. Maxwell, E.A.: Fallacies in Mathematics. Cambridge University Press, Cambridge (1959)
19. Krabbe, E.C.W.: Strategic maneuvering in mathematical proofs. Argumentation **22**, 453–468 (2008). https://doi.org/10.1007/s10503-008-9098-7
20. Ioannidis, J.P.A.: Why most published research findings are false. PLoS Med. **2**, e124 (2005). https://doi.org/10.1371/journal.pmed.0020124
21. Ioannidis, J.A.: Contradicted and initially stronger effects in highly cited clinical research. JAMA **294**, 218–228 (2005). https://doi.org/10.1001/jama.294.2.218
22. Koons, R.: Defeasible Reasoning (2013). http://plato.stanford.edu/archives/spr2014/entries/reasoning-defeasible/
23. Clark, T., Ciccarese, P.N., Goble, C.A.: Micropublications: a semantic model for claims, evidence, arguments and annotations in biomedical communications. J. Biomed. Semant. **5**, 28 (2014). https://doi.org/10.1186/2041-1480-5-28

24. Greenberg, S.A.: Understanding belief using citation networks. J. Eval. Clin. Pract. **17**, 389–393 (2011). https://doi.org/10.1111/j.1365-2753.2011.01646.x
25. Greenberg, S.A.: How citation distortions create unfounded authority: analysis of a citation network. BMJ **339**, b2680 (2009). https://doi.org/10.1136/bmj.b2680
26. Bench-Capon, T.J.M., Dunne, P.E.: Argumentation in artificial intelligence. Artif. Intell. **171**, 619–641 (2007). https://doi.org/10.1016/j.artint.2007.05.001
27. Besnard, P., Hunter, A.: Elements of Argumentation. MIT Press, Cambridge (2008)
28. Boella, G., Gabbay, D.M., Van Der Torre, L., Villata, S.: Support in abstract argumentation. In: Baroni, P., et al. (eds.) Computational Models of Argument. IOS Press, Amsterdam (2010)
29. Brewka, G., Polberg, S., Woltran, S.: Generalizations of dung frameworks and their role in formal argumentation. IEEE Intell. Syst. **29**, 30–38 (2014). https://doi.org/10.1109/MIS.2013.122
30. Carrera, Á., Iglesias, C.A.: A systematic review of argumentation techniques for multi-agent systems research. Artif. Intell. Rev. **44**(4), 509–535 (2015). https://doi.org/10.1007/s10462-015-9435-9
31. Cayrol, C., Lagasquie-Schiex, M.C.: Bipolar abstract argumentation systems. In: Rahwan, I., Simari, G.R. (eds.) Argumentation in Artificial Intelligence. Springer, Dordrecht (2009). https://doi.org/10.1007/978-0-387-98197-0_4
32. Cohen, A., Gottifredi, S., García, A.J., Simari, G.R.: An approach to abstract argumentation with recursive attack and support. J. Appl. Log. **13**, 509–533 (2015). https://doi.org/10.1016/j.jal.2014.12.001
33. Dung, P.M.: On the acceptability of arguments and its fundamental role in nonmonotonic reasoning, logic programming and n-person games. Artif. Intell. **77**, 321–357 (1995). https://doi.org/10.1016/0004-3702(94)00041-x
34. Oren, N., Norman, T.J.: Semantics for Evidence-Based Argumentation, p. 9. IOS Press, Amsterdam (2003)
35. Brewka, G., Woltran, S.: Abstract Dialectical Frameworks, p. 10 (2010)
36. Dung, P.M., Thang, P.M.: Representing the semantics of abstract dialectical frameworks based on arguments and attacks. Argum. Comput. **9**, 249–267 (2018). https://doi.org/10.3233/AAC-180427
37. Cayrol, C., Lagasquie-Schiex, M.-C.: Coalitions of arguments: a tool for handling bipolar argumentation frameworks. Int. J. Intell. Syst. **25**, 83–109 (2010). https://doi.org/10.1002/int.20389
38. Cayrol, C., Lagasquie-Schiex, M.-C.: Bipolarity in argumentation graphs: towards a better understanding. Int. J. Approximate Reasoning **54**, 876–899 (2013). https://doi.org/10.1016/j.ijar.2013.03.001
39. Gil, Y., et al.: PROV Model Primer: W3C Working Group Note 30 April 2013 (2013). https://www.w3.org/TR/prov-primer/
40. Lebo, T., et al.: PROV-O: The PROV Ontology W3C Recommendation 30 April 2013 (2013)
41. Moreau, L., et al.: PROV-DM: The PROV Data Model: W3C Recommendation 30 April 2013. World Wide Web Consortium (2013)
42. Soergel, D.A.W.: Rampant software errors may undermine scientific results. F1000Research **3**, 303 (2015). https://doi.org/10.12688/f1000research.5930.2
43. Neupane, J.B., Neupane, R.P., Luo, Y., Yoshida, W.Y., Sun, R., Williams, P.G.: Characterization of leptazolines A–D, polar oxazolines from the cyanobacterium Leptolyngbya sp., reveals a glitch with the "Willoughby–Hoye" scripts for calculating NMR chemical shifts. Org. Lett. **21**(20), 8449–8453 (2019). https://doi.org/10.1021/acs.orglett.9b03216
44. Miller, G.: A scientist's nightmare: software problem leads to five retractions. Science **314**, 1856–1857 (2006). https://doi.org/10.1126/science.314.5807.1856
45. Axelrod, V.: Minimizing bugs in cognitive neuroscience programming. Front. Psychol. **5**, 1435 (2014). https://doi.org/10.3389/fpsyg.2014.01435

46. Brown, A.W., Kaiser, K.A., Allison, D.B.: Issues with data and analyses: errors, underlying themes, and potential solutions. Proc. Natl. Acad. Sci. USA **115**, 2563–2570 (2018). https://doi.org/10.1073/pnas.1708279115
47. Goldberg, S.I., Niemierko, A., Turchin, A.: Analysis of Data Errors in Clinical Research Databases. **5**
48. Giglio, M., et al.: ECO, the evidence and conclusion ontology: community standard for evidence information. Nucleic Acids Res. **47**, D1186–D1194 (2019). https://doi.org/10.1093/nar/gky1036
49. Rocca-Serra, P., et al.: ISA software suite: supporting standards-compliant experimental annotation and enabling curation at the community level. Bioinformatics **26**, 2354–2356 (2010). https://doi.org/10.1093/bioinformatics/btq415
50. Bandrowski, A., et al.: The ontology for biomedical investigations. PLoS ONE **11**, e0154556 (2016). https://doi.org/10.1371/journal.pone.0154556
51. Velterop, J.: Nanopublications: the future of coping with information overload. LOGOS **21**, 119–122 (2010). https://doi.org/10.1163/095796511X560006
52. Gibson, A., van Dam, J., Schultes, E., Roos, M., Mons, B.: Towards computational evaluation of evidence for scientific assertions with nanopublications and cardinal assertions. In: Proceedings of the 5th International Workshop on Semantic Web Applications and Tools for Life Sciences (SWAT4LS), Paris, pp. 28–30 (2012)
53. Groth, P., Gibson, A., Velterop, J.: The anatomy of a nano-publication. Inf. Serv. Use **30**, 51–56 (2010). https://doi.org/10.3233/ISU-2010-0613
54. Schultes, E., et al.: The Open PHACTS Nanopublication Guidelines V1.8. EU Innovative Medicines Initiative—Open PHACTS Project RDF/Nanopublication Working Group (2012)
55. DeRoure, D., Goble, C.: Lessons from myExperiment: Research Objects for Data Intensive Research. Presented at the eScience Workshop (2009)
56. Bechhofer, S., Roure, D.D., Gamble, M., Goble, C., Buchan, I.: Research objects: towards exchange and reuse of digital knowledge. Presented at the Future of the Web for Collaborative Science (FWCS), 19th International World Wide Web Conference (WWW 2010) 26 April (2010)
57. Belhajjame, K., et al.: Using a suite of ontologies for preserving workflow-centric research objects. J. Web Semant. **32**, 16–42 (2015). https://doi.org/10.1016/j.websem.2015.01.003
58. Carragáin, E.Ó., Goble, C., Sefton, P., Soiland-Reyes, S.: A lightweight approach to research object data packaging (2019). https://doi.org/10.5281/ZENODO.3250687
59. Toulmin, S.E.: The Uses of Argument. Cambridge University Press, Cambridge (2003)
60. Verheij, B.: Evaluating arguments based on Toulmin's scheme. Argumentation **19**, 347–371 (2005). https://doi.org/10.1007/s10503-005-4421-z
61. Verheij, B.: The Toulmin argument model in artificial intelligence. Or: how semi-formal, defeasible argumentation schemes creep into logic. In: Rahwan, I., Simari, G. (eds.) Argumentation in Artificial Intellgence. Springer, Dordrecht (2009). https://doi.org/10.1007/978-0-387-98197-0_11
62. Aristotle: Rhetoric. Dover Publications, Mineola (2004)
63. Austin, J.L.: How to Do Things with Words. Harvard University Press, Cambridge (1962)
64. Levinson, M.A., et al.: FAIRSCAPE: a framework for FAIR and reproducible biomedical analytics. 2020.08.10.244947 (2020). https://doi.org/10.1101/2020.08.10.244947
65. OWL 2 Working Group: OWL 2 Web Ontology Language: W3C Recommendation 27 October 2009. World Wide Web Consortium, Cambridge (2009)
66. Al Manir, S., Niestroy, J., Levinson, M., Clark, T.: EVI: The Evidence Graph Ontology, OWL 2 Vocabulary, Zenodo (2021)
67. Guha, R.V., Brickley, D., Macbeth, S.: Schema.org: evolution of structured data on the web. Commun. ACM **59**(2), 44–51 (2016). https://doi.org/10.1145/2844544

68. Troupin, C., Muñoz, C., Fernández, J.G.: Scientific results traceability: software citation using GitHub and Zenodo. **4** (2018)

69. Niestroy, J., et al.: Discovery of signatures of fatal neonatal illness in vital signs using highly comparative time-series analysis. BioRXiv. 2021.03.26.437138 (2021). https://doi.org/10.1101/2021.03.26.437138

70. Niestroy, J., Levinson, M.A., Al Manir, S., Clark, T.: Evidence graph for: discovery of signatures of fatal neonatal illness in vital signs using highly comparative time-series analysis (2021). https://doi.org/10.18130/V3/HHTAYI

71. Niestroy, J., et al.: Replication data for: discovery of signatures of fatal neonatal illness in vital signs using highly comparative time-series analysis, V2 (2021). https://doi.org/10.18130/V3/VJXODP

72. Kunze, J., Rodgers, R.: The ARK Identifier Scheme (2008). https://escholarship.org/uc/item/9p9863nc

73. Bandrowski, A.E., Martone, M.E.: RRIDs: a simple step toward improving reproducibility through rigor and transparency of experimental methods. Neuron **90**, 434–436 (2016). https://doi.org/10.1016/j.neuron.2016.04.030

The PROV-JSONLD Serialization
A JSON-LD Representation for the PROV Data Model

Luc Moreau[⊠] and Trung Dong Huynh

Department of Informatics, King's College London,
Bush House, 30 Aldwych, London WC2B 4BG, UK
{luc.moreau,dong.huynh}@kcl.ac.uk

Abstract. Provenance is information about entities, activities, and people involved in producing a piece of data or a thing, which can be used to form assessments about the data or the thing's quality, reliability, or trustworthiness. PROV-DM is the conceptual data model that forms the basis for the W3C provenance (PROV) family of specifications. In this paper, we propose a new serialization for PROV in JSON called PROV-JSONLD. It provides a lightweight representation of PROV expressions in JSON, which is suitable to be processed by Web applications, while maintaining a natural encoding that is familiar with PROV practitioners. In addition, PROV-JSONLD exploits JSON-LD to define a semantic mapping that conforms to the PROV-O specification and, hence, the encoded PROV expressions can be readily processed as Linked Data. Finally, we show that the serialization is also efficiently processable in our evaluation. Overall, PROV-JSONLD is designed to be suitable for interchanging provenance information in Web and Linked Data applications, to offer a natural encoding of provenance for its targeted audience, and to allow for fast processing.

1 Introduction

Since their release in 2013, the PROV Recommendations [4] by the World Wide Web Consortium (W3C) have started being adopted by flagship deployments such as the Global Change Information System,[1] the Gazette[2] in the UK, and other Linked Datasets. PROV, which is used as the data model to describe the provenance of data, is made available in several different representations: PROV-N [13], PROV-XML [6], or in an RDF serialization using the PROV Ontology (PROV-O) [10]. The latter, arguably, is most suitable for Linked Data [5], given that it can readily be consumed by existing Semantic Web tools and comes with

---

[1] https://data.globalchange.gov.
[2] https://www.thegazette.co.uk.

T. D. Huynh—This work was partially supported by the UK Engineering and Physical Sciences Research Council (EPRSC Grant EP/S027238/1) and the US Department of Navy award (N62909-18-1-2079) issued by the Office of Naval Research Global. The United States Government has a royalty-free license throughout the world in all copyrightable material contained herein.

© Springer Nature Switzerland AG 2021
B. Glavic et al. (Eds.): IPAW 2020/IPAW 2021, LNCS 12839, pp. 51–67, 2021.
https://doi.org/10.1007/978-3-030-80960-7_4

the semantic grounding provided by PROV-O. Surprisingly, the PROV-JSON [7] serialization has gained traction, despite simply being a member submission to the W3C, and not having gone through the various stages of a standardization activity. The primary reason for this, we conjecture, is that many Web applications are built to be lightweight, working mainly with simple data formats such as JSON [2].

The very existence of all these serializations is a testament to the approach to standardization taken by the Provenance Working Group, by which a conceptual data model for PROV was defined, the PROV data model (PROV-DM) [12], alongside its mapping to different technologies, to suit users and developers. However, the family of PROV specifications lacks a serialization that is capable of addressing all of the following requirements.

R1 A serialization must support **lightweight** Web applications.

R2 A serialization must look **natural** to its targeted community of users.

R3 A serialization must allow for **semantic** markup and integration with linked data applications.

R4 A serialization must be processable in an **efficient** manner.

Surprisingly, none of the existing PROV serializations supports all these requirements simultaneously. While PROV-JSON is the only serialization to support lightweight Web applications, it does not have any semantic markup, its internal structure does not exhibit the natural structure of the PROV data structures, and its grouping of expressions per categories (e.g. all entities, all activities,...) is not conducive to incremental processing. The RDF serialization compatible with PROV-O has been architected to be natural to the Semantic Web community: all influence relations have been given the same directionality with respect to their time ordering, but the decomposition of data structures (essentially n-ary relations) into individual triples, which can occur anywhere in the serialization, is not conducive to efficient parsing. It is reasonable to say that the world has moved on from XML, while the PROV-N notation was aimed at humans rather than efficient processing.

Against that background, JSON-LD [15] allows a semantic structure to be overlaid over a JSON structure, thereby enabling the interpretation of JSON serializations as Linked Data. This was exploited in an early version of this work [8], which applied the JSON-LD approach to a JSON serialization of PROV. The solution, however, did not lead to a natural encoding of the PROV data structure, because a property occurring in different types of JSON objects had to be named differently so that it could be uniquely mapped to the appropriate RDF property; we observe here that what is natural in JSON is not necessarily natural in RDF, and vice-versa. The ability to define scoped contextual mappings was introduced in JSON-LD 1.1 [9] and is a key enabler of this work, allowing for the same natural PROV property names to be used in different contexts while still maintaining their correct mappings to the appropriate RDF properties.

Thus, this paper proposes PROV-JSONLD, a serialization of PROV that is compatible with PROV-DM and that addresses all of our four key requirements above. It is first and foremost a JSON structure so it supports lightweight

Web applications. It is structured in such a way that each PROV expression is encoded as a self-contained JSON object and, therefore, is natural to JavaScript programmers. Exploiting JSON-LD 1.1, we defined contextual semantic mappings, allowing a PROV-JSONLD document to be readily consumed as Linked Data that is conforming to the PROV Ontology. Finally, PROV-JSONLD allows for efficient processing since each JSON object can be readily mapped to a data structure, without requiring unbounded lookaheads, or search within the data structure.

In the remainder of this paper, we provide an illustration of PROV-JSONLD in Sect. 2; we then define its structure by means of a JSON Schema [1] in Sect. 3 and its JSON-LD semantic mapping in Sect. 4. We outline the interoperability testing we put in place to check its compatibility with the PROV data model in Sect. 5 and evaluate the efficiency of PROV-JSONLD processing in Sect. 6. Section 7 concludes the paper with an outline for future work.

2   Example

To illustrate the proposed PROV-JSONLD serialization, we consider a subset of the example of PROV-PRIMER [3], depicted in Fig. 1. It can be paraphrased as follows: agent Derek was responsible for composing an article based on a dataset.

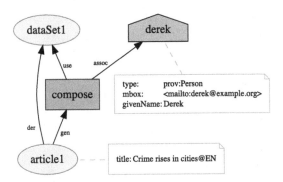

Fig. 1. Provenance expressing that Derek was responsible for composing an article based on a dataset.

The PROV-JSONLD representation of this example can be seen in Listing 1. At the top level, a PROV-JSONLD document is a JSON object with two properties @context and @graph, as per JSON-LD. A context contains mappings of prefixes to namespaces, and also an explicit reference to https://openprovenance. org/prov-jsonld/context.json, the JSON-LD 1.1 context defining the semantic mapping for PROV-JSONLD, which is described in Sect. 4. The @graph property has an array of PROV expressions as value. Each PROV expression itself is a JSON object with at least a @type property (for instance, prov:Entity, prov:Agent or prov:Derivation). Each of these PROV expressions provides a description for

```
1   {
2     "@context": [ {
3       "dcterms": "http://purl.org/dc/terms/",
4       "ex"     : "http://example/",
5       "foaf"    : "http://xmlns.com/foaf/0.1/"
6     }, "https://openprovenance.org/prov-jsonld/context.json" ],
7     "@graph" : [ {
8       "@type" : "prov:Entity",
9       "@id"   : "ex:dataSet1"
10    }, {
11      "@type" : "prov:Entity",
12      "@id"    : "ex:article1",
13      "dcterms:title": [
14        { "@value" : "Crime rises in cities", "@language" : "EN" }
15      ]
16    }, {
17      "@type"            : "prov:Derivation",
18      "generatedEntity" : "ex:article1",
19      "usedEntity"      : "ex:dataSet1"
20    }, {
21      "@type"           : "prov:Agent",
22      "@id"             : "ex:derek",
23      "foaf:mbox"       : [ { "@value" : "<mailto:derek@example.org>" } ],
24      "prov:type"       : [ "prov:Person" ],
25      "foaf:givenName"  : [ { "@value" : "Derek" } ]
26    }, {
27      "@type"    : "prov:Association",
28      "activity" : "ex:compose",
29      "agent"    : "ex:derek"
30    }, {
31      "@type"    : "prov:Activity",
32      "@id"      : "ex:compose"
33    }, {
34      "@type"    : "prov:Usage",
35      "activity" : "ex:compose",
36      "entity"   : "ex:dataSet1"
37    }, {
38      "@type"    : "prov:Generation",
39      "entity"   : "ex:article1",
40      "activity" : "ex:compose"
41    } ]
42  }
```

Listing 1: The PROV-JSONLD representation of Fig. 1.

a resource, some of which are identified by the @id property (for instance, ex:article1 or ex:derek). Some of the resources are anonymous and, therefore, do not have a property @id, for instance, the prov:Derivation relation between the dataset and the article (Line 17–19).

PROV expressions can be enriched with a variety of properties. Some of which are "reserved" such as `activity` and `agent` in a prov:Association. Others may be defined in a different namespace such as `foaf:givenName`, for which we expect the prefix `foaf` to be declared in the `@context` property. Finally, further PROV attributes are allowed, for instance, `prov:type` with an array of further types, to better describe the resource.

The property `@type` is mandatory and is associated with a single value, expected to be one of the predefined PROV expression types. From an efficiency viewpoint, this property is critical in determining which internal data structure a PROV expression should map to and, therefore, facilitates efficient processing. On the contrary, `prov:type` is optional and can contain as many types as required; their order is not significant.

3 PROV-JSONLD Schema

In this section, we provide an overview of the JSON schema [1] for PROV-JSONLD; the full schema is available at https://openprovenance.org/prov-jsonld/schema.json.

3.1 Preliminary Definitions

Some primitive types, namely `DateTime` and `QualifiedName`, occur in PROV serializations. We define their schema[3] as follows.

```
{ "DateTime": {
    "$id": "#/definitions/DateTime",
    "type": "string",
    "format": "date-time" },
  "QualifiedName": {
    "$id": "#/definitions/QualifiedName",
    "type": "string", "default": "",
    "pattern": "^[A-Za-z0-9_]+:(.*)$" },
}
```

In addition, we define typed values (`typed_value`) as JSON objects with properties `@value` and `@type` and string values `lang_string` as objects with properties `@value` and `@language`.

```
{ "typed_value": {
    "type": "object", "required": [ "@value", "@type" ],
    "properties": {
      "@value": { "type": "string" },
      "@type":  { "type": "string" }
    },
```

---

[3] The production rules for qualified names are more complex than the simple regular expression outlined here. A post-processor will need to check that qualified names comply with the definition in [13].

```
        "additionalProperties": false },
      "lang_string": {
        "type": "object", "required": [ "@value" ],
        "properties": {
          "@value":    { "type": "string" },
          "@language": { "type": "string" }
        },
        "additionalProperties": false }
}
```

We also define types for collections of property values, which can be arrays of values (`ArrayOfValues`) or arrays of labels (`ArrayOfLabelValues`).

```
{ "ArrayOfValues": {
    "$id": "#/definitions/ArrayOfValues", "type": "array",
    "items": {
      "anyOf": [
        { "$ref": "#/definitions/QualifiedName" },
        { "$ref": "#/definitions/typed_value" },
        { "$ref": "#/definitions/lang_string" } ]
    }
  },
  "ArrayOfLabelValues": {
    "$id": "#/definitions/ArrayOfLabelValues", "type": "array",
    "items": { "$ref": "#/definitions/lang_string" }
  }
}
```

With these preliminary definitions in place, we can now present the specification of the core data structures of PROV-JSONLD.

3.2   Encoding a PROV Expression

Each PROV expression is serialized into a single JSON object in a `@graph` array. For instance, Listing 2 shows the JSON schema for a prov:Entity expression in PROV-JSONLD. All the constituents of an expression become properties of the object as follows:

– The **identifier** (if present) becomes the identifier of the object (`@id` property). For prov:Entity, prov:Activity, and prov:Agent expressions, the `@id` property is *required* while it is *optional* for all other PROV expressions.
– The **type** of the PROV expression, e.g. prov:Activity, prov:Derivation, becomes the *only* value for the object's `@type` property, which is *always required*. Additional types, if any, are added to an array held by the `prov:type` property.

```
1   {
2     "prov:Entity": {
3       "type": "object", "required": [ "@type", "@id" ],
4       "properties": {
5         "@type":              { "pattern": "prov:Entity" },
6         "@id":                { "$ref": "#/definitions/QualifiedName" },
7         "prov:type":          { "$ref": "#/definitions/ArrayOfValues"},
8         "prov:location":      { "$ref": "#/definitions/ArrayOfValues" },
9         "prov:label":         { "$ref": "#/definitions/ArrayOfLabelValues"}
10      },
11      "patternProperties": {
12        "^[A-Za-z0-9_]+:(.*)$": { "$ref": "#/definitions/ArrayOfValues" }
13      },
14      "additionalProperties": false }
15  }
```

Listing 2: The JSON schema for prov:Entity.

- Other formal constituents of the PROV expression are encoded as properties
  of the object using the same property name as defined in PROV-DM. All
  those properties are *optional*. For example, the JSON object for a prov:Activity
  may have the properties startTime and/or endTime, for which DateTime string
  values are expected; while the object for a prov:Derivation expression may have
  the properties activity, generation, usage, generatedEntity, and usedEntity,
  for which QualifiedName string values are expected.
- The object may contain **additional attributes** which are encoded as the
  object's properties, such as a location (property prov:location), a label (property prov:label), or any other properties with an *explicit* prefix.

3.3   Encoding a PROV Document and a PROV Bundle

A PROV document is encoded as a JSON object which must contain a property
@type with the value prov:Document, a JSON-LD context @context, and an array
of PROV expressions as the value of the property @graph. The names of the
properties @context and @graph are specified by JSON-LD [9].

A PROV bundle is encoded in the same way as a PROV document except
that the JSON object for the bundle must contain a property @type with the
value prov:Bundle and additionally an identifier (property @id). Listing 3 shows
the JSON schema of a prov:Bundle object in PROV-JSONLD. A bundle contains
a list of statements (see Listing 4, definition prov:Statement), which can be one of
the defined PROV expressions as per Sect. 3.2. Documents, however, can contain
statements and/or bundles (see Listing 4, definition prov:StatementOrBundle).

```
1   { "prov:Bundle": {
2       "type": "object",
3       "required": [ "@type", "@id", "@graph", "@context" ],
4       "properties": {
5         "@type":    { "pattern": "prov:Bundle" },
6         "@id":      { "$ref": "#/definitions/QualifiedName" },
7         "@context": { "$ref": "#/definitions/Context" },
8         "@graph":   {
9           "type": "array",
10          "items": { "$ref": "#/definitions/prov:Statement" } } },
11      "additionalProperties": false }
12  }
```

Listing 3: JSON schema for prov:Bundle.

```
1   { "prov:Statement": {
2       "oneOf": [
3         { "$ref": "#/definitions/prov:Entity" },
4         { "$ref": "#/definitions/prov:Activity" },
5         { "$ref": "..." },
6         { "$ref": "#/definitions/prov:Communication" }
7       ]
8     },
9     "prov:StatementOrBundle": {
10      "oneOf": [
11        { "$ref": "#/definitions/prov:Statement" },
12        { "$ref": "#/definitions/prov:Bundle" }
13      ] }
14  }
```

Listing 4: JSON schema for prov:Statement and prov:StatementOrBundle; 14 other statements are abbreviated in Line 5 to save space.

4   PROV-JSONLD Context

JSON-LD contexts define mappings between terms[4] in a JSON document and IRIs (Internationalized Resource Identifier) [9] and, thus, enable the JSON document to be parsed as Linked Data. Using this mechanism, we define the PROV-JSONLD context in order for terms in a PROV-JSONLD document to be mapped to appropriate PROV properties and classes as defined by PROV-O (when read by a JSON-LD-compliant consumer). Due to the limited space, we present only some typical examples of term mappings in this section. The full context is available at https://openprovenance.org/prov-jsonld/context.json.

---

[4] A term is a short-hand string that expands to an IRI, a blank node identifier, or a keyword [9].

4.1   Default Context Elements

The following JSON properties have a *default* meaning *unless* they are rede-
fined in a specific context of a PROV-JSONLD document: `entity`, `activity`
and `agent` respectively map to the properties `prov:entity`, `prov:activity`, and
`prov:agent`. In addition, the JSON properties `prov:role`, `prov:type`, `prov:label`
and `prov:location` have the same meaning in *all* contexts of a PROV-JSONLD
document and respectively map to `prov:hadRole`, `rdf:type`, `rdfs:label`, and
`prov:atLocation`.

```
{ "entity":         { "@type": "@id", "@id": "prov:entity" },
   "activity":      { "@type": "@id", "@id": "prov:activity" },
   "agent":         { "@type": "@id", "@id": "prov:agent" },
   "prov:role":     { "@type": "@id", "@id": "prov:hadRole" },
   "prov:type":     { "@type": "@id", "@id": "rdf:type" },
   "prov:label":    {                 "@id": "rdfs:label" },
   "prov:location": { "@type": "@id", "@id": "prov:atLocation" }
}
```

4.2   Contexts for PROV Elements

JSON objects with types `prov:Entity` and `prov:Agent` can be mapped directly to
the corresponding classes defined by PROV-O without any extra specific mapping apart from the default above. JSON objects with type `prov:Activity`, however, can additionally have the JSON properties `startTime` and `endTime`, which
map to the RDF data properties `prov:startedAtTime` and `prov:endedAtType`,
respectively, and have a range of type `xsd:dateTime`.

```
{ "prov:Activity": {
    "@id": "prov:Activity",
    "@context" : {
      "startTime":{"@type": "xsd:dateTime", "@id": "prov:startedAtTime"},
      "endTime":  {"@type": "xsd:dateTime", "@id": "prov:endedAtTime"} }
  }
}
```

4.3   Contexts for PROV Relations

The ontology PROV-O [10] defines the Qualification Pattern, which restates
a binary property between two resources by using an intermediate class that
represents the influence between the two resources. This new instance, in turn,
can be annotated with additional descriptions of the influence that one resource
had upon another. Figure 2, for example, shows the Qualification Pattern defined
for class prov:Usage in PROV-O. For each PROV relation expression, we apply its
Qualification Pattern and encode the relation as a resource in PROV-JSONLD.
The mapping below supports the Qualification Pattern of Fig. 2. The JSON
properties `activity` and `time` map to the object property `prov:qualifiedUsage`
and the data property `prov:atTime`, respectively.

```
{ "prov:Usage": {
    "@id": "prov:Usage",
    "@context": {
      "activity": { "@type": "@id", "@reverse": "prov:qualifiedUsage" },
      "time":     { "@type": "xsd:dateTime", "@id": "prov:atTime" } } }
}
```

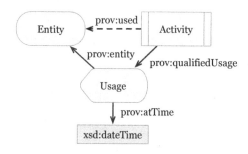

Fig. 2. The qualification pattern for class prov:Usage defined by PROV-O [10].

Note that the context above applies only to objects with the @type property having the value prov:Usage thanks to the support for *type-scoped contexts* by JSON-LD 1.1 [9]. For such objects, the above context for prov:Usage is in effect *in addition to* the default context in Sect. 4.1 and overrides the default mapping for the term activity, replacing it with a reverse mapping to prov:qualifiedUsage. The default mapping for the term entity (mapping it to prov:entity), however, still applies. Along with the additional definition for the term time, they complete the JSON-LD context for prov:Usage (Fig. 2).

We follow the same convention for all the remaining PROV relations. Table 1 provides the mappings to the qualification properties for the reverse terms defined in the type-scoped contexts. Note that while PROV-O does not define a Qualification Pattern for Specialization, Alternate, and Membership relations, for uniformity and usability reasons, we adopt similar mappings as other PROV relations, via a Qualification Pattern. However, the mappings are to new classes and properties in the PROV extension namespace (denoted by the prefix provext). See the following section for some interoperability considerations.

5   Interoperability Considerations

IC1 There are differences between PROV-DM and PROV-O in terms of the level of requirements set on some expressions. For instance, PROV-DM mandates the presence of an entity in a generation, whereas PROV-O defines an activity as optional. Compliance requirements are not the same in PROV-O as one could define a qualified generation with an activity but without an entity. Experience shows that there may be good reasons why a generation may

Table 1. PROV-JSONLD reverse terms defined in type-scoped contexts and their corresponding qualification properties.

PROV-O classes	PROV-JSONLD terms	Qualification properties
prov:Generation	`entity`	`prov:qualifiedGeneration`
prov:Derivation	`generatedEntity`	`prov:qualifiedDerivation`
prov:Invalidation	`entity`	`prov:qualifiedInvalidation`
prov:Attribution	`entity`	`prov:qualifiedAttribution`
prov:Usage	`activity`	`prov:qualifiedUsage`
prov:Start	`activity`	`prov:qualifiedStart`
prov:End	`activity`	`prov:qualifiedEnd`
prov:Association	`activity`	`prov:qualifiedAssociation`
prov:Communication	`informed`	`prov:qualifiedCommunication`
prov:Delegation	`delegate`	`prov:qualifiedDelegation`
prov:Influence	`influencee`	`prov:qualifiedInfluence`
provext:Specialization	`specificEntity`	`provext:qualifiedSpecialization`
provext:Alternate	`alternate1`	`provext:qualifiedAlternate`
provext:Membership	`collection`	`provext:qualifiedMembership`

not refer to an entity; for instance, because the recorded provenance is not "complete" yet, and further provenance expressions still need to be asserted, received, or merged; in the meantime, we still want to be able to process such provenance, despite being "incomplete". Thus, in PROV-JSONLD, the presence of an entity and an activity in a generation expression is *recommended*, while other properties are optional, and only its `@type` property is *required*.

IC2 In PROV-DM, all relations are n-ary except for specialization, alternate and membership, which are binary, meaning that no identifier or extra properties are allowed for these. In PROV-O, this design decision translates to the lack of qualified relations for specialization, alternate and membership. In PROV-JSONLD, in order to keep the regular structure of JSON objects and the natural encoding of relations, but also to ensure the simplicity and efficiency of parsers, these three relations are encoded using the same pattern as for other relations. Therefore, their mapping to RDF via the JSON-LD context relies on a PROV extension namespace (denoted by the prefix `provext`) in which classes for Specialization, Alternate, and Membership are defined. The PROV-JSONLD serialization also allows for identifier and properties to be encoded for these relations.

IC3 The notion of a PROV document is not present in PROV-DM or PROV-O, but is introduced in PROV-N as a housekeeping construct, and is defined in PROV-XML as the root of a PROV-XML document. A document in PROV-JSONLD is also a JSON object, allowing for a JSON-LD `@context` property to be specified.

IC4 PROV-JSONLD does not introduce constructs for some PROV subtypes (prov:Person, prov:Organization, prov:SoftwareAgent, and prov:Collection) and sub-relations (prov:Quotation, prov:PrimarySource, and prov:Revision). Instead, the example of Sect. 2 illustrates how they can be accommodated within the existing structures. We copy below an agent expression of type `prov:Person`

(Line 5) and a derivation of type prov:Revision (Line 11). These subtypes and
subrelations are specified inside the **prov:type** property. PROV-XML offers
a similar way of encoding such subtypes and subrelations, alongside specialized structures. We opted for this single approach to ensure the simplicity
and efficiency of parsers.

```
1   { "@graph" : [
2       { "@type" : "prov:Agent",
3         "@id" : "ex:derek",
4         "foaf:mbox" : [ { "@value" : "<mailto:derek@example.org>" } ],
5         "prov:type" : [ "prov:Person" ],
6         "foaf:givenName" : [ { "@value" : "Derek" } ]
7       },
8       { "@type" : "prov:Derivation",
9         "generatedEntity" : "ex:dataSet2",
10        "usedEntity" : "ex:dataSet1",
11        "prov:type" : [ "prov:Revision" ]
12      } ]
13  }
```

IC5 The interoperability of the PROV-JSONLD serialization can be tested in
different ways: In a roundtrip testing, consisting of the serialization of an
internal representation in some programming language to PROV-JSONLD,
followed by deserialization from PROV-JSONLD back to the same programming language, the source and target representations are expected to be
equal. Likewise, in a roundtrip testing, consisting of the serialization of an
internal representation in some programming language to PROV-JSONLD,
followed by a conversion of PROV-JSONLD to another RDF representation
such as Turtle [14], followed by a reading of the Turtle representation back to
the same programming language, the source and target representations are
also expected to be equal. Both interoperability tests have been implemented
in the Java-based ProvToolbox, with:

- The first roundtrip testing is implemented in https://github.com/
  lucmoreau/ProvToolbox/blob/master/modules-core/prov-jsonld/src/
  test/java/org/openprovenance/prov/core/RoundTripFromJavaJSONLD
  11Test.java
- The second roundtrip testing is implemented in https://github.com/
  lucmoreau/ProvToolbox/blob/master/modules-legacy/roundtrip/src/
  test/java/org/openprovenance/prov/core/roundtrip/RoundTrip
  FromJavaJSONLD11LegacyTest.java.

6   Implementation and Evaluation

We have introduced PROV-JSONLD as a PROV serialization that is lightweight,
natural, semantic and efficient. So far, this paper has focused on the first three
characteristics. The purpose of this section is to discuss its performance.

The PROV-JSONLD serialization is implemented in ProvToolbox,[5] a JVM-based library for processing PROV standardized representations. The library can build representations of the PROV data model in Java and can convert such data structures to PROV-JSONLD, PROV-N, and PROV-JSON, and vice-versa.

From an implementation viewpoint, each PROV expression has an associated class implementing it, which we refer to as JAVA-PROV. For instance, the JAVA-PROV class for a PROV Generation has fields for an activity and an entity, and further optional fields.

```java
public class WasGeneratedBy implements
  org.openprovenance.prov.model.WasGeneratedBy, HasAttributes {

  QualifiedName activity;
  QualifiedName entity;
  Optional<QualifiedName> id=Optional.empty();
  Optional<XMLGregorianCalendar> time=Optional.empty();
  List<org.openprovenance.prov.model.LangString> labels=new LinkedList<>();
  List<org.openprovenance.prov.model.Location> location=new LinkedList<>();
  List<org.openprovenance.prov.model.Other> other = new LinkedList<>();
  List<org.openprovenance.prov.model.Type> type = new LinkedList<>();
  List<org.openprovenance.prov.model.Role> role = new LinkedList<>();

  // constructors, accessors and mutators ...
}
```

Serialization/Deserialization to/from PROV-JSONLD is performed by the library Jackson[6], which can be configured by means of mix-ins: in the interface below, the sister interface JLD_WasGeneratedBy allows for configuration annotation for Jackson to be mixed-in with the definition of the JAVA-PROV definition of WasGeneratedBy, while keeping the original JAVA-PROV code intact. For instance, for each field, the mix-in has the opportunity to control specialized methods for serialization or deserialization. It also specifies an order in which the JSON properties are expected to be serialized.

```java
@JsonPropertyOrder({ "@id", "entity", "activity", "atTime" })
@JsonInclude(JsonInclude.Include.NON_NULL)
public interface JLD_WasGeneratedBy extends JLD_Generic, HasRole {

  @JsonDeserialize(using = CustomQualifiedNameDeserializer.class)
  public QualifiedName getEntity();

  @JsonDeserialize(using = CustomQualifiedNameDeserializer.class)
  public QualifiedName getActivity();

  XMLGregorianCalendar getTime();
}
```

---

[5] https://lucmoreau.github.io/ProvToolbox/.

[6] https://github.com/FasterXML/jackson.

A PROV document consists of a sequence of statements or bundles. Given that a JAVA-PROV statement is declared by an interface, the Jackson deserializer is able to determine the necessary constructor to invoke by relying on the @type property, automatically inserted at serialization time, by the declaration below. It makes explicit, e.g., how prov:Usage class should be parsed when encountering @type value "prov:Usage".

```
@JsonPropertyOrder({ "@context", "@graph"})
public interface JLD_Document {
  @JsonProperty("@context")
  Namespace getNamespace();

  @JsonTypeInfo(use=JsonTypeInfo.Id.NAME,
                include=JsonTypeInfo.As.PROPERTY,
                property="@type")
  @JsonSubTypes({
    @JsonSubTypes.Type(value = WasGeneratedBy.class,
                                           name = "prov:Generation"),
    @JsonSubTypes.Type(value = Used.class,     name = "prov:Usage"),
    @JsonSubTypes.Type(value = Activity.class, name = "prov:Activity"),
    @JsonSubTypes.Type(value = Agent.class,    name = "prov:Agent"),
    @JsonSubTypes.Type(value = Entity.class,   name = "prov:Entity"),
    // all other statements and bundles ...
  })
  @JsonProperty("@graph")
  List<StatementOrBundle> getStatementOrBundle();
}
```

Our investigation of the performance of PROV-JSONLD focuses on deserialization, which consists of reading a PROV-JSONLD serialization and constructing the corresponding JAVA-PROV representation, using the kind of classes described above. To compare the performance, we use an alternative set of mix-in configurations also to allow (de)serialization for PROV-JSON. We also compare with the PROV-N (de)serialization: the serialization is written by handcrafted code, whereas the deserialization is implemented using the ANTLR grammar. We are not interested in measuring the cost of inputs and outputs; therefore, our benchmarks generate serializations in a memory buffer, and vice-versa, deserialization operates on an input memory buffer.

Two further points of comparison were used for the evaluation. First, a native JSON parser, without any customization code, generates native Java objects (consisting of Java Maps for JSON objects and Java arrays for JSON sequences) from a PROV-JSONLD serialization. Such internal representations based on Java native objects are not as conducive to processing as the JAVA-PROV classes above, since types are not made explicit, and therefore cannot exploit the Java object-oriented style with its inheritance and static typing. Second, a copy procedure performs a deep copy of a JAVA-PROV data structure, which involves the creation of the JAVA-PROV data structure and the necessary checks and initializations, to make it ready for subsequent processing.

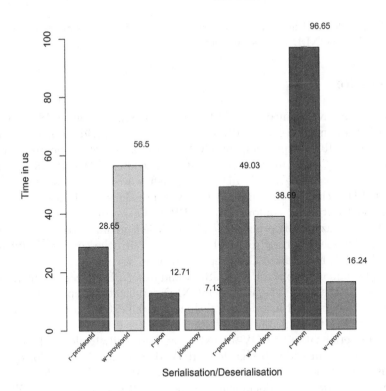

Fig. 3. (De)Serialization benchmark: **r-provjsonld**: reading time from PROV-JSONLD to JAVA-PROV; **w-provjsonld**: writing time from JAVA-PROV to PROV-JSONLD; **r-json**: reading time from PROV-JSONLD to native Java objects; **jdeepcopy**: time for deep copy of JAVA-PROV; **r-provjson**: reading time from PROV-JSON to JAVA-PROV; **w-provjson**: writing time from JAVA-PROV to PROV-JSON; **r-provn**: reading time from PROV-N to JAVA-PROV; **w-provn**: writing time from JAVA-PROV to PROV-N.

The results of the benchmarking operations are displayed in Fig. 3. We can see that the efficiency of **r-provjsonld** (28.65 μs) which is barely 45% over the **r-json** + **jdeepcopy** (i.e. 19.84 μs). This result is very good as there are additional operations included in **r-provjsonld** but not in **r-json** or **jdeepcopy**, such as indexing and preparing prefix and namespace mappings.

The PROV-JSONLD reading time (**r-provjsonld**) significantly outperforms PROV-N reading time (**r-provn**), which is penalized by currently relying on an intermediary abstract syntax tree before constructing JAVA-PROV.

We were surprised how the handcrafted PROV-N writer **w-provn** outperforms any of JSON serializations **w-provjsonld** and **w-provjson**. We have not been able to ascertain the origin of this difference. We conjecture that the handcrafted technique of **w-provn** could be applied to PROV-JSONLD and give a similar performance.

Overall, the plot in Fig. 3 demonstrates a serialization/deserialization technique for PROV-JSONLD that is efficient.

7   Conclusion

In this paper, we have defined the PROV-JSONLD serialization, a JSON and Linked Data representation for the PROV data model. It provides a lightweight representation of PROV expressions in JSON, which is suitable to be processed by Web applications, while maintaining a natural encoding that is familiar with PROV practitioners. Using JSON-LD 1.1, we define a semantic mapping for PROV-JSONLD such that the encoded PROV expressions can be readily processed as Linked Data that conforms to the PROV-O specification. Finally, we show that the serialization is processable in an efficient manner with our implementation in the open-source ProvToolbox library. With the combined advantages of both JSON and Linked Data representations, we envisage that PROV-JSONLD will gradually replace PROV-JSON and other PROV-compliant RDF serializations. To that end, the PROV-JSONLD serialization reported in this paper is being documented in a formal technical specification to be submitted to World Wide Web Consortium [11].

As a JSON serialization, PROV-JSONLD can be readily exploited by existing JSON stores to provide storage for PROV documents. ProvToolbox, for instance, is exploiting this opportunity by using MongoDB,[7] a document-oriented database for JSON documents, to persist PROV documents. While JSON stores offer generic query capabilities for JSON documents, in the future, it would be useful to define a query language that exploits the structure and semantics of PROV-JSONLD. Likewise, learning from MongoDB and its BSON binary encoding of JSON, an efficient, compact binary encoding of PROV-JSONLD could be specified.

As illustrated by the different compliance requirements discussed in **IC1** (Sect. 5), the various PROV serializations do not interoperate fully. At the W3C, the Provenance Working group attempted to maintain an informal mapping between PROV-DM and its encoding in RDF (as per PROV-O). This was a manual task without any tool support and, therefore, error-prone and hard to maintain. The JSON-LD context used by PROV-JSONLD appears to be a promising mechanism to systematically encode these mappings and to help iron out outstanding interoperability issues.

References

1. Andrews, H., Wright, A., Hutton, B.: JSON schema: a media type for describing JSON documents. Internet draft, Internet Engineering Task Force (IETF) (2019). https://tools.ietf.org/html/draft-handrews-json-schema-02

---

[7] https://www.mongodb.com.

2. Bray, T.: The JavaScript object notation (JSON) data interchange format. Request for Comments 8259, Internet Engineering Task Force (IETF) (2017). https://tools.ietf.org/html/rfc8259

3. Gil, Y., Miles, S.: PROV model primer. W3C Working Group Note, World Wide Web Consortium (April 2013). http://www.w3.org/TR/2013/NOTE-prov-primer-20130430/

4. Groth, P., Moreau, L.: PROV-overview. An overview of the PROV family of documents. W3C Working Group Note, World Wide Web Consortium (April 2013). http://www.w3.org/TR/2013/NOTE-prov-overview-20130430/

5. Heath, T., Bizer, C.: Linked Data: Evolving the Web into a Global Data Space, Synthesis Lectures on the Semantic Web: Theory and Technology, vol. 1. Morgan & Claypool (2011). https://doi.org/10.2200/S00334ED1V01Y201102WBE001

6. Hua, H., Tilmes, C., Zednik, S.: PROV-XML: the PROV XML schema. W3C Working Group Note, World Wide Web Consortium (April 2013). http://www.w3.org/TR/2013/NOTE-prov-xml-20130430/

7. Huynh, T.D., Jewell, M.O., Keshavarz, A.S., Michaelides, D.T., Yang, H., Moreau, L.: The PROV-JSON serialization. W3C Member Submission, World Wide Web Consortium (April 2013). https://www.w3.org/Submission/2013/SUBM-prov-json-20130424/

8. Huynh, T.D., Michaelides, D.T., Moreau, L.: PROV-JSONLD: a JSON and linked data representation for provenance. In: Mattoso, M., Glavic, B. (eds.) IPAW 2016. LNCS, vol. 9672, pp. 173–177. Springer, Cham (2016). https://doi.org/10.1007/978-3-319-40593-3_15

9. Kellogg, G., Champin, P.A., Longley, D.: JSON-LD 1.1: a JSON-based serialization for linked data. W3C Recommendation, World Wide Web Consortium (2020). https://www.w3.org/TR/2020/REC-json-ld11-20200716/

10. Lebo, T., Sahoo, S., McGuinness, D.: PROV-O: the PROV ontology. W3C Recommendation, World Wide Web Consortium (2013). http://www.w3.org/TR/2013/REC-prov-o-20130430/

11. Moreau, L., Huynh, T.D.: The PROV-JSONLD serialization: a JSON-LD representation for the PROV data model. Editor's draft, King's College London (2020). https://openprovenance.org/prov-jsonld/

12. Moreau, L., Missier, P.: PROV-DM: the PROV data model. W3C Recommendation, World Wide Web Consortium (2013). http://www.w3.org/TR/2013/REC-prov-dm-20130430/

13. Moreau, L., Missier, P.: PROV-N: the provenance notation. W3C Recommendation, World Wide Web Consortium (2013)

14. Prud'hommeaux, E., Carothers, G.: RDF 1.1 Turtle. W3C Recommendation, World Wide Web Consortium (2014). http://www.w3.org/TR/2014/REC-turtle-20140225/

15. Sporny, M., Longley, D., Kellogg, G., Lanthaler, M., Lindström, N.: A JSON-based serialization for linked data. W3C Recommendation, World Wide Web Consortium (2014). https://www.w3.org/TR/2014/REC-json-ld-20140116/

Security

Proactive Provenance Policies for Automatic Cryptographic Data Centric Security

Shamaria Engram, Tyler Kaczmarek[✉], Alice Lee, and David Bigelow

MIT Lincoln Laboratory, Lexington, USA
{shamaria.engram,tyler.kaczmarek,alice.lee,dbigelow}@ll.mit.edu

Abstract. Data provenance analysis has been used as an assistive measure for ensuring system integrity. However, such techniques are typically reactive approaches to identify the root cause of an attack in its aftermath. This is in part due to the fact that the collection of provenance metadata often results in a deluge of information that cannot easily be queried and analyzed in real time. This paper presents an approach for proactively reasoning about provenance metadata within the Automatic Cryptographic Data Centric (ACDC) security architecture, a new security infrastructure in which all data interactions are considered at a coarse granularity, similar to the Function as a Service model. At this scale, we have found that data interactions are manageable for the proactive specification and evaluation of *provenance policies*—constraints placed on provenance metadata to prevent the consumption of untrusted data. This paper provides a model for proactively evaluating provenance metadata in the ACDC paradigm as well as a case study of an electronic voting scheme to demonstrate the applicability of ACDC and the provenance policies needed to ensure data integrity.

1 Introduction

Data provenance provides a comprehensive history of data and the manipulations it has underwent from its inception to its latest state. Analysis of this history can provide significant insight into a datum's integrity and authenticity for forensic analysts and security administrators. However, due to the mass of data being produced in computing environments, manual analysis of provenance metadata is a daunting task. Automated provenance analysis techniques exist but generally provide a reactive evaluation in the aftermath of a security incident (e.g., [20]).

DISTRIBUTION STATEMENT A. Approved for public release. Distribution is unlimited.

This material is based upon work supported by the Under Secretary of Defense for Research and Engineering under Air Force Contract No. FA8702-15-D-0001. Any opinions, findings, conclusions or recommendations expressed in this material are those of the author(s) and do not necessarily reflect the views of the Under Secretary of Defense for Research and Engineering.

© Springer Nature Switzerland AG 2021
B. Glavic et al. (Eds.): IPAW 2020/IPAW 2021, LNCS 12839, pp. 71–87, 2021.
https://doi.org/10.1007/978-3-030-80960-7_5

This retrospective approach to data provenance analysis has proven valuable in several security contexts (e.g., diagnosing an attacker's point of entry to a system). Nevertheless, given the ubiquity of online services, many of which operate in an outsourced distributed environment, there is a need for a proactive approach to data provenance analysis. Proactively evaluating a datum's provenance record before consumption is especially applicable to operations within cloud environments, where end users, who outsource their data to be processed by cloud applications, should have some level of assurance about their data's integrity. Runtime analysis of whole-system provenance has recently gained attention in the literature but does so at a fine-grained level, which does not translate cleanly to a distributed system [24].

The ability to proactively specify properties of provenance metadata, to aid in security enforcement decisions, can have a significant impact on a distributed environment's overall security posture. This paper presents an approach for proactively reasoning about provenance metadata within the Automatic Cryptographic Data Centric (ACDC) security architecture, a distributed architecture that upends the current system-centric paradigm by taking a data-centric approach to security. Rather than protecting systems that store data, ACDC puts the focus directly on protecting data itself both at rest and in motion while simultaneously ensuring that data is used in only authorized and auditable ways. Data protection goals include confidentiality, integrity, and availability throughout all uses of the data, including not only storage and transmission but also sharing and computation, on devices and networks that may be partially compromised.

ACDC allows application developers to proactively express policies over provenance metadata to be enforced before data is consumed by an individual process. We call such policies *provenance policies*. ACDC can prevent the consumption of untrusted data by providing the following capabilities: 1) secure packaging of data with associated integrity and confidentiality policies at the network's edge, 2) enforcement of integrity and confidentiality policies throughout the data's entire lifespan, and 3) a thorough record of data provenance to account for every manipulation. To the best of our knowledge, this paper presents the first effort to provide a proactive approach for data provenance evaluation within a data-centric security architecture.

Our core contributions are as follows:

1. We introduce the ACDC architecture for data-centric security (Sect. 2),
2. We describe a formal approach for reasoning about provenance policies proactively based on a mathematical semantics of provenance metadata (Sect. 3), and
3. We demonstrate the applicability of ACDC and proactive provenance policy evaluation by providing a case study of an end-to-end, coercion-resistant voting system (Sect. 4).

Section 5 provides a summary of related work and Sect. 6 concludes and provides directions for future work.

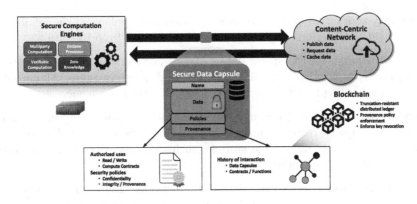

Fig. 1. ACDC core component architecture

2   The ACDC FaaS Paradigm

This section introduces the Automatic Cryptographic Data-Centric (ACDC) security paradigm and describes each of the components that make up an ACDC network. As shown in Fig. 1, ACDC puts all data into named, secure data capsules, where each capsule is associated with an owner. These capsules contain cryptographically enforced access-control policies that define who can access and use the capsules' associated data. Each capsule also contains its provenance as captured within the ACDC system, allowing authorized parties to assess a capsule's integrity before acting upon it. ACDC provides flexibility to data owners by allowing them to 1) cryptographically authorize functions to run on their data, and 2) specify which secure computation techniques are allowed to process their data (e.g., multiparty computation (MPC) or secure enclaves), which enables data owners to consider the tradoffs between security, functionality, and performance. These capabilities allow mutually distrusting data owners to securely collaborate and share their data in a controlled environment. Lastly, ACDC uses content-centric networking (CCN) [17] to route and transmit data capsules by their name rather than by the systems storing such data, thus enabling capsules' cryptographic mechanisms to protect data wherever capsules go on the network.

An instance of an ACDC network (closed or Internet-wide) consists of the following components:

Nodes. ACDC nodes may be a set of dedicated servers each running ACDC software. Each node may also have a set of supporting servers that provide data for specific ACDC functionality using unspecified (back-end) protocols. In general, all ACDC nodes use a common ACDC core library. The library itself makes no distinction based on the node type, though the capabilities of an individual node can dictate many different types.

Data Capsules. As previously mentioned, all data is stored in named, secure capsules. All capsules are digitally signed for authenticity and integrity, and the internal data of each capsule is encrypted for confidentiality. Each data capsule may contain an optional output confidentiality policy, which defines the confidentiality restrictions imposed on any data derived from its data.

Capsule Storage. ACDC stores data capsules persistently, allowing nodes to publish new capsules, fetch existing capsules, and delete capsules. All capsules are named according to a CCN-compatible ACDC naming scheme.

Function as a Service. FaaS allows nodes to perform (or serve) one or more functions in a query/response model. In general, FaaS is expected to use the same naming schemes as capsule storage, such that any request can be static (Capsule Storage) or dynamic (FaaS).

Secure Execution Environments. ACDC provides environments for secure function execution (e.g., secure enclaves such as Intel SGX or MPC).

Keys. ACDC uses cryptographic keys for confidentiality, integrity, and authenticity.

Policies. ACDC has two types of policies: 1) confidentiality policies, and 2) integrity policies (i.e., provenance policies). The confidentiality policies are attribute-based encryption policies [10] that define the attributes needed to decrypt a data capsule and thus cryptographically enforce access control. Attributes are terms that may refer to a principal's characteristics (e.g., a role or identity) or proof of taking an action (e.g., validating a capsule's provenance). Provenance policies define a capsule's expected provenance and should be checked before a capsule is used as input to a function (discussed at length in Sect. 3).

Contracts. Contracts define functions and give restrictions, limiting nodes to perform computations on data capsules under a given set of conditions. For example, a contract may restrict who can perform computations, require provenance checks via a provenance policy (detailed in following sections), or require key revocation checks.

All contracts are expected to provide an output confidentiality policy, which defines confidentiality restrictions to impose on the output data of the function. However, each function argument may have its own output confidentiality policy, in which case the policies must be composed, thereby accumulating all the restrictions from each policy (i.e., the contract and each function argument's output confidentiality policy).

3   ACDC Provenance Model

To reason about provenance within an ACDC architecture, we follow the W3C PROV Data Model [6] in characterizing the elements of the model into 3 main types: entities, activities, and agents. We further refine the model by extending the entity type to contain 3 subtypes and the agent type to contain 2 subtypes. An entity can be either a *key entity*, a *contract entity*, or a *data entity* and an agent can be either an *account agent* or a *node agent*.

Table 1. The effect of the additional subtypes on provenance relations introduced by ACDC to the PROV data model.

Relation	Source	Destination	Meaning
WasAttributedTo	Entity (any subtype)	Node agent	The entity was created by execution on the node agent
		Account agent	The entity was sealed under the account agent's key(s)
WasDerivedFrom	Entity (any subtype)	Contract entity	The entity was created based on rules specified in the contract
		Data entity	The entity is dependent on the data entity
		Key entity	The key entity was needed to either wrap the source entity or unwrap an input entity
Used	Activity	Contract entity	The contract entity defined the activity's execution
		Data entity	The data entity was input to the activity
		Key entity	The activity performed some cryptographic function using the key entity
ActedOnBehalfOf	Node agent	Account agent	The node agent performed a computation on behalf of the account agent
WasAssociatedWith	Activity	Node agent	The activity describing the computation was performed by the node agent

Key entities represent cryptographic keys belonging to an agent, contract entities represent ACDC contracts, and data entities represent all other types of data. Account agents represent the users in a computing environment and node agents represent a secure execution environment (e.g., an sgx enclave). Activities represent a computation that uses, manipulates, or generates entities. Node agents act on behalf of account agents; conversely, account agents *cannot* act on behalf of node agents. Because node agents represent environments where computations are performed, activities can only be associated with node agents. Table 1 summarizes the valid types for provenance relations affected by our additional subtypes.

To illustrate this new distinction between entity and agent subtypes, consider the provenance of a scenario in which a user has introduced some data into the ACDC ecosystem at the network's edge, shown in Fig. 2. To introduce this data, the data must be encapsulated because all data in ACDC is stored in secure capsules. The sgx enclave is a node agent which acts on behalf of Bob who is an account agent. The encapsulate computation is an activity associated with the sgx enclave. The plaintext is a data entity, the encapsulate contract is a contract entity specifying how the function should input and output entities, Key_{SGX} is a key entity attributed to the sgx enclave for secure computation, and Key_B is a key entity attributed to account agent Bob. The secure capsule is a data entity generated by the encapsulate activity, derived from the contract, key, and data entities, and is attributed to account agent Bob.

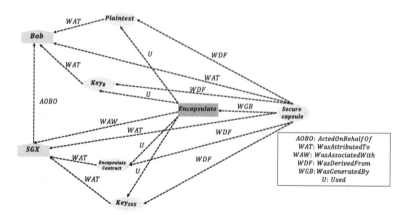

Fig. 2. A provenance graph of a user who has encapsulated some data

To reason about the provenance of a distributed ACDC environment, we specify the environment at a high level of abstraction as a 6-tuple $D = (\mathcal{E}_k, \mathcal{E}_c, \mathcal{E}_d, G_n, G_a, \mathcal{A})$, where $\mathcal{E}_k$ is a finite set of key entities ranged over by metavariable ε_k, $\mathcal{E}_c$ is a finite set of contract entities ranged over by metavariable ε_c, $\mathcal{E}_d$ is a finite set of data entities ranged over by metavariable ε_d, G_n is a finite set of node agents ranged over by metavariable g_n, G_a is a finite set of account agents ranged over by metavariable g_a, and $\mathcal{A}$ is a finite set of activities ranged over by metavariable a.

The set of all possible entities $\mathcal{E} = \mathcal{E}_k \cup \mathcal{E}_c \cup \mathcal{E}_d$ is the union of all entity subtypes, and the set of all possible agents $G = G_n \cup G_a$ is the union of all agent subtypes. Because provenance is represented by a labeled, directed acyclic graph, $V = \mathcal{E} \cup G \cup \mathcal{A}$ denotes the set of all possible vertices, $E \subset V \times V$ denotes the set of all possible edges, L denotes the set of all possible labels (relations) and is the union of all relations, and L^E denotes the set of all possible graph labeling functions where $l : E \rightarrow L$ is a function that inputs an edge and outputs the label corresponding to that edge, indicating the causal relationship between the source and destination nodes.

The set of all provenance graphs of a distributed environment D is denoted by $2^V \times 2^E \times L^E$. A provenance policy is a predicate $P : 2^V \times 2^E \times L^E \rightarrow \{true, false\}$. ACDC provenance policies determine whether a particular subgraph is contained in the provenance graph under consideration. It is not always the case that the entire provenance record for a distributed environment be evaluated against a policy. For example, a provenance policy can be evaluated at runtime to ensure that data was generated via the expected pathways before using the data as input for a computation. In this case, a contract will specify a provenance policy to be evaluated over the function's inputs; therefore, only the provenance associated with the input data is relevant for policy evaluation, making it unnecessary and inefficient to evaluate the policy on the entire provenance record. Consequently, for each distributed environment there is a one-to-many relationship between the distributed environment and the number of provenance graphs it contains. In this paper, we refer to an *event* as a provenance subgraph containing an activity with all of its immediate input and output entities along with their attributions. In a larger distributed environment, Fig. 2 would be considered the *Encapsulate* event.

Provenance policies are specified as boolean predicates so that large, complex policies can be composed from simpler policies. For example, let's consider a scenario where Bob would like to use his secure capsule in a computation, but would like to verify that his secure capsule was properly encapsulated (i.e., encapsulated with only his data and key). A policy for this situation might ensure that: (1) the encapsulate function used Bob's data and key, (2) if the encapsulate function used any data and cryptographic keys, then they can only be Bob's data and key or the node acting on Bob's behalf key, (3) the secure capsule is only derived from Bob's key and plaintext data and no other account agent's key and data, and (4) the secure capsule was computed using the encapsulate contract. To note the importance of precise policy specification, it may not be easy to distinguish the difference between the informal specification of concern (1) and concern (2). Concern (1) only ensures that the encapsulate function used Bob's data and key but does not preclude the function from using any one else's data and key. The second concern ensures that if the encapsulate function used any data or cryptographic keys, then the data and keys can only belong to Bob or the node acting on Bob's behalf. Formally, given a provenance graph $(V', E', l') \in 2^V \times 2^E \times L^E$, Bob can specify the following policies:

$$P_1(V', E', l') \iff \exists \varepsilon_k \in V' : (Encapsulate, \varepsilon_k) \in E' \wedge l'(Encapsulate, \varepsilon_k) = Used,$$

$$P_2(V', E', l') \iff \exists \varepsilon_d \in V' : (Encapsulate, \varepsilon_d) \in E' \wedge l'(Encapsulate, \varepsilon_d) = Used,$$

$$\begin{aligned} P_3(V', E', l') \iff \ &\forall \varepsilon_k \in V' : ((Encapsulate, \varepsilon_k) \in E' \wedge l'(Encapsulate, \varepsilon_k) = Used) \\ &\Rightarrow (((\varepsilon_k, Bob) \in E' \wedge l'(\varepsilon_k, Bob) = WasAttributedTo) \\ &\vee (\exists g_n \in V' : ((\varepsilon_k, g_n) \in E' \wedge l'(\varepsilon_k, g_n) = WasAttributedTo) \\ &\wedge ((g_n, Bob) \in E' \wedge l'(g_n, Bob) = ActedOnBehalfOf))), \end{aligned}$$

$$\begin{aligned} P_4(V', E', l') \iff \ &\forall \varepsilon_d \in V' : ((Encapsulate, \varepsilon_d) \in E' \wedge l'(Encapsulate, \varepsilon_d) = Used) \\ &\Rightarrow ((\varepsilon_d, Bob) \in E' \wedge l'(\varepsilon_d, Bob) = WasAttributedTo), \end{aligned}$$

$$\begin{aligned} P_5(V', E', l') \iff \ &\exists \varepsilon_d \in V' : (SecureCapsule, \varepsilon_d) \in E' \\ &\wedge l'(SecureCapsule, \varepsilon_d) = WasDerivedFrom, \end{aligned}$$

$$\begin{aligned} P_6(V', E', l') \iff \ &\exists \varepsilon_k \in V' : (SecureCapsule, \varepsilon_k) \in E' \\ &\wedge l'(SecureCapsule, \varepsilon_k) = WasDerivedFrom, \end{aligned}$$

$$\begin{aligned} P_7(V', E', l') \iff \ &\forall \varepsilon_k \in V' : ((SecureCapsule, \varepsilon_k) \in E' \\ &\wedge l'(SecureCapsule, \varepsilon_k) = WasDerivedFrom) \\ &\Rightarrow (((\varepsilon_k, Bob) \in E' \wedge l'(\varepsilon_k, Bob) = WasAttributedTo) \\ &\vee (\exists g_n \in V' : ((\varepsilon_k, g_n) \in E' \wedge l'(\varepsilon_k, g_n) = WasAttributedTo) \\ &\wedge ((g_n, Bob) \in E' \wedge l'(g_n, Bob) = ActedOnBehalfOf))), \end{aligned}$$

$$\begin{aligned} P_8(V', E', l') \iff \ &\forall \varepsilon_d \in V' : ((SecureCapsule, \varepsilon_d) \in E' \\ &\wedge l'(SecureCapsule, \varepsilon_d) = WasDerivedFrom) \\ &\Rightarrow ((\varepsilon_d, Bob) \in E' \wedge l'(\varepsilon_d, Bob) = WasAttributedTo), \end{aligned}$$

$$\begin{aligned} P_9(V', E', l') \iff \ &(SecureCapsule, EncapsulateContract) \in E' \\ &\wedge l'(SecureCapsule, EncapsulateContract) = WasDerivedFrom. \end{aligned}$$

The overall provenance policy can be composed as the conjunction of policies $P_1 - P_9$. Specifying policies in this way allows analyst to reason about small, simple policies. Logical connectives can then be used to compose these simple policies into larger, more complex policies.

4   A Case Study on Detecting Voter Fraud in E-Voting

This section presents a case study of an e-voting scenario within an ACDC architecture and provenance policies that may prevent illegal ballots from being cast. As recent voting elections have been under scrutiny by both the media and general public [9], we believe that ACDC equipped voting machines can provide significant benefits and increase public confidence in the integrity of voting elections.

Table 2. Entities in an ACDC E-voting environment

Entities	Description
VoterID	Data entity describing a unique identifier corresponding to the identity of the voter (e.g., voter registration)
DREKey	Key entity describing the cryptographic key needed for secure computation by the voting machine
KeyGenContract	Contract entity describing the KeyGen function and confidentiality and integrity policies
VoterKey	Key entity describing the cryptographic key generated by KeyGen
SelectContract	Contract entity describing the Select function and confidentiality and integrity policies
E-Ballot$_e$	Data entity describing an empty electronic ballot
E-Ballot$_c$	Data entity describing completed electronic ballot
PrintContract	Contract entity describing the Print function and confidentiality and integrity policies
P-Ballot	Data entity describing the paper ballot
VerifyContract	Contract entity describing the Verify function and confidentiality and integrity policies
V-Bits$_u$	Data entity describing unselected verification bits corresponding to yes and no
V-Bits$_s$	Data entity describing the selected verification bit corresponding to either yes or no
CountContract	Contract entity describing the Count function and confidentiality and integrity policies
Result	Data entity describing all recorded votes
PrintReceiptContract	Contract entity describing the PrintReceipt function
Receipt	Data entity describing a receipt provided to a voter as confirmation that their vote was counted
ExitContract	Contract entity describing the Exit function and confidentiality and integrity policies

Table 3. Activities in an ACDC E-voting environment

Activities	Description
KeyGen	Produces a cryptographic key used to protect the confirmation number on both the P-Ballot and Receipt
Select	Produces a completed electronic ballot
Print	Produces a paper ballot
Verify	Produces a verification bit indicating whether the voter approves or denies the correct recording of their vote
Count	Produces an aggregated result of all previous votes plus the newly cast vote
PrintReceipt	Produces a voter confirmation receipt
Exit	Quits the voting process

Table 4. Agents in an ACDC E-voting environment

Agents	Description
Voter	Account agent describing a physical user acting in the role of someone casting a ballot
DRE	Node agent describing an ACDC equipped voting machine with a secure enclave for secure computation, which also includes a printer for a Voter-Verified Paper Audit Trail (VVPAT)

4.1 ACDC E-Voting Scenario

Within an ACDC architecture all voting may take place electronically on ACDC equipped voting machines. For illustration purposes, we assume these voting machines can perform similarly to Direct Recording Electronic (DRE) voting machines with a Voter-Verified Paper Audit Trail (VVPAT) [28]. However, ACDC equipped voting machines perform all computations securely (e.g., in a secure enclave) and the internal data of all capsules is encrypted. Tables 2, 3 and 4 describe the provenance objects in such an ACDC voting network.

In this scenario, a voter's ballot is successfully cast after the following steps: (1) a voter enters their unique *VoterID* into the ACDC equipped voting machine, (2) the voting machine invokes a key generation function in which a cryptographic key is generated that will be attributed to the corresponding voter, (3) the voter will then be presented with an electronic ballot in which they can manually enter their selections, (4) a paper ballot, containing a cryptographically protected confirmation number, will then be generated and displayed through a viewing glass for a limited amount of time, in which a user can verify whether they approve the recorded selections, (5) after the user verifies that their vote has been correctly recorded, the machine securely stores the paper ballot for a VVPAT, (6) the machine then electronically counts the new result by including the newly cast vote, and (7) the machine then provides a printed receipt to the voter, which includes a cryptographically protected confirmation number that matches the confirmation number of the paper ballot and exclaims that their vote has been counted. The encrypted confirmation number on the receipt provided to the voter can be used at a later date by the voter to ensure that their vote was correctly included in the election result [7].

To formalize, let $VM = (\mathcal{E}_k, \mathcal{E}_c, \mathcal{E}_d, G_n, G_a, \mathcal{A})$ be a distributed environment of ACDC equipped electronic voting machines where,

- $\mathcal{E}_k$ is a finite set of key entities, where each key entity describes a key belonging to either a voter or a voting machine,
- $\mathcal{E}_c$ is the finite set of contract entities where the possible contracts are *Key-GenContract*, *SelectContract*, *PrintContract*, *VerifyContract*, *CountContract*, *PrintReceiptContract*, and *ExitContract*,
- $\mathcal{E}_d$ is a finite set of data entities,
- G_n is a finite set of node agents, where each node is an ACDC equipped voting machine,
- G_a is a finite set of account agents, where each account is a physical user of an ACDC equipped voting machine, and

– $\mathcal{A}$ is a finite set of activities, where the possible activities are *KeyGen, Select, Print, Verify, Count, PrintReceipt,* and *Exit*.

This environment consists of a set of provenance graphs $2^V \times 2^E \times L^E$ where $V = \mathcal{E}_k \cup \mathcal{E}_c \cup \mathcal{E}_d \cup G_n \cup G_a \cup \mathcal{A}$ is the set of all possible vertices, $E \subset V \times V$ is the set of all possible edges, and L^E is the set of all possible labeling functions. We assume that in a scenario where a provenance-based enforcement mechanism is tasked with enforcing a provenance policy at a function execution, the mechanism is able to query the provenance record to obtain the relevant provenance graph $(V', E', l') \in 2^V \times 2^E \times L^E$. For this particular case study, a mechanism can query the provenance record for all provenance associated with a particular voter. Such an assumption is reasonable because an input-enabled mechanism will be enabled to query the necessary provenance by a voter inputting their *VoterID*; this requirement can be specified by the contract for a specific function. In this scenario, the provenance graph being evaluated will only contain one account agent, namely the present voter.

4.2   Voter Fraud Scenarios

To demonstrate the applicability of ACDC provenance for reasoning about voter fraud in an e-voting context, we consider 2 real scenarios in which voters have committed fraud and present provenance policies that might be enforced by ACDC voting machines to prevent such fraud. Additionally, we present a scenario in which a user may try to manipulate the voting machine and how provenance policies can aid in reasoning about such manipulation. These scenarios include: 1) a voter attempting to cast multiple votes [1,27], 2) an ineligible voter attempting to cast a vote [1,26], and 3) a voter attempting to cast multiple votes by exiting the system just before a receipt is printed.

Duplicate Voting. Consider a scenario in which a user, say Alice, is legitimately registered to vote in two states. Although it is not a crime for Alice to be registered in two states, it is a crime, according to state law, for her to cast more than one vote in the same election [2]. In this scenario, Alice has intentions on participating in early voting in state 1 and voting on election day in state 2. Because Alice has a legitimate *VoterID* for state 1, her vote will be counted and will result in a provenance record showing that she has cast a legitimate vote. When Alice attempts to vote on election day in state 2, based on her provenance record, the voting machine should not allow her to cast another ballot. The simplest check would be to determine whether Alice has already received a receipt indicating that she has already cast a ballot. To do so, we can express a provenance policy that defines the expected provenance of a printed receipt. This policy can be checked at the execution of the *KeyGen* activity, as specified by the *KeyGenContract*, when Alice attempts to cast a second ballot. Formally, given a provenance graph $(V', E', l') \in 2^V \times 2^E \times L^E$ that corresponds to all provenance metadata associated with Alice, we can determine whether Alice has been attributed a printed receipt if the following policy P evaluates to true

$$
\begin{aligned}
P(V', E', l') \iff & \ \exists\, \varepsilon_d, a, g_a \in V' : ((a, PrintReceiptContract) \in E' \\
& \wedge\ l'(a, PrintReceiptContract) = Used) \\
& \wedge\ ((\varepsilon_d, a) \in E' \wedge l'(\varepsilon_d, a) = WasGeneratedBy) \\
& \wedge\ ((\varepsilon_d, PrintReceiptContract) \in E' \\
& \wedge\ l'(\varepsilon_d, PrintReceiptContract) = WasDerivedFrom) \\
& \wedge\ ((\varepsilon_d, g_a) \in E' \wedge l'(\varepsilon_d, g_a) = WasAttributedTo)).
\end{aligned}
$$

If the policy evaluates to true over the given provenance graph, then the voting machine can take the necessary actions of preventing Alice from casting a second ballot (e.g., exiting the system).

Ineligible Voting. In the US 2012 election a convicted felon successfully voted in the election, in a state that prohibits convicted felons from voting, by providing false information on the voter registration form [26]. Consider a scenario in which Bob, who is a convicted felon, falsely indicates that he is not a convicted felon on his voter's registration form and is approved to vote and is provided a legitimate *VoterID*. Because US convicted felon records are public record, this record can be considered as a blacklist of account agents in an ACDC voting network. Although a user may have a valid *VoterID*, voting machines can ensure that they are not acting on behalf of blacklisted account agents. However, to make this determination, Bob will first have to enter his *VoterID* into the voting machine, thereby generating provenance of a voting machine acting on his behalf. When the voting machine invokes the *KeyGen* function, the function will first use the *KeyGenContract* to determine how it will process entities. The contract can specify a provenance policy stating that the function should proceed iff the voting machine for which it is associated with is not acting on behalf of a blacklisted account agent. Formally, given Bob's provenance graph $(V', E', l') \in 2^V \times 2^E \times L^E$ we can determine if Bob is a convicted felon if

$$
\begin{aligned}
\exists G_{a_{blacklist}} \subseteq G_a : P(V', E', l') \iff & \ \exists g_{a_{blacklist}} \in G_{a_{blacklist}} : \\
& \ \exists g_n \in V' : (g_n, g_{a_{blacklist}}) \in E' \\
& \ \wedge\ l'(g_n, g_{a_{blacklist}}) = ActedOnBehalfOf.
\end{aligned}
$$

If this policy evaluates to true, then it will be known that the voting machine is acting on behalf of a blacklisted user; therefore, this user should not be allowed to cast a vote according to state law.

Manipulating an ACDC Voting Machine. Consider a scenario in which a malicious voter, Mallory, is aware of the workflow of the voting machine and attempts to manipulate a voting machine into allowing her to vote multiple times by preventing the attribution of a receipt for her vote. In this scenario, Mallory may be able to exit the voting process right after the *Count* function executes but before the *PrintReceipt* function executes. When Mallory attempts to vote again her provenance record will not indicate that she has been attributed a receipt for voting. To detect this scenario, we can specify a policy to detect the execution of each function to determine how far Mallory may have gotten in the voting process. Due to space limitations, we only show a policy to detect the execution of the *KeyGen* function. The other policies can be found in the extended version of this paper [11]. Formally, given a provenance graph $(V', E', l') \in 2^V \times 2^E \times L^E$ we can specify the following policy for the *KeyGen* function—the other policies can be specified similarly:

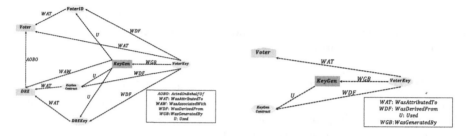

Fig. 3. KeyGen provenance event.   **Fig. 4.** Policy subgraph

$$
\begin{aligned}
P(V', E', l') \iff & \exists \, \varepsilon_k, a, g_a \in V' : ((a, KeyGenContract) \in E' \\
& \land \, l'(a, KeyGenContract) = Used) \\
& \land \, ((\varepsilon_k, a) \in E' \land l'(\varepsilon_k, a) = WasGeneratedBy) \\
& \land \, ((\varepsilon_k, KeyGenContract) \in E' \\
& \land \, l'(\varepsilon_k, KeyGenContract) = WasDerivedFrom) \\
& \land \, ((\varepsilon_k, g_a) \in E' \land l'(\varepsilon_k, g_a) = WasAttributedTo)
\end{aligned}
$$

Informally, such policies can evaluate whether each of the possible contracts were used by activities that generated entities, if so, the generated entities should be derived from the specified contract and attributed to the account agent under consideration. Figure's 3 and 4 illustrate the *KeyGen* event and the subgraph specified by the policy, respectively. These policies can be composed to form a single policy to be evaluated at the *KeyGen* activity whenever a voter attempts to begin the voting process. Because we employ a separation of concerns and specify policies for each functional execution, the mechanism enforcing such policies can determine how far Mallory may have gotten in the voting process by determining which policies fail. In our scenario, since Mallory's provenance record indicates that she completed all steps except for the *PrintReceipt* function, if she attempts to vote on the same machine as her originally counted vote, then the machine can continue its process and print a receipt with a confirmation number based on her *VoterKey*. If Mallory attempts to vote on another machine, then the machine can simply exit, perhaps notifying Mallory to return to the original machine for a receipt.

4.3   Challenges of Voting Provenance

Due to the increase of technology used in voting elections where the technology can malfunction [12], is possibly vulnerable to attacks [3], and may be hacked [4],

it is important to be able to verify the trustworthiness of results reported by voting machines. Data provenance collection is one viable solution to ensure trustworthy results. However, in a democratic election it is important to only reveal
the final result of the election while keeping individual votes secret. Auditing the
provenance record of a DRE voting machine in a traditional provenance architecture can reveal the results of individual ballots and can attribute ballots to
specific voters.

Prior work has examined protection mechanisms for provenance storage systems in which the leakage of the provenance record is potentially more sensitive
than the leakage of the data for which the provenance corresponds (e.g., [5,8]).
However, such solutions are system-centric, relying on protection mechanisms
of the storage system. If the system is breached by an unauthorized agent, the
provenance record may be exposed. Therefore, the security of the provenance
record relies on the strength of security placed on the physical storage system.

We argue that a data-centric approach is more suitable and may provide better security guarantees in scenarios where both the data and provenance record
of such data can reveal sensitive information. Analyzing provenance records in
an ACDC e-voting network, where all data capsules contain encrypted data, does
not suffer from the drawbacks of analyzing provenance records in a traditional
system-centric architecture because an ACDC provenance record is a causal
record of named encrypted data rather than a causal record of named plaintext
data. Therefore, the only information that may be revealed by an ACDC voting
provenance record is that a specific user cast a vote but not what or who the
particular user voted for. We do not consider revealing that a particular user
cast a vote as a limitation of this architecture because this fact is inherent to
any voting system in practice.

5   Related Work

Several frameworks have been proposed for analyzing provenance metadata but
do so reactively and in retrospect, relying on either human analysis or the use of
automated tools that may rely on machine learning techniques to characterize
provenance graphs. Reactive security has benefits in areas such as identifying the
root cause of an attack [19] and security auditing to ensure compliance with company policies [25]. While useful, these security practices do not actively prevent
security mishaps. Proactive security practices should also be used in conjunction
with reactive security practices. However, because proactive security policies are
specified with the intent of being enforced, such policies must be based on precise
and unambiguous reasoning instead of human intuition. Relevant to this work is
proactive reasoning about data provenance, which has received little attention
in the literature.

Much work related to data provenance has focused in the areas of provenance
collection (e.g., [21]) and secure storage of provenance metadata (e.g., [22]). Both
of these areas are foundational to provenance-aware systems; however, in the
context of security, it is equally important to continually analyze provenance

metadata at runtime to gain insight into and maintain a computing environment's overall security posture.

Due to the large amounts of data that provenance collection systems can capture, relying on human analysis is impractical and error prone [15]. Automated tools aim to simplify and make the analysis of provenance metadata more efficient; however, many do so at a loss in precision. Huynh et al. [16] present an automated analysis technique that relies on network analysis and machine learning techniques, it is shown that their analysis technique is able to classify provenance graphs into predetermined categories with high accuracy. FRAP-puccino [14] is a provenance-based intrusion detection framework that aims to distinguish benign from anomalous behavior using a machine learning approach. Although machine learning techniques improve the efficiency with which provenance graphs can be analyzed, in high security contexts, such techniques have at least two drawbacks: (1) the classification categories do not provide well-defined properties of the graphs, and (2) the classification categories cannot provide formal guarantees about data due to the possibility of false positives and false negatives.

CamQuery [24] is a framework for the runtime analysis of whole system provenance. Because analysis takes place at runtime, the framework takes a proactive approach to policy specification over provenance metadata by expressing policies in a programmable graph processing framework inspired by GraphChi [18] and GraphX [13]. Our approach differs from CamQuery in that we present a formal approach for reasoning about provenance policies in a distributed environment, which is based on a mathematical semantics of provenance graphs.

Lemay et al. [20] present a framework for automated analysis of provenance by using graph grammars as a way to characterize provenance graphs. However, because the class of graphs parseable by such grammar is restricted to regular grammars, precision is lost and some graphs become parseable that the analyst may not intend to be; therefore, this approach is not amenable to security policy specification in which the policy must be precise and unambiguous.

Park et al. [23], present a model for provenance-based access control in which policies are specified using propositional logic as an underlying formalism. This approach can provide formal guarantees about data that conforms to the policy. However, the approach presented in [23] is specific to the access-control domain. In this paper, we have provided a more general and expressive framework for reasoning about provenance policies in a distributed, data-centric environment by using predicate logic as an underlying formalism.

6   Conclusion and Future Work

In summary, this paper presented a new data-centric paradigm that provides capabilities for rigorous provenance analysis over distributed systems. A formal approach for reasoning about, and the proactive specification of, provenance policies was introduced. Additionally, we provided a case study that examined the provenance policies necessary to ensure integrity of an ACDC-equipped electronic voting system without sacrificing capabilities for post-factum auditing that traditional provenance techniques provide. We believe that the migration from the current server-centric security paradigm is key to not only enabling the collection of coarsely-grained provenance that is suitable for proactive policy evaluation, but also defends against catastrophic compromises of data records within a given system. In this regard, there are two primary directions for future work stemming from this initial policy design and evaluation. First, the expansion of the ACDC framework. Securing data as a first-class citizen is an approach that has a myriad of benefits that prevent many of the pitfalls that have led to catastrophic data breaches in systems today. Second, there is independent advancement of provenance policies in the Function as a Service (FaaS) execution model. Such an expansion could enable clients of services such as AWS lambda to untangle the currently inscrutable chain of custody for inputs and products used in FaaS-style execution. This may entail the introduction of a distributed truncation-resistant store and provenance hooks into FaaS job specifications, but could be handled entirely on the clients' end.

References

1. A sampling of election fraud cases from across the country. https://www.heritage.org/sites/default/files/voterfraud_download/VoterFraudCases_5.pdf. Accessed 10 Jan 2020
2. Double voting (2018). https://www.ncsl.org/research/elections-and-campaigns/double-voting.aspx. Accessed 10 Jan 2020
3. Appel, A.W., et al.: The New Jersey voting-machine lawsuit and the AVC advantage DRE voting machine. In: Electronic Voting Technology Workshop/Workshop on Trustworthy Elections (2009)
4. Bannet, J., Price, D.W., Rudys, A., Singer, J., Wallach, D.S.: Hack-a-vote: security issues with electronic voting systems. IEEE Secur. Privacy **2**(1), 32–37 (2004)
5. Bates, A., Mood, B., Valafar, M., Butler, K.: Towards secure provenance-based access control in cloud environments. In: Proceedings of the third ACM Conference on Data and Application Security and Privacy, pp. 277–284. ACM (2013)
6. Belhajjame, K., et al.: PROV-DM: the PROV data model. Technical report (2012). http://www.w3.org/TR/prov-dm/
7. Bernhard, M., et al.: Public evidence from secret ballots. In: Krimmer, R., Volkamer, M., Braun Binder, N., Kersting, N., Pereira, O., Schürmann, C. (eds.) E-Vote-ID 2017. LNCS, vol. 10615, pp. 84–109. Springer, Cham (2017). https://doi.org/10.1007/978-3-319-68687-5_6
8. Braun, U.J., Shinnar, A., Seltzer, M.I.: Securing provenance. In: Proceedings of the 3rd USENIX Workshop on Hot Topics in Security (2008)
9. Cassidy, C.A., Long, C.: Voting officials under scrutiny amid heavy election turnout (2018). https://apnews.com/8af093ef14954d3293fae718c37f3eb3. Accessed 10 Jan 2020
10. Chase, M.: Multi-authority attribute based encryption. In: Vadhan, S.P. (ed.) TCC 2007. LNCS, vol. 4392, pp. 515–534. Springer, Heidelberg (2007). https://doi.org/10.1007/978-3-540-70936-7_28

11. Engram, S., Kaczmarek, T., Lee, A., Bigelow, D.: Proactive provenance policies for automatic cryptographic data centric security. arXiv preprint arXiv:submit/ 3769967 (2021)
12. Friedersdorf, C.: An embarrassment of glitches: a wealthy country should be able to conduct a national election with fewer problems than the united states experiences in the 2018 midterms (2018). https://www.theatlantic.com/ideas/archive/2018/ 11/voting-machines/575044/. Accessed 10 Jan 2020
13. Gonzalez, J.E., Xin, R.S., Dave, A., Crankshaw, D., Franklin, M.J., Stoica, I.: Graphx: graph processing in a distributed dataflow framework. In: 11th USENIX Symposium on Operating Systems Design and Implementation, pp. 599–613 (2014)
14. Han, X., Pasquier, T., Ranjan, T., Goldstein, M., Seltzer, M.: Frappuccino: fault-detection through runtime analysis of provenance. In: Workshop on Hot Topics in Cloud Computing (2017)
15. Hassan, W.U., Aguse, L., Aguse, N., Bates, A., Moyer, T.: Towards scalable cluster auditing through grammatical inference over provenance graphs. In: Network and Distributed Systems Security Symposium (2018)
16. Huynh, T.D., Ebden, M., Fischer, J., Roberts, S., Moreau, L.: Provenance network analytics. Data Mining Knowl. Discov. **32**(3), 708–735 (2018)
17. Jacobson, V., Smetters, D.K., Thornton, J.D., Plass, M.F., Briggs, N.H., Braynard, R.L.: Networking named content. In: Proceedings of the 5th International Conference on Emerging Networking Experiments and Technologies, pp. 1–12 (2009)
18. Kyrola, A., Blelloch, G., Guestrin, C.: GraphChi: large-scale graph computation on just a PC. In: 10th USENIX Symposium on Operating Systems Design and Implementation, pp. 31–46 (2012)
19. Lee, K.H., Zhang, X., Xu, D.: High accuracy attack provenance via binary-based execution partition. In: Network and Distributed System Security Symposium (2013)
20. Lemay, M., Hassan, W.U., Moyer, T., Schear, N., Smith, W.: Automated provenance analytics: a regular grammar based approach with applications in security. In: 9th USENIX Workshop on the Theory and Practice of Provenance (2017)
21. Liang, X., Shetty, S., Tosh, D., Kamhoua, C., Kwiat, K., Njilla, L.: Provchain: a blockchain-based data provenance architecture in cloud environment with enhanced privacy and availability. In: Proceedings of the International Symposium on Cluster, Cloud and Grid Computing, pp. 468–477. IEEE Press (2017)
22. Liang, X., Zhao, J., Shetty, S., Li, D.: Towards data assurance and resilience in IoT using blockchain. In: IEEE Military Communications Conference, pp. 261–266. IEEE (2017)
23. Park, J., Nguyen, D., Sandhu, R.: A provenance-based access control model. In: International Conference on Privacy, Security and Trust, pp. 137–144. IEEE (2012)
24. Pasquier, T., et al.: Runtime analysis of whole-system provenance. In: Proceedings of the 2018 ACM SIGSAC Conference on Computer and Communications Security, pp. 1601–1616. ACM (2018)
25. Pasquier, T., Singh, J., Powles, J., Eyers, D., Seltzer, M., Bacon, J.: Data provenance to audit compliance with privacy policy in the internet of things. Pers. Ubiquit. Comput. **22**(2), 333–344 (2018)
26. Trischitta, L.: 'I voted early' sticker leads to arrest, fraud charges (2013). https:// www.sun-sentinel.com/news/fl-xpm-2013-02-22-fl-felon-voter-fraud-pompano-20130222-story.html. Accessed 10 Jan 2020

27. Vielmetti, B.: Shorewood man sentenced to jail for multiple votes in several elections. https://archive.jsonline.com/news/crime/shorewood-man-sentenced-to-jail-for-multiple-votes-in-several-elections-b99677321z1-370317801.html. Accessed 10 Jan 2020

28. Wack, J.P.: Draft Standard for Voter Verified Paper Audit Trails in DRE Voting Systems (DRE-VVPAT): Supplement to the 2002 Voting Systems Standard (2005). https://www.nist.gov/system/files/documents/itl/vote/VVPAT-Addendum-jpw-3-2-051.pdf. Accessed 10 Jan 2020

Provenance-Based Security Audits and Its Application to COVID-19 Contact Tracing Apps

Andreas Schreiber[1(✉)], Tim Sonnekalb[2], Thomas S. Heinze[2],
Lynn von Kurnatowski[1], Jesus M. Gonzalez-Barahona[3], and Heather Packer[4]

[1] Institute for Software Technology, German Aerospace Center (DLR),
Cologne and Weßling, Germany
`andreas.schreiber@dlr.de`
[2] Institute of Data Science, German Aerospace Center (DLR), Jena, Germany
[3] Universidad Rey Juan Carlos, Fuenlabrada, Spain
[4] University of Southampton, Southampton SO17 1BJ, UK

Abstract. Software repositories contain information about source code, software development processes, and team interactions. We combine the provenance of development processes with code security analysis results to provide fast feedback on the software's design and security issues. Results from queries of the provenance graph drives the security analysis, which are conducted on certain events—such as commits or pull requests by external contributors. We evaluate our method on Open Source projects that are developed under time pressure and use Germany's COVID-19 contact tracing app 'Corona-Warn-App' as a case study.

Keywords: Program analysis · Provenance · Software security ·
Repository mining · Open source software · COVID-19

1 Introduction

The COVID-19 pandemic raises challenges for scientists of many disciplines. Information technology help to fight the pandemic with software systems, AI models, and other technologies [12,19,20], which must be developed under time pressure [3], with high quality, and with accepted concepts for data security and privacy.

For example, apps for mobile devices that support *contact tracing* of infected persons are useful to identify local COVID-19 hot-spots and find other persons, who are potentially infected, too [4]. For contact tracing, several architectures are possible and have been discussed—sometimes with significant controversy— in many countries. Two favoured approaches are centralized and decentralized architectures; both using Bluetooth Low Energy for contact identification. Apple and Google developed an *Exposure Notification API*[1] as extension of their

---

[1] https://www.apple.com/covid19/contacttracing/.

© Springer Nature Switzerland AG 2021
B. Glavic et al. (Eds.): IPAW 2020/IPAW 2021, LNCS 12839, pp. 88–105, 2021.
https://doi.org/10.1007/978-3-030-80960-7_6

operating systems iOS and Android, which developers of exposure notification apps can use for privacy-preserving contact tracing.

Because exposure notification apps are an important contemporary topic with serious real-life context, we use the German decentralized exposure notification app *Corona-Warn-App*[2] (CWA; see Sect. 2) for a *case study* towards continuous evaluation with regards to security by automated analysis [17,33]. The CWA is an Open Source software, which is by far not always the case for a governmental software. Its software repositories contain significant process information in addition to the source code itself. Especially for Open Source projects, the team composition and development process is transparent and traceable and can be evaluated at any point of time.

We structure our contributions towards an *automated, provenance-driven security audit methodology and infrastructure for software projects* as follows:

- Some insights into the development of the Corona-Warn-App, to give some context (Sect. 2).
- Our method for querying the development process by using provenance (Sect. 3).
- An overview of static code analysis, which we use for our purpose (Sect. 4).
- Our method for combining information from process provenance with static code analysis for some specific revisions of the source code (Sect. 5).
- As as case study for demonstrating the methodology, some intentionally simple example queries to the *CWA server* repository (Sect. 6).

An in-depth analysis of the CWA is beyond the scope of this paper.

2 Development of the "Corona-Warn-App"

The development of the Corona-Warn-App gets special attention during the COVID-19 pandemic; the development had to be done in a short time frame: development started in April 2020 and the app was released on 16th June, 2020for Android and iOS. CWA is developed by SAP and Telekom using a transparent and open development process. CWA has a decentralized architecture, accompanied by centrally-managed Java-based server applications to distribute findings about infected users and store test results uploaded by the laboratories.

CWA development history is publicly available from 13 repositories (some of them auxiliary), including data[3] since 29th April, 2020, for source code changes (15166 git commits; Fig. 1), issue tracking (2560 GitHub issues) and code review (5780 GitHub pull requests)[4]. The human team participating in the development is composed of 306 persons authoring code changes, working on the documentation, filing issues, testing, etc. Taking into account the short time span, this amounts to much effort, and suggests that most of the real activity is in these public repositories.

---

[2] https://github.com/corona-warn-app.

[3] Data source: https://cauldron.io/project/3860.

[4] All numbers are as of 10th March, 2021.

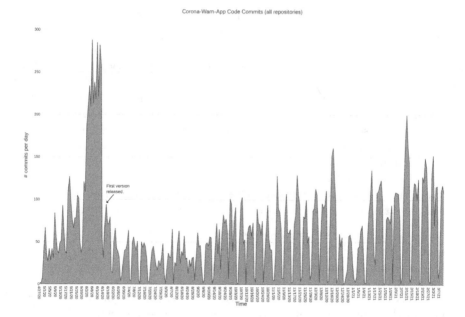

Fig. 1. Code commits for the Corona-Warn-App repositories over time.

The analysis of the software development context for applications, by retrieving metadata from software repositories, has been an active area of research since the early 2000s [28,40]. During this time several tools have been developed to get some metrics about the software development process and the team building it. We use GRIMOIRELAB[5], a toolset for retrieving data from software development repositories, storing it, and performing analytics (via its SaaS instance CAULDRON[6]), to produce statistics for the CWA. In this case, the context analysis ensures that the data analyzed for provenance is likely real (e.g., it is not likely that the analyzed repositories are not "dump repositories," where code is copied from time to time, while the real activity happens elsewhere), and gives an idea of the volume of activity caused by the project. In a more complete analysis, software development analytics may complement our provenance analysis by providing insights about how the different actors behave in the project, and how their contributions are related and processed.

3   Provenance of Repositories

Software development is a highly complex process involving a wide range of responsibilities and people. In addition the complexity of the software itself grows over time. To cope with this, different tools are used to support the development

---

[5] GRIMOIRELAB: http://chaoss.github.io/grimoirelab.
[6] CAULDRON: https://cauldron.io.

process. During the entire software development process, all these support tools produce several types of data. These large amounts of data, which are generated before, during, and after the development of a software, can be analyzed using *provenance* [22].

Provenance analysis focusing on the development of open source software projects provides insight into the interactions of people. These interactions can fall into different categories. The most notable interactions in the development of track and trace software for COVID-19 are those that scrutinize the nature of the data collected and stored. These are hard to evaluate for automated processing with respect to privacy and security concerns. This can be evident in the provenance by the number of people collaborating outside of the development team, the number of developers, and the issues reported. While these types of measures cannot guarantee the ethics of the software, it does provide an indication that it has been evaluated by humans.

3.1   Generating Retrospective Provenance for Git Repositories

To analyze the development process, we extract *retrospective provenance* [21] from repositories and store it in a graph database for further analysis (Fig. 2) [29]. To extract provenance from **git**-based projects we use tools, which crawl the **git** repositories and additional information, such as issues or pull requests (GIT2PROV [5,38] and GITHUB2PROV [26]). The provenance is generated as a file in PROV-JSON format and then stored in a Neo4j graph database. While GitHub already provides visualizations for their hosted projects, the GITHUB2PROV model supports bespoke visualizations that benefit from complex queries across the model's graph structure, which are not achievable using GitHub's API.

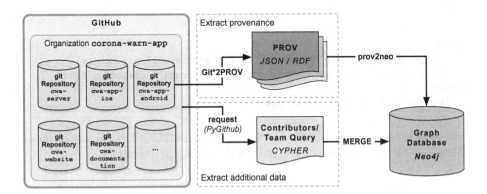

Fig. 2. Extracting provenance from git repositories using GITHUB2PROV and additional information using the GitHub API.

3.2   Using and Analyzing Provenance—An Example

To analyze the provenance graph, many *visual* and *analytical* methods exist; including graph visualization or semantic reasoning. We illustrate querying and using the provenance graph for a simple query for the *CWA Server* repository: *"Which files have commits by team members as well as external contributors?"*

After extracting the provenance, we generate a CYPHER query, that adds information about contributors roles. We retrieve member information via the GitHub API and store it in Python lists of team members and external contributors, which we insert in a CYPHER template. The following Python snippet adds a new relationship between team members and the files where they contributed during development:

```
link_team_query = """
MATCH
  (n:Agent)-[:wasAttributedTo]-(e:Entity)-[:specializationOf]-(f:Entity)
WHERE
  n.`prov:label` IN {team}
MERGE
  (n)-[r:CONTRIBUTES_TO {{role: 'team'}}]->(f)
""".format(team=team,)
```

This CYPHER query creates new directed relations between persons [Agent] and files [Entity] with an attribute "role" ∈ {"team","contributor"}; for example, the relation for team members who made a change to any of the file's revision is:(:Agent)-[:CONTRIBUTES_TO {role: 'team'}]->(:Entity). This additional relation within the graph database simplifies further queries regarding impacts of team members vs. external contributors (Fig. 3).

Then we query for files, where team members and external contributors made changes at any of the files revisions:

```
MATCH
  (team_member:Agent)-[:CONTRIBUTES_TO {role: 'team'}]->(f:Entity)<-
  [:CONTRIBUTES_TO {role: 'contributor'}]-(external_contributor:Agent)
RETURN
  team_member,f,external_contributor
```

Instead of using the extra database relation CONTRIBUTES_TO, it would also possible to create more complex CYPHER queries with sub-queries for

The query result is exported, either for visualization (Fig. 4) or as input for the static code analysis (Sects. 4, 5 and 6).

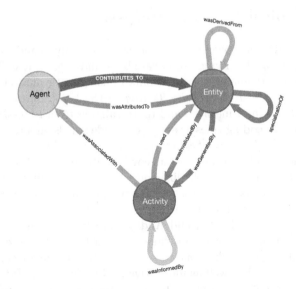

Fig. 3. The meta graph of the property graph in Neo4j for the extended provenance graph: all PROV classes elements and relations that are generated by GITHUB2PROV as well as the additional database relation CONTRIBUTES_TO.

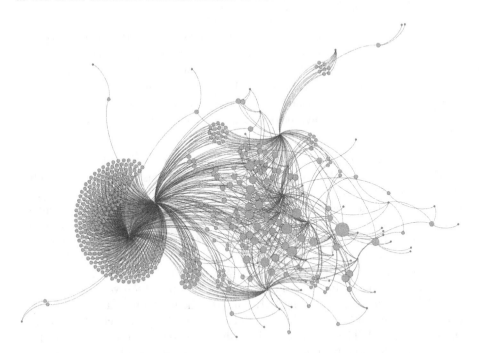

Fig. 4. Source code files (●) and contributors (●) for the cwa-server project. Red edges indicate file changes by team members (●——→●). Blue edges indicate file changes by external contributors (●——→●). (Color figure online)

4   Code Audit with Static Analysis

Static code analysis is a proven method for program analysis and can be used as an early indicator for identifying pre-release bugs and defects as well as vulnerabilities [23]. In security analysis, the discipline of using static analysis tools is also known as *Static Application Security Testing (SAST)* [25]. Static code analysis spans a wide spectrum of methods and tools, ranging from *linters*, which check adherence of code to coding rules or absence of code smells on a textual and syntactical level, to *full-fledged verification tools*, which formally prove specific properties of the code. Checked properties can cover multiple aspects of program code, including unreachable code, smells like code duplication, null pointer/reference errors, concurrency bugs, incorrect API usage, and taint-related problems like data leaks and code injection vulnerabilities.

SAST tools for Java, Kotlin, and Android are included in our analysis, as these are the dominant programming languages for CWA. Because a single tool is not enough [9,25], more than one tool is used for each language. We include simple linters like *PMD* as well as more advanced tools such as *Infer* and *Xanitizer* (Table 1). Except Xanitizer, all tools are open source and freely available.

Table 1. Used static analysis tools.

Static analysis tool	Tool category	Reference
Flowdroid	Taint analysis	https://blogs.uni-paderborn.de/sse/tools/
Xanitizer	Taint analysis	https://www.rigs-it.com/xanitizer/
Infer	Formal verification	https://fbinfer.com/
Spotbugs/FindSecBugs	Coding rules	https://spotbugs.github.io/
Detekt	Coding rules	https://detekt.github.io/detekt/
PMD	Linter, code smells	https://pmd.github.io/

The differences of the tools become also apparent when considering the number of reports per tool. We provide the number of warnings reported by the linter PMD and by the more specialized SAST scanner Xanitizer for the `cwa-server` repository over time (Fig. 5)[7]. The number of the linter's reports simply increase conjointly with the growth of the code base during the repository's continuing development. The picture for Xanitizer is more complex (Fig. 5b)—for example a drop in the number of reported warnings when a SAST-supported pull request review was installed in May 2020 (issues #13/14 in `cwa-server`).

SAST tools can be integrated at various points in the software development lifecycle (e.g., while coding using IDE plugins, when committing to a developer repository, either in batch mode or at diff-time, or when conducting designated quality assurance). The utility of static analysis is known to be influenced by factors such as false-positive ratio, understandable and actionable analysis results,

---

[7] Spikes in the graphs during 08/20–09/20 are due to parallel branch development.

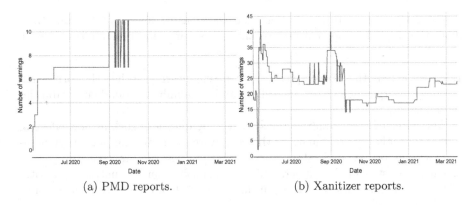

(a) PMD reports. (b) Xanitizer reports.

Fig. 5. PMD and Xanitizer analysis warnings for the `cwa-server` repository over time.

and integration with developer workflow [16,32]. Experiences in large-scale application of static analysis shows, that integration with developer workflow and reporting bugs as soon as possible is in particular important [6,14].

The CWA project employs standard best practices for (secure) software development. As a part of that, SAST-supported code review for auditing the quality and security of external contributions (i.e., pull requests), was configured. For example, *SonarCloud* found a bug, which would have otherwise been introduced into the code base of the repository `cwa-app-android` by pull request #876 [33]. The bug was signaled by *SonarScanner* when reviewing the pull request[8].

5 Provenance-Driven Code Analysis

For conducting a security analysis of the CWA and its development process, we integrate the extracted provenance (Sect. 3) with bugs or vulnerabilities as reported by the selection of static analysis tools (Sect. 4). In our infrastructure, we therefore consider individual commit snapshots in the history of the CWA repositories [33]. According to the respective repository, we run certain static analysis tools on a snapshot, track their reported findings and save them into a database for later analysis.

Due to the various involved static analysis tools and their differing report formatting and output granularity, the tools' findings need to be consolidated such that, for example, duplicated findings can be identified. The tools' reports are therefore parsed to extract the locations and types of found bugs or vulnerabilities; the latter is additionally normalized using the *Common Weakness Enumeration* (CWE)[9] and other bug ontologies. Interlinking the tools findings with provenance information is done via the respective snapshot's *commit hash*.

---

[8] cf. https://github.com/corona-warn-app/cwa-app-android/pull/876.

[9] https://cwe.mitre.org/.

Using the combined information then allows us to answer various questions about the CWA development process and how security has been addressed, such as:

1. Classical hypotheses of empirical software engineering, such as the correlation of repository metrics (e.g., code churn and the number of found vulnerabilities or bugs) [24].
2. The usage of static analysis tools, answering questions such as how effective certain tools—or combinations thereof—were in uncovering bugs or vulnerabilities [9] or how understandable and usable their reports were [16].
3. Characteristics of the vulnerability management can be analyzed quantitatively, using metrics such as mean time to fix [13], or qualitatively, using fault tree analysis.

The general principle of our provenance-driven code analysis is to select relevant or "interesting" activities Activity (e.g., commits or releases) during the development process by querying the provenance database and then to query the SAST database on the provenance query results. In detail, we conduct the following steps (Fig. 6):

Step 1: Query the (using CYPHER for a distinct list of commits Activity .
Step 2: Clean—and optionally filter—the query result to get a clean list of commit hashes.
Step 3: Query the SAST database for each of the commit hashes from Step 2.
Step 4: Analyze the results from Step 3. For example, by summarizing, classifying, or visualizing them.

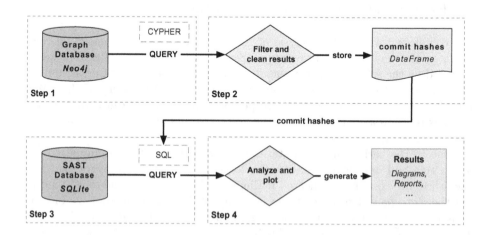

Fig. 6. The four steps of the provenance-driven code analysis.

In practice, we use Python to submit the CYPHER query to Neo4j and store the result in a Pandas `DataFrame`, on which we do Step 2. Then, we submit an SQL query on the SAST database using Pandas' `read_sql_query` method for each of the commit hashes, which returns—for example—the number of warnings reported for changed files during the related commits.

6   Case Study: Corona-Warn-App

In this section, we present examples for queries and results for the *CWA Server* repository[10], which is the implementation of the server for encryption keys for the Corona-Warn-App (i.e., part of the backend infrastructure). The `cwa-server` development started from the beginning of the whole CWA project[11]. The repository has 1042 commits (by team members and external contributors), 983 pull/merge requests (976 closed), and 251 issues (247 closed) with 1411 comments. 99 authors (i.e., git users) contributed to the development.

As an example, we investigate the correlation between the role of a contributor and the number of warnings that the code analysis tools reported after a git commit. We extracted the provenance from the `cwa-server` using GitHub2PROV, which led to a property graph with 49914 nodes and 110265 relations in Neo4j (see Packer et al. [26] for a description of the PROV model).

For **Step 1**, we use the CYPHER query from Sect. 3.2, which already returns files Entity where both team members and external contributors made changes at any of the files revisions, and extend it with a subquery (CYPHER clause "CALL") to return the actual commits Activity . Specifically, the following CYPHER query gets all commits for external contributions:

```
MATCH
    (external_contributor:Agent)-[:CONTRIBUTES_TO {role: 'contributor'}]
    ->(file:Entity)
CALL {
    WITH external_contributor, file
    MATCH (f:Entity)-[:wasGeneratedBy]->(commit:Activity)-
        [:wasAssociatedWith]->(c:Agent)
    WHERE c = external_contributor
    RETURN DISTINCT commit
}
RETURN
    file.`prov:label` AS filename,
    external_contributor.`prov:label` as contributor,
    commit.`prov2neo:identifier` AS commit
```

This query returns 34091 distinct file changes in total with contributions to 596 files by 50 external contributors in 407 unique commits.

---

[10] https://github.com/corona-warn-app/cwa-server.

[11] All numbers are as of 10th March, 2021.

The following Python code does **Steps 1–3**, which include the SQL query on the SAST database:

```python
# Query Neo4j, store results in Pandas DataFrame (Step 1)
df = graph_db.run(query).to_data_frame()

# Clean query results (Step 2)
df["commit"]= df["commit"].str.replace('result:commit-', '')

# Iterate over retrieved commit hashes, query SAST database (Step 3)
warnings = pd.DataFrame(columns=['commit', 'warnings'])
for commit_hash in query_result_df.commit.unique():
    df = pd.read_sql_query("""
            SELECT count(*)
            FROM warning
            WHERE warning.run IN
                (SELECT run.id
                FROM run
                WHERE run.snapshot = '{commit_hash}');
    """.format(commit_hash=commit_hash), sast_db)
    warnings = warnings.append({'commit': commit_hash,
        'warnings': df.get('count(*)')[0]},ignore_index=True)

# do something with results here... (Step 4)
```

As a result, we show the distribution of the number of warnings per commit actions as a histogram plot (Fig. 7). The plot shows the distribution of how many commits with the given number of warnings were made by external contributors and by team members. While for many commits the number of security warnings is similar for both contributor roles, external contributors provoke clearly visible more warnings per commit; around 45 more warnings compared to team members.

The predominance of commits with more than 20 accumulated static analysis warnings (Fig. 7) coincides with the development of SAST warnings over time with PMD and Xanitizer (Fig. 5). This result is well explainable by the usual ratio of false positive warnings for SAST tools, which is in particular high for linters or lightweight tools [14,32], and shows the need for tool selection and configuration.

Another example for a result that can be queried with an according SQL query, is the difference in the number of warnings caused by commits—compared to the previous revision (Fig. 8). The result visually shows: for most commits, the number of warning does not change at all. For a few commits, the number of warnings changes slightly between ±5. For some commits, the difference is higher around ±15.

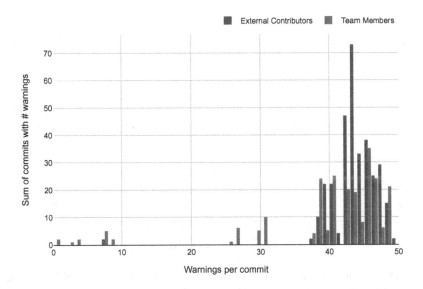

Fig. 7. Distribution of number of all SAST warnings for commits.

Most commits do not significantly change the number of accumulated SAST warnings, but stay in the range of adding or removing up to 5 warnings. This is again in line with our expectations, as the CWA project introduced SAST checking early in the development process, thus certainly preventing a number of SAST warnings a priori, and a sampling of commits showed that for most commits it is not very large. However, this could be further researched by analyzing the size of the commits' code diffs in more detail. There are though some outliers on both ends (Fig. 8). These are partially explainable by special effects (e.g., the initial setup of the project) but certainly make up interesting questions for further investigation. For instance, whether or not issues[12] calling for community-effort in "brushing up" the code base can be associated to commits showing a drop in the number of SAST warnings.

7   Related Work

While we consider the development process and security of the implementation of the CWA, most of current research on the security of contact tracings apps sheds light on their architectural design and discusses thereby implied attacks and possible mitigations. Ahmed et al. [1] give a comprehensive overview on the topic, also including contact tracing solutions other than CWA.

The initial development of the CWA took place as a controversial discussion about centralized and decentralized architectures [2,8,36,37]. Originally,

---

[12] For example, https://github.com/corona-warn-app/cwa-server/issues/269.

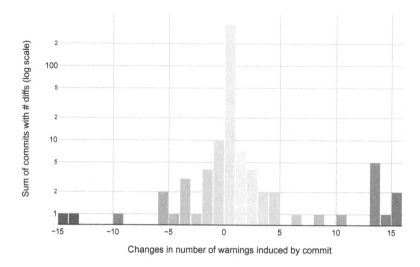

Fig. 8. Distribution of change in the number of SAST warnings caused by commits; compared to previous revision (logarithmic scale). The chart shows results for change by external contributors only.

the German contact tracing app was planned as centralized protocol in line with the *PEPP-PT*[13] initiative. However, the CWA adopted its current decentralized design based on *DP-3T*[14] and the *Exposure Notification Framework* from Apple and Google.

Vaudenay [36] investigates the decentralized protocol of the DP-3T solution and possible attack scenarios on the communication. He concludes, that there are downsides in the design of decentralized protocols, and that, counterintuitively, a decentralized solution causes more threats compared to a well-designed centralized protocol. Gvili [8] also showed several risks and attacks for the initial proposal of the Exposure Notification Framework. Security and privacy of centralized and decentralized architectures have since been discussed (e.g., [36,37]). Baumgärtner et al. [2] categorized attacks on security and privacy for contact tracing app solutions from a methodological point of view. They discussed the different architectures, conducted an experimental study on relay as well as deanonymization attacks, and where able to create a movement profile of a person in the real world.

Starting with Kuhn et al. [18], there have also been approaches to provide formal foundations for the discussion of security of contact tracing apps. In this vein, Kammüller and Lutz [15] provide a formal analysis of the CWA app protocol and respective attacks using attack trees.

Similar to our work, Hatamian et al. [11] and Sun et al. [34] investigate the security of contract tracing apps using dynamic and static analysis, among

---

[13] https://github.com/PEPP-PT.
[14] https://github.com/DP-3T.

others. While both studies include a wide range of contact tracing apps, the CWA app was not part in them. For static analysis, Sun et al. [34] analyzed the apps' Android APK binary packages using tools similar to us and were able to find multiple vulnerabilities, e.g., the use of weak cryptographic algorithms, leakage of sensitive information, or plain coding of passwords. They even found trackers and malware in some of the apps. Hatamian et al. [11] provide an in-depth analysis of the security and privacy of early-deployed contact tracing apps, including a review of their privacy policy, conformance to GDPR, dynamic and static analysis. They confirmed the results of Sun et al. [34]. In contrast to our work, both studies do not consider the development process of the contact tracing apps.

Comparable to our approach, Trautsch et al. [35] conduct a longitudinal study of bugs, as identified by static analysis tools, and compared them to other development artifacts (i.e., bug reports in an issue tracker). They consider 54 engineered software projects of the Apache Software Foundation over a course of 17 years in their respective commit history, though just PMD as a single static analysis tool. In this way, their work considers a much more extended time frame and many software projects, compared to the development of the CWA app in our study.

Wang et al. [39] analyzed the activities of much-contributing developers to open source projects in an empirical study and looked also on other repository artifacts besides the code. They investigated the communication between developers and quality of software with increasing contribution.

Other works focus on runtime analysis of software systems for systems security. For example, Pasquier et al. [27] provide a solution for inline, realtime provenance analysis for applications such as data loss prevention, intrusion detection, or regulatory compliance. Hassan et al. [10] incorporated data provenance into endpoint detection and response tools to detect advanced persistent threats.

8   Conclusions and Future Work

We described our method for a provenance-driven security analysis of software hosted on git hosting services: We extract provenance using GitHub2PROV, query the provenance graph for "interesting" activities, and analyze the results of static code analysis for these revision created during these "interesting" activities. We *demonstrated the methodology* on a contemporary relevant application, the German Corona-Warn-App—we intentionally did not provide the detailed analysis of the project.

Many functionalities for security checking and providing metrics on the development process are part of GitHub already—for example, developers can setup *Code scanning alerts* for projects by enabling GitHub *Actions* with pre-defined workflows (e.g., for tools such as XANITIZER). However, we see more benefit for provenance graphs, which contain actions, entities, and agents from processes outside of GitHub; such as communication patterns between developers on other platforms or results from online monitoring and observability sources for deployed software.

Using a provenance-based approach for the analysis of software development processes and practices allows us therefore to conduct a holistic and integrated analysis. In this way, the approach is in particular able to integrate code at the core of GitHub with other artifacts, as well as with meta data. We have exemplified the approach for contributor types and their respective commits, but many more use cases are possible. For instance, correlating the numbers of defect reports in an issue tracker with SAST warnings can be readily demonstrated in our approach, thus contrasting code quality and usage of static analysis, and as another example, analyzing the role of specific issues on the number of SAST warnings and code quality in detail (Sect. 6).

In the future, we apply our method on various software projects where security of the software product is essential. This includes developing tools and visualizations for developers to investigate how software is developed, the processes used, and the details around how security issues are identified and fixed.

Additionally to the analysis of open source projects on GitHub, we work on the analysis of *Inner Source* projects hosted on instances of GitLab, which many organization use for code hosting. For that, we develop GitLab2PROV [30] and apply it to large aerospace software systems development.

A more holistic future work—especially during pandemics—is to combine the results of security audits for apps and services that deal with personal data, medical data, self-tracking ("Quantified Self") data etc. with audits on data privacy and transparency. That extends our previous work on provenance of personal data [31].

Future work in code analysis is to capture code insertions and deletions of individual commits by *diff trees* [7]. This would enable us to enrich the provenance information; not just with the static code view, via the analysis of commit snapshots, but also with a dynamic view. As a result, sources and fixes of vulnerabilities identified by static analysis could be better researched.

References

1. Ahmed, N., et al.: A survey of COVID-19 contact tracing apps. IEEE Access **8**, 134577–134601 (2020)
2. Baumgärtner, L., et al.: Mind the gap: security & privacy risks of contact tracing apps (2020)
3. Carroll, N., Conboy, K.: Normalising the "new normal": changing tech-driven work practices under pandemic time pressure. Int. J. Inf. Manag. **55**, 102186 (2020)
4. Dar, A.B., Lone, A.H., Zahoor, S., Khan, A.A., Naaz, R.: Applicability of mobile contact tracing in fighting pandemic (COVID-19): issues, challenges and solutions. Comput. Sci. Rev. **38**, 100307 (2020)
5. De Nies, T., et al.: Git2PROV: exposing version control system content as W3C PROV. In: Proceedings of the 12th International Semantic Web Conference (Posters & Demonstrations Track), ISWC-PD 2013, vol. 1035, pp. 125–128. CEUR-WS.org (2013)
6. Distefano, D., Fähndrich, M., Logozzo, F., O'Hearn, P.W.: Scaling static analyses at Facebook. Commun. ACM **62**(8), 62–70 (2019)

7. Falleri, J., Morandat, F., Blanc, X., Martinez, M., Monperrus, M.: Fine-grained and accurate source code differencing. In: ACM/IEEE International Conference on Automated Software Engineering, ASE 2014, September 15–19, 2014, pp. 313–324. ACM, Vasteras (2014)
8. Gvili, Y.: Security analysis of the COVID-19 contact tracing specifications by Apple Inc. and Google Inc., Cryptology ePrint Archive, Report 2020/428 (2020)
9. Habib, A., Pradel, M.: How many of all bugs do we find? A study of static bug detectors. In: Proceedings of the 33rd ACM/IEEE International Conference on Automated Software Engineering, ASE 2018, Montpellier, France, September 3–7, 2018, pp. 317–328. ACM (2018)
10. Hassan, W.U., Bates, A., Marino, D.: Tactical provenance analysis for endpoint detection and response systems. In: 2020 IEEE Symposium on Security and Privacy (SP), pp. 1172–1189 (2020)
11. Hatamian, M., Wairimu, S., Momen, N., Fritsch, L.: A privacy and security analysis of early-deployed COVID-19 contact tracing Android apps. Empir. Softw. Eng. **26**(3), 36 (2021)
12. He, W., Zhang, Z.J., Li, W.: Information technology solutions, challenges, and suggestions for tackling the COVID-19 pandemic. Int. J. Inf. Manag. **57**, 102287 (2021)
13. Hewett, R., Kijsanayothin, P.: On modeling software defect repair time. Empir. Softw. Eng. **14**, 165–186 (2009)
14. Johnson, B., Song, Y., Murphy-Hill, E.R., Bowdidge, R.W.: Why don't software developers use static analysis tools to find bugs? In: Notkin, D., Cheng, B.H.C., Pohl, K. (eds.) 35th International Conference on Software Engineering, ICSE 2013, San Francisco, CA, USA, May 18–26, 2013, pp. 672–681. IEEE Computer Society (2013)
15. Kammüller, F., Lutz, B.: Modeling and analyzing the corona-virus warning app with the Isabelle infrastructure framework. In: Garcia-Alfaro, J., Navarro-Arribas, G., Herrera-Joancomarti, J. (eds.) DPM/CBT -2020. LNCS, vol. 12484, pp. 128–144. Springer, Cham (2020). https://doi.org/10.1007/978-3-030-66172-4_8
16. Krishnamurthy, R., Heinze, T.S., Haupt, C., Schreiber, A., Meinel, M.: Scientific developers v/s static analysis tools: vision and position paper. In: Proceedings of the 12th International Workshop on Cooperative and Human Aspects of Software Engineering, CHASE@ICSE 2019, Montréal, QC, Canada, 27 May 2019, pp. 89–90. IEEE/ACM (2019)
17. Krishnamurthy, R., Meinel, M., Haupt, C., Schreiber, A., Mäder, P.: DLR secure software engineering: position and vision paper. In: Proceedings of the 1st International Workshop on Security Awareness from Design to Deployment, SEAD 2018, pp. 49–50. ACM (2018)
18. Kuhn, C., Beck, M., Strufe, T.: Covid notions: towards formal definitions–and documented understanding–of privacy goals and claimed protection in proximity-tracing services. CoRR abs/2004.07723 (2020)
19. Mbunge, E.: Integrating emerging technologies into COVID-19 contact tracing: opportunities, challenges and pitfalls. Diabetes Metab. Syndr.: Clin. Res. Rev. **14**(6), 1631–1636 (2020)
20. Mbunge, E., Akinnuwesi, B., Fashoto, S.G., Metfula, A.S., Mashwama, P.: A critical review of emerging technologies for tackling COVID-19 pandemic. Hum. Behav. Emerg. Technol. **3**(1), 25–39 (2021)

21. McPhillips, T., Bowers, S., Belhajjame, K., Ludäscher, B.: Retrospective provenance without a runtime provenance recorder. In: Proceedings of the 7th USENIX Conference on Theory and Practice of Provenance, TaPP 2015. USENIX Association, USA (2015)

22. Moreau, L., et al.: The provenance of electronic data. Commun. ACM **51**(4), 52–58 (2008)

23. Nagappan, N., Ball, T.: Static analysis tools as early indicators of pre-release defect density. In: Proceedings of 27th International Conference on Software Engineering, 2005, ICSE 2005, pp. 580–586. ACM (2005)

24. Nagappan, N., Ball, T.: Use of relative code churn measures to predict system defect density. In: 27th International Conference on Software Engineering (ICSE 2005), 15–21 May 2005, pp. 284–292. ACM, St. Louis (2005)

25. Oyetoyan, T.D., Milosheska, B., Grini, M., Soares Cruzes, D.: Myths and facts about static application security testing tools: an action research at telenor digital. In: Garbajosa, J., Wang, X., Aguiar, A. (eds.) XP 2018. LNBIP, vol. 314, pp. 86–103. Springer, Cham (2018). https://doi.org/10.1007/978-3-319-91602-6_6

26. Packer, H.S., Chapman, A., Carr, L.: GitHub2PROV: provenance for supporting software project management. In: 11th International Workshop on Theory and Practice of Provenance (TaPP 2019). USENIX Association, Philadelphia (June 2019)

27. Pasquier, T., et al.: Runtime analysis of whole-system provenance. In: Proceedings of the 2018 ACM SIGSAC Conference on Computer and Communications Security, CCS 2018, pp. 1601–1616. ACM, New York (2018)

28. Robles, G., Gonzalez-Barahona, J.M., Merelo, J.J.: Beyond source code: the importance of other artifacts in software development (a case study). J. Syst. Softw. **79**(9), 1233–1248 (2006). Fourth Source Code Analysis and Manipulation Workshop (SCAM 2004)

29. Schreiber, A., de Boer, C.: Modelling knowledge about software processes using provenance graphs and its application to git-based version control systems. In: 42nd International Conference on Software Engineering Workshops. IEEE/ACM, Seoul, Republic of Korea (May 2020)

30. Schreiber, A., de Boer, C., von Kurnatowski, L.: GitLab2PROV–provenance of software projects hosted on GitLab. In: 13th International Workshop on Theory and Practice of Provenance (TaPP 2021). USENIX Association (July 2021)

31. Schreiber, A., Struminski, R.: Visualizing the provenance of personal data using comics. Computers **7**(1), 12 (2018)

32. Smith, J., Do, L.N.Q., Murphy-Hill, E.R.: Why can't Johnny fix vulnerabilities: a usability evaluation of static analysis tools for security. In: Sixteenth Symposium on Usable Privacy and Security (SOUPS) (2020)

33. Sonnekalb, T., Heinze, T.S., von Kurnatowski, L., Schreiber, A., Gonzalez-Barahona, J.M., Packer, H.: Towards automated, provenance-driven security audit for git-based repositories: applied to Germany's Corona-Warn-App. In: Proceedings of the 3rd ACM SIGSOFT International Workshop on Software Security from Design to Deployment (SEAD 2020). ACM, New York (2020)

34. Sun, R., Wang, W., Xue, M., Tyson, G., Camtepe, S., Ranasinghe, D.C.: An empirical assessment of global COVID-19 contact tracing applications. In: Proceedings of the 43rd International Conference on Software Engineering (ICSE 2021) (June 2021)

35. Trautsch, A., Herbold, S., Grabowski, J.: A longitudinal study of static analysis warning evolution and the effects of PMD on software quality in apache open source projects. Empir. Softw. Eng. **25**(6), 5137–5192 (2020)

36. Vaudenay, S.: Analysis of DP3T: between scylla and charybdis. Cryptology ePrint Archive, Report 2020/399 (2020)
37. Vaudenay, S.: Centralized or decentralized? The contact tracing dilemma. Cryptology ePrint Archive, Report 2020/531 (2020)
38. Verborgh, R., Magliacane, S., Schreiber, A., Korolev, V.: GIT2PROV: improved error handling (July 2020). https://doi.org/10.5281/zenodo.3942169
39. Wang, Z., Feng, Y., Wang, Y., Jones, J.A., Redmiles, D.: Unveiling elite developers' activities in open source projects. ACM Trans. Softw. Eng. Methodol. **29**(3), 1–35 (2020)
40. Zimmermann, T., Weisgerber, P., Diehl, S., Zeller, A.: Mining version histories to guide software changes. In: Proceedings of the 26th International Conference on Software Engineering, ICSE 2004, pp. 563–572. IEEE (2004)

Provenance Types, Inference, Queries and Summarization

Notebook Archaeology: Inferring Provenance from Computational Notebooks

David Koop[✉]

Northern Illinois University, DeKalb, IL, USA
dakoop@niu.edu

Abstract. Computational notebooks allow users to persist code, results, and explanations together, making them important artifacts in understanding research. However, these notebooks often do not record the full provenance of results because steps can be repeated, reordered, or removed. This can lead to inconsistencies between what the authors found and recorded, and what others see when they attempt to examine those results. However, these notebooks do offer some clues that help us infer and understand what may have happened. This paper presents techniques to unearth patterns and develop hypotheses about how the original results were obtained. The work uses statistics from a large corpora of notebooks to build the probable provenance of a notebook's state. Results show these techniques can help others understand notebooks that may have been archived without proper preservation.

Keywords: Notebook · Provenance · Archaeology

1 Introduction

As computational notebooks replace paper scratchpads, there are similarities to the type of work involved in understanding and utilizing these notes. While some notetakers carefully order and prepare their notes, others archive very raw notes with arrows indicating reordering, strikethroughs indicating deletions, and extra pages inserted to provide added details. These may be rewritten, but this takes time which may not be invested due to a low likelihood that the notes will be consulted. Computational notebooks exhibit similar patterns with some that are well-polished and designed for others to read and reuse, while others are scratchwork that may never be revisited. However, when one needs to reexamine past results (especially older results or those from others), these raw notes can present a challenge.

One of the more difficult situations is when a notebook contains results from multiple sessions, work from different time periods or from different contributors. Akin to having pages from multiple investigations combined together, understanding often requires not only ordering but also separating the pieces according to the different sessions. Unfortunately, there often is not a recorded history

© Springer Nature Switzerland AG 2021
B. Glavic et al. (Eds.): IPAW 2020/IPAW 2021, LNCS 12839, pp. 109–126, 2021.
https://doi.org/10.1007/978-3-030-80960-7_7

of exactly when each action was taken. Sometimes, notebooks have dated entries or pages with ordered numbering, but uncollated notebook pages crammed in a folder are not uncommon. While the format of today's computational notebooks is different, similar challenges remain. Computational notebooks can be shared for collaboration, analyses may be split in different notebooks, and some results may be outdated. The order of additions, changes, and executions, is hinted at by cell execution counts, but using these counts to surmise events is not straightforward.

Our goal of *understanding* the past is different from successfully *executing* the notebook. This goal is also important for those wishing to reuse the notebook, but we are curious about the provenance of the notebook–all the steps taken in manipulating the notebook, including the executions of individual cells. In many cases, a top-down execution strategy allows the notebook to successfully execute, but it can conflict with the *actual* execution order indicated by cell's execution counts. In addition, a successful run may still lead to different results; the results saved in a notebook may not match those generated even when the execution is successful [20, 27].

This paper uses collections of notebooks along with notebook session histories to build an understanding of common patterns in notebook use. From this information, we construct an algorithm that fills in gaps of its execution provenance using the breadcrumbs a notebook provides. For example, the common practice, reinforced by the interface, of executing cells in consecutive order helps us fill in gaps in the provenance indicated by the saved notebook cell positions and execution counts. Our inferred provenance is necessarily more uniform that the actual provenance because some operations cannot be derived from only saved notebooks; we cannot determine if a cell was moved to a different location. In addition, where cells have changed or been deleted, we must project the provenance onto the current state of the notebook.

To infer provenance, we use a corpus of notebooks and a separate collection of histories of executed code from notebooks. In addition to looking to model user interactions with notebooks, we find some interesting results showing users commonly revisit and reexecute notebooks across multiple sessions and some differences between how users structure their code. To evaluate potential provenance inference algorithms, we use static code analysis to highlight dependencies that are or are not satisfied in the constructed provenance. The many difficulties we found suggests notebooks would benefit from improved provenance tracking. At the same time, the ability to produce plausible provenance from the limited information can be useful in better understanding the millions of already published notebooks.

2   Related Work

A *computational notebook* is a sequence of code and text blocks called cells. Generally, a user executes individual code cells one at a time, going back to edit and re-execute cells as desired. This is in contrast to scripts where all code is executed at once. In addition, new cells may be later inserted between existing, already-computed cells, so it possible that the semantics of a variable change. There exist a variety of different computational notebook environments [1,2, 9,16,17,24,28], all of which use text and code cells with computational results shown inline. Generally, these environments serve to mimic paper notebooks that document a scientist's work and include text, computations, and visualizations. Notebooks persist *input code, output results, and explanatory text*, providing a single record of an analysis and any discoveries. This contrasts with other computing where source code, outputs, and explanation are stored in separate documents.

Despite this encapsulation of research artifacts, the reproducibility of notebook results has drawn considerable concern. Recent studies on the reproducibility of notebooks provide evidence that current practices fall short; even for those notebooks where dependencies are specified and cell order is unambiguous, hidden dependencies and out-of-order execution can hinder reproducibility [20,27]. Work has also been done to help diagnose non-reproducible notebooks and reconstruct execution schemes by examining the dependencies between code cells [27]. Other solutions seek to modify the execution semantics of notebooks in order to improve reproducibility in the future. Nodebook [15] and Datalore [5] enforce in-order execution semantics on notebooks, and reactivepy restricts cells to single definitions to allow reactive execution [21]. Dataflow notebooks make dependencies between cells clearer, allowing the system to reactively update dependent cells as well as determine when cells are stale or up-to-date [13]. NBSafety uses static analysis techniques to highlight cells that may be stale, helping users see the effects of code changes without modifying the normal interaction or execution in notebooks [14]. Other research has shown that around 1 in 13 cells are duplicated in notebooks [12]. While provenance may also aid in reproducing results, our goal is different–to infer history from saved notebooks.

There has also been study of problems with the current modes of use in notebooks [4], and there has been work to improve usability. In particular, techniques help users better understand navigation of the existing notebook structure, something which can aid in inferring provenance. For messy notebooks, techniques have been developed to fold blocks of cells [22] or help users gather only those cells germane to a particular artifact [7]. It can also be important for users to understand how their actions affect the evolution of a notebook, and interfaces that present such information augment users' memories [10,11]. In real-time collaboration settings where users are working on a shared notebook, users tend to require some level of coordination, and understanding other users' contributions is often complicated by the non-linear structure of notebook work [26].

There are a number of solutions for tracking provenance in scripts [19], and some specific features and work to address provenance in notebooks. IPython tracks the history of all code that was run in a session in a user-level SQLite database [18]. This history is available in a notebook to document the provenance of executed code, but it is not stored with the notebook. Jupyter [9] also creates checkpoints that keep snapshots of a notebook through time, although these

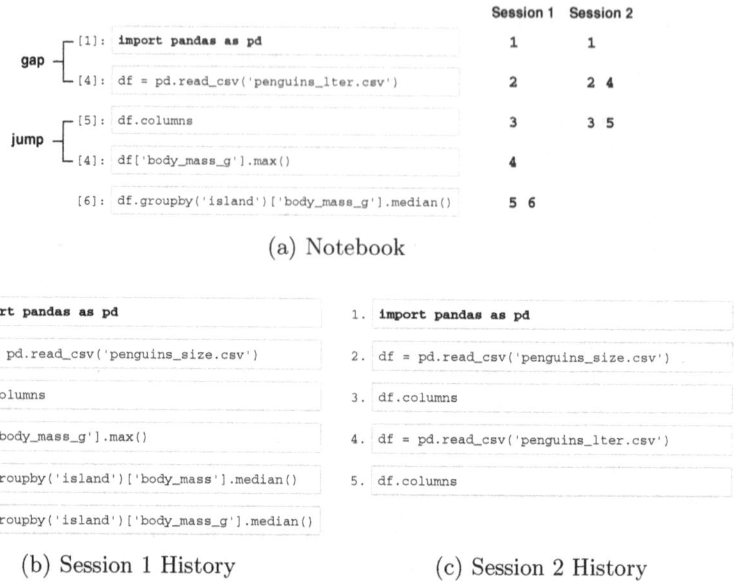

(a) Notebook

(b) Session 1 History

(c) Session 2 History

Fig. 1. The notebook records the final state, after edits to cells, while the session histories record the code at each cell execution.

are generally overwritten. Other opportunities to improve the provenance of notebooks includes storing the provenance directly with notebook results [25].

In many settings including with workflows, there has been work to infer provenance, whether that be to improve its granularity [3] or its precision [6]. ProvenanceCurious infers data provenance from annotated scripts, using the abstract syntax tree to build the provenance graph [8]. Our work deals with less well-defined data in that we seek to infer likely provenance given limited information, knowing much can be missing, about the final notebook state including cell positions and execution counts.

3   Definitions

A *computational notebook* is a sequence of code and text blocks called *cells* (see Fig. 1a). A *code cell* contains any number of lines of executable code, while a *markdown cell* contains text that is often explanatory and rendered from markdown syntax. Our work will focus on Jupyter notebooks [9] written in IPython [18], but many of the concepts and ideas will translate to other systems. In Jupyter, cells are ordered by *position* which indicates their location in the notebook; we can associate a numeric index to track this (one at the top, increasing down the page). There are a number of ways a user can modify a notebook; a user may add a new cell, delete cells, move cells to new position, edit a cell, or execute cells. Any operations involving multiple cells can be decomposed into operations on a single cell. Other more complex operations like copy-and-paste can similarly be decomposed into delete/add/edit operation chains. Note that many of these operations modify the structure of a notebook in a way that can cause headaches in inferring past provenance.

Jupyter uses a web-based front-end to facilitate editing and execution, but the actual computation is done by a back-end *kernel*. Different kernels exist for various programming languages, but we will concentrate on Python, the most commonly used with Jupyter. When Jupyter creates a new connection between the notebook and the kernel, a new *session* begins. Sessions are closely linked to the kernel, tracking the code that is run and the outputs that are generated. Each session has a global counter that is used to tag code, cells, and outputs, upon a cell execution. The notebook records this number for the executed cell as its *execution count*, and the *session history* separately records the code and count in a database (see Fig. 1) This counter is reset to one each time a new session begins, meaning the same execution count can appear for different cells in the same notebook. In addition, a cell's execution count is overwritten any time it is executed, and can be deleted completely if the notebook's outputs are cleared. The execution count hints at a global *execution order*: provided each session is assigned a monotonically increasing identifier, the session identifier plus the execution count provides global timestamp for all cells in a notebook. Unfortunately, session identifiers are not recorded, leading to ambiguity of the existing execution counts.

Then, an execution count k is *missing* when no cell has such an execution count and there exists a cell with execution count $\ell > k$. A *gap* (also known as a skip [20]) is a consecutive sequence of missing counts, and thus has a *length* (see Fig. 1a). When two cells have been executed in order, the signed difference between the positions of the first and second cells is the *jump* (see Fig. 1a). No meaningful jump occurs when this value is 1, signifying the cells were executed in a top-down manner without the user refocusing on a different cell. Putting these together, we define a *gap-jump* when we have both a gap and a jump. More precisely, given two cells with positions i and j and execution counts k and ℓ, respectively, such that there is no cell in the notebook with an execution count m, $k < m < \ell$, the *gap-jump* measure is a tuple $(\ell - k, j - i)$. In a top-down execution, $\ell = k + 1$ and $j = i + 1$, leading to a gap-jump measure of $(1, 1)$. A gap-jump of $(2, 1)$ often arises when a user executes the same cell twice, for example, after fixing a typo. A gap-jump of $(1, 2)$ might indicate a user skipping the execution of a cell in a later session. Note that these quantities represent differences so similar gap-jumps can occur in different times and locations for different notebooks.

3.1   Provenance

The *provenance* of a notebook is the sequence of all cell actions–the ordered steps that led to the notebook's state. While there is more state information that is stored with the notebook (which cells are collapsed, whether output exists, other cell metadata), we will ignore those because they do not affect the order or execution of cells. In general, this provenance information is not stored in the notebook, meaning for the majority of notebooks that do not use some versioning scheme as an extension to Jupyter, we do not know what this provenance is. The remainder of this paper seeks to present information that is useful in analyzing notebooks and solutions that use this data to infer potential provenance.

The *execution provenance* of a notebook is the chronological record of code cell executions, that is each cell (including its code and position) that was executed. Note that markdown cells and unexecuted code cells are omitted from this provenance. This history matches what IPython records in its history.sqlite database, but is not stored with the notebook in most cases. Specifically, when a cell is executed twice but was edited in between executions, the execution provenance records the cell code for each execution. Because the notebook only stores the most recent edit to each cell, this full provenance is impossible to infer. Instead, we will focus on the *projected* execution provenance which substitutes the "closest" cell to stand-in for the state of the cell executed in the past. For a cell that was edited, the closest cell remains that same cell, regardless of where it was moved to. For a cell that was deleted, the closest cell could be any, either one that fits well into the sequence or simply the cell that was executed after it. Recall that only executed cells figure into this provenance. With the projected provenance, we can re-execute the notebook in a manner that approximates the original execution. With no reexecutions or deletes, the projected provenance is the same as the original execution provenance. Given a saved, executed notebook, our goal is to infer this projected execution provenance.

4   Data and Statistics

Because we are inferring the provenance, we need to make decisions about how a notebook was *likely* executed based only on its final state. To do this, we will lean on a corpus of notebooks as well as one of session history collected from the GitHub online repository. With a diverse set of notebooks, we can gain an understanding of the distribution of various notebook features like gaps and jumps, and the session histories provide more detail on how cells are modified and re-executed. This will allow us to derive some general patterns related to notebook use, reuse, and editing. These will be used to inform an algorithm that seeks to infer the projected provenance.

4.1   Notebooks

A number of studies have harvested notebooks from GitHub for research [20,23], and these notebooks have shown significant diversity ranging from polished, explanatory documents to single-use scratchwork; ranging from a handful of cells to hundreds; and ranging from programming cheat sheets to in-depth machine learning experiments. We have employed similar strategies to existing work, obtaining new notebooks by querying GitHub for the distinguishing `.ipynb` file extension. From a corpus of millions of notebooks collected through February 2021, we randomly sampled 100,000 notebooks. To focus on IPython, and in particular notebooks that use Python 3, we filtered notebooks based on that metadata. Checking that notebooks that could be meaningfully loaded, we were left with 65,119 notebooks, and of these, 58,276 have at least one executed cell.

Gaps and Jumps. The easy case for inferring provenance is when we have no gaps or jumps in a notebook. In this case, the cells have been executed in positional order–that is from the top to the bottom of the notebook. There were 17,587 notebooks (30.18%) that fell into this category, something achieved by running all cells consecutively in a notebook. In the remaining notebooks, we may have some that involve multiple sessions. We know we have a notebook that has been used in multiple sessions when the same execution count appears twice; this is sufficient but not necessary. For those notebooks assumed to be single-session, we can count the number of gaps and jumps, and gap-jumps. The standard execution of two cells in top-down order, a gap of 1 and jump of 1 is by far the most common, occurring almost 80% of the time. Another 10% have larger gaps but no jump, likely indicating repeated execution of the second cell. About 3% of those pairs with a larger gap have actual jumps.

Sessions. An important issue in understanding how the execution counts relate to the provenance of a notebook lies in how many sessions a notebook has been used in. Recall that the execution count restarts at one in each new session so we cannot estimate how many cells may have been executed in total without first knowing how many sessions there were. We can conservatively estimate this number by finding the maximum number of repeats of an execution count in a notebook. Based on this cardinality, most (87.56%) of the notebooks have only a single *detectable* session, 10.06% have at least two sessions, and 1.66% have at least three. We can also compute a lower bound for the number of cells that must have been executed by summing the maximum execution count for each number of repeats. For example, consider a notebook with execution counts $[1, 6, 4, 5, 2, 4, 6, 1, 2, 3, 4]$. Because we have three 4s, and two 6s, the notebook had at least $4 + 6 + 6 = 16$ executed cells; the last 6 is added because it is the maximum execution count among those counts that appear at least once. Calculating this lower bound for all notebooks, there is one notebook where at least 10,916 cells were executed, but the median is 27. Note that this is usually *more* than the number of cells in the notebook. To that end, we can examine the ratio of executed cells in the notebook versus our lower bound of those executed. Using the example data, this ratio is 11/16 0.69. Interestingly, the interquartile range of this ratio is wide, from 0.15 to 0.89, indicating different modes of interaction in notebooks. Low ratios indicate many reruns of cells while higher ratios may indicate single executions or a session where the notebook was reexecuted.

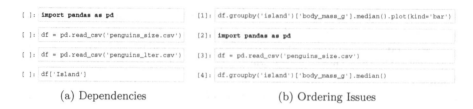

(a) Dependencies   (b) Ordering Issues

Fig. 2. In (a), the last cell is *dependent* on an earlier cell that defines `df`. Because there are two such cells, the dependency is *ambiguous*. In (b), suppose the cells are executed in positional order. Then, the first cell has *unbound* symbols (`df`) that are later defined, meaning the cell is *out of order*.

Static Code Dependencies. In addition to the cell positions and execution counts, we have the code of each cell. While this work does not seek to execute the cells, we can employ static code analysis to inform our understanding of relationships between cells, similar to techniques used by Osiris [27] and NBSafety [14]. Because it is a dynamic language, it more difficult to statically analyze Python code, but we can make some progress in investigating dependencies between cells. Specifically, the language makes it possible to differentiate between definitions and references of a particular identifier (or name). We care about those definitions that are made in one cell and then referenced in a different cell because this indicates a dependency between cells that can be used as a partial ordering. It is not foolproof as there are many potential ways to influence the global namespace, but this should cover most common cases. This also allows us to determine when cell references are potentially ambiguous–that is when two different cells assign to or define a particular name. When a third cell references this name, it is possible that reference is to either of the cells.

Function implementations, which do not access particular names until executed present challenges because a name in a global namespace need not be defined when the function is defined but must exist when the function is run. Because of this, it is possible that another cell defines the global after the function, but this is still valid because the function is not executed until after that definition.

We define four types of symbol dependencies which also lead to potential relationships between cells. Specifically, any code cell that has a referenced symbol that was not first defined in that cell has a likely dependency on another cell. In this case, we call the symbol and cell *dependent*. When that referenced symbol is defined/assigned in more than one cell, the symbol or cell is *ambiguously dependent* (see Fig. 2a). These two definitions are unrelated to the order cells were executed in. The dependency, ambiguous or otherwise, exists regardless of any specified execution order. We found that most notebooks (94.76%) had at least one dependency, although more than half (53.58%) had zero ambiguous dependencies. Among those with ambiguous dependencies, the average ratio of ambiguously dependent cells to total cells was about a quarter (25.49%). Again, this shows different variable definition patterns, hinting that some users may be keenly aware of issues with defining a variable more than once.

The second pair of definitions are related to execution order, meaning we can use these to evaluate inferred execution provenance. Given an ordering of cells, when a cell references a symbol that has not been defined/assigned in a cell earlier in the ordering, we have a *unbound* symbol. (We specifically exclude builtin symbols in these calculations.) This may mean the symbol is later defined, or it may mean the symbol is *never* defined. There also may be cases where the symbol would be added to the namespace by a wildcard import or some other code. The subset of those symbols that are later defined are the classified as *out-of-order* (see Fig. 2b). The number of out-of-order cells will serve as a metric to evaluating how well our provenance inference technique works.

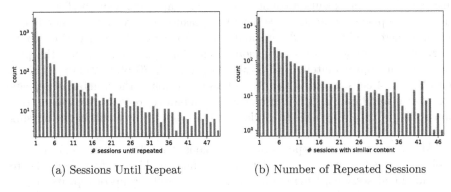

(a) Sessions Until Repeat   (b) Number of Repeated Sessions

Fig. 3. In the session history, we find evidence that users revisit notebooks. Usually, this is soon after the previous session (a), and many notebooks are revisited many times (b).

4.2 History

Inspired by Macke et al.'s use of IPython session history as a proxy for user behavior [14], we take a similar approach to understand execution patterns. Note that this assumes that the mode of interaction is via notebook, but it is possible this history is recorded from console-based IPython interactions as well. We will assume the code represents input from cells. Because the session history contains all executed code, we have a more complete record of executed cells, and can better see how often and when cells are re-executed. The patterns from these histories will help us determine when to infer repeated executions in our provenance reconstruction.

We downloaded all history .sqlite files from GitHub, and found 570 unique files with 86,711 sessions, many of which were empty. We were able to extract code from 43,529 sessions. We eliminated sessions with 10 or fewer lines (27,328) and those with 100 or more (2,058), the latter due to the number of possible checks required. In the 14,143 sessions, we found 977,728 "cells". (IPython calls these lines despite many being composed of multiple lines, but cells of notebooks become lines in the history database.)

Because we were not concerned about the actual execution of the cells, errors or outdated code are fine. Our goal is to find all repeated executions. To do so, we test all combinations of cells in the same session for similarity. Following Macke et al., we classify two strings as similar if the Levenshtein distance between them, normalized by dividing by the maximum length of the two strings, is less than 0.2, that is roughly 80% of the code is the same [14]. Running this repeat detection across all sessions, we found 222,202 likely repeated cells. Note that this does not mean that all of these cells were (modified and) re-executed as there may also be duplicate cells [12].

Importantly, this allows us to estimate the probability of a (1, 0) gap-jump, that is a change in execution count of 1 (no real gap), and a jump of 0, staying in the same place. Recall that we have no measure of this from the notebooks because there could be no data about jumps of 0 as the re-execution would overwrite the previous cell's execution count. The next cell matches the previous cell in approximately 10% of all repeats (102,580 of 1,024,508). This is out of 447,244 cells analyzed (for 23% of all executions); the number of repeats exceeds the number of cells because we count all pairs of repeats. We will use this probability of repeating cells to guide decisions about how to fill in the missing gaps.

We can also look for repeats *across* sessions; this shows how often a notebook was revisited in a later session. To accomplish this, we first de-duplicate the individual sessions, leaving only one copy of each group of repeats. Then, we compare earlier sessions with later ones. If the later session repeats at least 50% of the cells from the earlier session (repeats measured via the same Levenshtein distance criteria), we classify it as a revisit of the notebook. If, at any time after comparing ten lines from the first session, we have less than 10% overlap, we quit checking for overlaps. We only searched for repeats within 50 sessions due to computational time, but found 5,163 sessions repeated, some multiple times. The results show that most repeats occur quickly, often within the first 10 sessions (see Fig. 3a). In addition, many sessions are repeated multiple times with a significant number of notebooks being revisited over 20 times (see Fig. 3b).

5 Algorithm

Our goal is to infer projected execution provenance, the order in which we should execute the notebook's current cells to best emulate all of the past executions of notebook cells. Again, we will use the position and execution counts to guide decisions, but also the patterns and frequencies that were gathered from the GitHub notebooks and session data. Because multiple sessions introduce added complexity, we will be begin by examining the single-session case, and then discuss how this can be extended for the multi-session case.

Worst Case. Note that even with the best algorithm, it is possible to have wildly different actual provenance than that inferred by this model. For example, each cell could be executed repeatedly in a separate session, allowing any possible execution count that has no relationship to the other cells in the notebook. They may also be moved to reorder their positions. Given the history data, this is likely an extremely rare occurrence, but it is possible, as with an archaeological dig, that the most likely explanation given all evidence is not correct. Someone trying to deliberately obfuscate the provenance of a notebook can very likely succeed.

5.1   Base Algorithm

The base algorithm strictly follows the order implied by the execution counts. We don't know what happens with any gaps so we can fill them in with repeated executions of the cell at the end of the gap. While this seems reasonable, and we will see a nice extension to the multi-session case, the results (see Sect. 6) show this to be a somewhat poor strategy, as many symbol definition-reference pairs are out of order. The reason lies with the probability of repeated execution being *lower* than that of the standard $(1, 1)$ gap-jump. For example, if Fig. 1 showed execution counts $[1, 6, 7, 4, 5]$, it is most plausible that the user executed all five cells in order and then went back to execute the second and third cell again. The base algorithm would instead jump from the first cell to the second-to-last, likely missing declarations or computations.

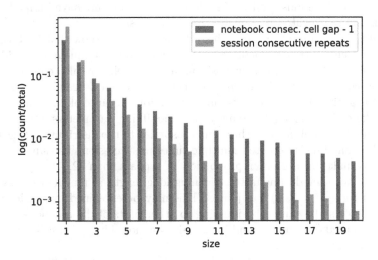

Fig. 4. Comparing the gap (≥ 2) between two adjoining cells in notebooks to the number of repeats of the same code in session history. A gap of n can be caused by $n - 1$ repeats of the second cell.

Extension to Multiple Sessions. This base algorithm does, however, provide a nice path to determine how to segment a multi-session notebook. Recall that we can obtain a lower-bound on the number of sessions by finding the count of the mode (the maximum number of repeats for an execution count). Given this, we can start from an alignment of all the sessions at this mode, and use a greedy approach to find the best next step in each session. Specifically, given the next possible step, we look up the relative frequencies of the induced gap-jump, picking the highest one. The step can be in either direction (to the next lower or higher execution count) as the process is the same. Continuing this process allows us to assign each cell to a session, at the same time building the projected provenance. Note that the order of the sessions is difficult to ascertain because there is nothing in this algorithm that considers when executed cells may have been reexecuted–this is only implicitly captured in the gap-jump data.

5.2 Informed Algorithm

In the single session case where we assume the entire notebook state was generated in one session, any gaps mean that we have executed a cell twice or executed a now-deleted cell. Since re-executing a cell often does not change state, we will assume that all gaps are re-executions, rather than deleted cells. (Any code that modifies a variable based on its current value may be problematic here; it may be possible to flag such cells.) Then, the problem is finding the best path through cells that have execution counts *higher* than the specified number. Here, we can leverage the distribution of jumps, but we must also consider the endpoint of the gap, the cell we must end at. In addition, the user may have jumped to the final cell and re-executed it as many times as necessary.

From the data from the session history database, we know that both consecutive cell executions and immediate re-executions appear frequently. In addition, if we see two cells that adjoin in position, and the cells are also consecutive by execution count, the gap between those cells may often be caused by multiple executions of the second cell. This may come about because of trial-and-error in getting the code correctly by fixing typos, modifying parameters, etc. Figure 4 shows that the distribution of these gaps is similar to the distribution of sessions where the same line is executed multiple times in succession. The single repeats in sessions make up a greater proportion of repeats than $(2, 1)$ gap-jumps in notebooks, but then decline faster, meaning long length-m repeats are *less common* than $(m - 1 \gg 2, 1)$ gap-jumps. This may be explained by the idea that the gaps can also be caused by jumping to other parts of the notebook that are later re-executed or removed, and it may also be more likely that cells tried once or twice are later deleted.

Our goal is to come up with likely execution provenance to fill in the gaps. From the notebook data, we know that a $(1, 1)$ gap-jump is most likely. In addition, the frequency of jumps of 1–that the next cell in execution count is also the next cell positionally, is about 9 out of 10 (89.56%). Thus, we expect mostly top-down order (and without other information are best to assume this), but this must mesh with the notebook. A negative jump—executing a cell earlier in the

---

Algorithm 1. Informed Provenance Algorithm

---

function FILLPROVENANCE(C)

   $order \leftarrow []$ ▷ initialize result

   $C \leftarrow \{\text{Cell}(pos = 0, count = 0)\} \cup C$ ▷ add dummy cell

   sortByPosition(C)   ▷ c_i is at position i

   for $c_i, c_j \in$ paired(sortedByCount(C)) **do**

      $gap \leftarrow count(c_j) - count(c_i)$

      if $gap = 1$ **then**

         $order.\text{append}(c_j)$

      else

         $n = \min_{s \geq 0}\{s \mid \forall k \in [s, j]\ count(c_k) \geq count(c_j)\}$

         $m = \max_{t \leq |C|}\{t \mid \forall \ell \in [i, t]\ count(c_\ell) \geq count(c_j)\}$

         if $j > i$ **then**

            $posGap \leftarrow \min(j - i - 1, gap - 1)$

         else

            $posGap \leftarrow gap - 1$

         $numBefore \leftarrow \min(posGap, j - n)$

         $numAfter \leftarrow \min(posGap - numBefore, m - i)$

         $numRepeats \leftarrow posGap - numBefore - numAfter$

         for $k \in i + 1, i + numAfter$ **do**

            $order.\text{append}(c_k)$

         for $k \in j - numBefore, j - 1$ **do**

            $order.\text{append}(c_k)$

         for $\ell \in 1, numRepeats + 1$ **do**   ▷ always do once so c_j is added

            $order.\text{append}(c_j)$

   return $order$

---

notebook, requires a negative jump at some point in the execution provenance (since we are ignoring moves). We can maximize the number of consecutive executions as cell numbering permits, but need to make at least one jump. Thus, our best strategy may be to move forward as much as possible with a single jump. Since this may still not cover the entire gap, we can repeat the final cell until reaching the desired execution count.

More formally, we wish to determine the projected execution provenance for the gap defined by cells c_i and c_j which have positions i and j and $count(c_j) - count(c_i) > 1$. We will attempt to use all cells that come after c_i or before c_j *and* have execution counts greater than c_j's. Formally, we want cells $\{c_k\}$ with $count(c_k) > count(c_j)$ and either $k < j$ or $k > i$. If the size of candidates, $\{c_k\}$, is greater than the size of the gap, we use those positionally before c_j first and then those after c_i (the jump happens earlier). If there are too few candidates, we choose to repeat c_j as many times as necessary, drawing on the session history data showing repeats to be a common occurrence. In between those executions, we will need to jump if the cells are positionally out-of-order, $j < i$, or if the gap is smaller than the jump, $j - i > count(c_j) - count(c_i)$. See Algorithm 1 for details, and Fig. 5 for an example showing how a gap in the provenance is filled by the algorithm.

variables		i			m			n	j		
pos	...	3	4	5	6	7	8	9	10	11	...
count	...	13	22	23	24	7	8	21	19	20	...
inferred	...	13	14	15	16	7	8	17	18	20	...
			22	23	24			21	19		

Fig. 5. Filling in the gap between c_3 and c_{10}. These cells are the third and tenth in the notebook and have execution counts of 13 and 19, respectively. This means $gap = 19 - 13 = 6$, and we need to decide which five cells were executed during steps 14 through 18. The algorithm assigns counts to cells with execution counts higher than 19 following c_3 ($numAfter = 3$) and preceding c_{10} ($numBefore = 1$), and then assigns c_{10} to repeat once ($numRepeats = 1$). The inferred execution order shows that some cells (e.g. c_4) are executed more than once.

Extension to Multiple Sessions. The extension to the multiple session case brings the possibility of having a cell with a *lower* execution count being run in a previous session at a higher execution count. We can attack this by first assigning each cell to a session, but then we have to find a way to order the sessions so that we know which cells will eventually be re-run (and their execution count overwritten). One option here is to assume that later sessions will be more contiguous. Assuming this can be solved, the algorithm continues as in the single session case, allowing gaps to be filled by inferring executions of not only cells whose execution counts are greater but also cells in later sessions. A second option is to thread this with the cell-session assignments, as in the base algorithm. Here, we will rank assignments of cells to sessions based on the provenance they induce. For example, in Fig. 1, assigning the third and fourth cells to the same session forces less frequent jumps than assigning the second and third to the same session instead (as was the case).

6   Evaluation

We used the code dependency measures defined in Sect. 4 to evaluate how well our provenance captures a realistic execution history without attempting to run the code. Other work has attempted to reexecute entire notebooks, classifying them as reproducible when the execution succeeds and the results match. This work is subject to a number of variables including data availability, library and package dependencies, and execution order [20,27]. Our work focuses on execution order in a way that is agnostic to the results of the code. We lean on the static code analysis to find those identifiers that are defined out of order in order to test our approach. Again, this analysis looks at the names that appear across cells. Any name that is referenced before it is introduced would be out of order.

We choose to compare three different techniques using the code dependency metrics. First, we take the top-down approach–simply execute all executed cells in positional order. Second, we examine the base approach that goes not by position but by the stored execution counts. Finally, we compare with the informed algorithm that attempts to fill in gaps with other cell executions.

There were 1,519,914 cells in the notebooks. The top-down approach has only 2,196 out-of-order cells, compared with 39,386 for the base algorithm, and 26,619 for the advanced algorithm. The top-down median number of out-of-order cells per notebook was 1 compared with 2 for the other approaches. Perhaps surprisingly, both algorithms do significantly worse as measured by out-of-order executions than top-down execution. Note, however, that the single-session advanced algorithm does improve significantly on the base algorithm. Reflecting on this further, the actual execution is often messier than the top-down order, and may result in more similar results.

One notebook that has problems with out-of-order cells under the inferred provenance has definitions (imports) as the first cell but an execution count of 141, followed by a second cell with count 132, before cells with the count sequence 2, 3, 4, 5. The algorithm assumes that the second cell was the first execution (1), leaving the actual first cell until much later. Most likely, this second cell was inserted later, something that would be difficult to determine without other information. Around 100 notebooks have fewer out-of-order cells using our algorithm than the top-down execution. One of these has a cell with a plot as output that was executed last yet featured as the first cell. Again, the cell may have been moved, but following the execution counts here provides what is likely more accurate provenance.

7   Discussion

The data we have gathered helps shine a light on patterns of notebook interaction, allowing us to infer the provenance of a particular notebook. However, there are several limitations. First, because we cannot determine if a cell was removed or a cell was added or moved, our inferred provenance necessarily lacks some of the actions that a user might take. Second, we do not have data that links session histories with notebooks. The session histories do not record notebook locations or filenames, and it is unclear how to effectively link the session histories on GitHub to existing notebooks. The histories are maintained in a separate area of the filesystem (a "dot" directory in a user's home directory), and that is generally not included in the same repository as published notebooks, if any published notebooks exist.

Improving Evaluation. A true recording of the provenance would be beneficial in better profiling notebooks. This would help better tie data from notebooks and session histories together, as well. Extensions that version notebooks and their cells are very useful for this purpose [11], but the vast majority of notebooks lack this information. Another opportunity may be those who version their notebooks using conventional tools like git. Even though these will lack the granularity of a system that tracks all operations on a notebook, they would allow improved inference of changes in the notebook as adds, moves, and deletions may be more effectively estimated.

Using All Cells. Notebooks contain more than code cells, but we have restricted most of the discussion of provenance to code. Literate programming emphasizes a combination of code with text, and this text is included in markdown cells in Jupyter. While some notebooks have more text than others, for those that do, we may be able to use information about the position of this text to determine logical sections of a notebook which may aid is session partitioning. In addition, the calculations of gaps and jumps ignore markdown cells, but having such cells in between may affect the probability of a particular repeated execution or jump, thus improving the algorithm.

Using Code Dependencies. Both Osiris and NBSafety look to static code dependencies in order to derive more likely execution sequences and flag stale cells, respectively. We instead use these code dependencies to evaluate provenance reconstructed via statistical trends of gaps, jumps, and repeats. We expect that code dependencies can be used to improve this provenance construction, but if we optimize for that, we lose our ability to evaluate the proposed algorithm. A possible solution is to use execution of the notebooks, comparing output values directly. This is prone to the other issues mentioned earlier, including missing data and dependency issues, but may provide enough results to judge the efficacy of a hybrid solution.

Determining Sessions. Our method to determine sessions looks reasonable in that it segments the notebook in meaningful pieces most of the time. However, it induces more issues with out-of-order cells than top-down execution. This is not totally unexpected, as we expect most users to execute cells in top-down fashion so cell execution counts that are out of order are actually more likely to have been reexecuted than simply executed in a random fashion. Thus, when execution counts are missing, it is actually more likely that the cell was repeated (or potentially moved) than it was executed in a haphazard fashion.

Localized Predictions. Our model for inferring provenance uses global distributions for guidance, but different users have different approaches to notebook use [23]. Those with few but lengthy cells that function more like scripts will be editing and re-editing single cells over and over while those with many shorter cells will likely be executing cells in sequence more often. In addition, even among the same users, notebooks used for exploration may be structured differently than those used for explanation. It may be useful, then, to classify notebooks or users according to particular styles in order to better infer provenance. We also expect that in later sessions, many of the cells have fewer immediate re-executions. Often, the first execution of a cell raises an exception due to a typo, a missed import, or some flawed logic, leading a user to correct that problem. Thus, some repeats may be less likely if we know the code was executed in a previous session. Another opportunity for improving predictions is understanding the content of the cell; cells importing dependencies may be executed and updated more often and with a greater probability of a jump.

8   Conclusion

We have presented methods to infer provenance from static notebooks based on knowledge gained from examining the large corpora of notebooks and session histories. These methods take a step forward in the very difficult problem of meaningfully understanding how a user interacted with a notebook. A future direction is to examine how well this computed provenance meshes with the actual results.

While we present some evidence that provenance can be inferred, the frequent ambiguities point to a need for improved provenance in notebooks. While it has been shown that many notebooks have reproducibility issues, this paper demonstrates that even with further analysis of partially-known steps rooted in statistical analysis of notebook and session data, there is not enough data to provide the type of provenance that would enable greater understanding of how a user arrived at particular conclusions and where they may have changed course. Since there are millions of notebooks that already exist, this work addresses the challenges from the past while prompting action for the future.

Acknowledgements. This material is based upon work supported by the National Science Foundation under Grant SBE-2022443.

References

1. Apache Zeppelin. http://zeppelin.apache.org
2. Beaker Notebook. http://beakernotebook.com
3. Bowers, S., McPhillips, T., Ludäscher, B.: Declarative rules for inferring fine-grained data provenance from scientific workflow execution traces. In: Groth, P., Frew, J. (eds.) IPAW 2012. LNCS, vol. 7525, pp. 82–96. Springer, Heidelberg (2012). https://doi.org/10.1007/978-3-642-34222-6_7
4. Chattopadhyay, S., Prasad, I., Henley, A.Z., Sarma, A., Barik, T.: What's wrong with computational notebooks? Pain points, needs, and design opportunities. In: Proceedings of the 2020 CHI Conference on Human Factors in Computing Systems, pp. 1–12 (2020)
5. Datalore. https://datalore.jetbrains.com
6. Dey, S., Belhajjame, K., Koop, D., Song, T., Missier, P., Ludäscher, B.: UP & DOWN: improving provenance precision by combining workflow-and trace-level information. In: 6th USENIX Workshop on the Theory and Practice of Provenance (TaPP 2014) (2014)
7. Head, A., Hohman, F., Barik, T., Drucker, S.M., DeLine, R.: Managing messes in computational notebooks. In: Proceedings of the 2019 CHI Conference on Human Factors in Computing Systems, p. 270. ACM (2019)
8. Huq, M.R., Apers, P.M., Wombacher, A.: ProvenanceCurious: a tool to infer data provenance from scripts. In: Proceedings of the 16th International Conference on Extending Database Technology, pp. 765–768 (2013)
9. Jupyter. http://jupyter.org
10. Kery, M.B., Myers, B.A.: Interactions for untangling messy history in a computational notebook. In: 2018 IEEE Symposium on Visual Languages and Human-Centric Computing (VL/HCC), pp. 147–155 (October 2018). https://doi.org/10.1109/VLHCC.2018.8506576

11. Kery, M.B., John, B.E., O'Flaherty, P., Horvath, A., Myers, B.A.: Towards effective foraging by data scientists to find past analysis choices. In: Proceedings of the 2019 CHI Conference on Human Factors in Computing Systems, CHI 2019, pp. 92:1–92:13. ACM, New York (2019). https://doi.org/10.1145/3290605.3300322, http://doi.acm.org/10.1145/3290605.3300322

12. Koenzen, A.P., Ernst, N.A., Storey, M.A.D.: Code duplication and reuse in Jupyter notebooks. In: 2020 IEEE Symposium on Visual Languages and Human-Centric Computing (VL/HCC), pp. 1–9. IEEE (2020)

13. Koop, D., Patel, J.: Dataflow notebooks: encoding and tracking dependencies of cells. In: 9th Workshop on the Theory and Practice of Provenance (TaPP 2017) (2017)

14. Macke, S., Gong, H., Lee, D.J.L., Head, A., Xin, D., Parameswaran, A.: Fine-grained lineage for safer notebook interactions. Proc. VLDB Endow. **14**(6), 1093–1101 (2021)

15. Nodebook. https://github.com/stitchfix/nodebook

16. North, S., Scheidegger, C., Urbanek, S., Woodhull, G.: Collaborative visual analysis with rcloud. In: 2015 IEEE Conference on Visual Analytics Science and Technology (VAST), pp. 25–32. IEEE (2015)

17. Observable. https://observablehq.com

18. Pérez, F., Granger, B.E.: IPython: a system for interactive scientific computing. Comput. Sci. Eng. **9**(3), 21–29 (2007)

19. Pimentel, J.F., Freire, J., Murta, L., Braganholo, V.: A survey on collecting, managing, and analyzing provenance from scripts. ACM Comput. Surv. (CSUR) **52**(3), 1–38 (2019)

20. Pimentel, J.F., Murta, L., Braganholo, V., Freire, J.: A large-scale study about quality and reproducibility of Jupyter notebooks. In: Proceedings of the 16th International Conference on Mining Software Repositories, pp. 507–517. IEEE Press (2019)

21. reactivepy. https://github.com/jupytercalpoly/reactivepy

22. Rule, A., Drosos, I., Tabard, A., Hollan, J.D.: Aiding collaborative reuse of computational notebooks with annotated cell folding. Proc. ACM Hum.-Comput. Interact. **2**(CSCW), 150 (2018)

23. Rule, A., Tabard, A., Hollan, J.D.: Exploration and explanation in computational notebooks. In: Proceedings of the 2018 CHI Conference on Human Factors in Computing Systems, CHI 2018, pp. 32:1–32:12. ACM, New York (2018). https://doi.org/10.1145/3173574.3173606, http://doi.acm.org/10.1145/3173574.3173606

24. Sage Developers: SageMath, the Sage Mathematics Software System (2017). http://www.sagemath.org

25. Samuel, S., König-Ries, B.: Provbook: provenance-based semantic enrichment of interactive notebooks for reproducibility. In: International Semantic Web Conference (P&D/Industry/BlueSky) (2018)

26. Wang, A.Y., Mittal, A., Brooks, C., Oney, S.: How data scientists use computational notebooks for real-time collaboration. Proc. ACM Hum.-Comput. Interact. **3**(CSCW), 39 (2019)

27. Wang, J., Tzu-Yang, K., Li, L., Zeller, A.: Assessing and restoring reproducibility of Jupyter notebooks. In: 2020 35th IEEE/ACM International Conference on Automated Software Engineering (ASE), pp. 138–149. IEEE (2020)

28. Wolfram Research Inc.: Mathematica. https://www.wolfram.com/mathematica/

Efficient Computation of Provenance
for Query Result Exploration

Murali Mani$^{(\boxtimes)}$ ⓘ, Naveenkumar Singaraj, and Zhenyan Liu

University of Michigan Flint, Flint, MI 48502, USA
{mmani,nsingara,zhenyanl}@umich.edu

Abstract. Users typically interact with a database by asking queries
and examining the results. We refer to the user examining the query
results and asking follow-up questions as *query result exploration*. Our
work builds on two decades of provenance research useful for *query
result exploration*. Three approaches for computing provenance have
been described in the literature: lazy, eager, and hybrid. We investigate
lazy and eager approaches that utilize constraints that we have identified in the context of query result exploration, as well as novel hybrid
approaches. For the TPC-H benchmark, these constraints are applicable to 19 out of the 22 queries, and result in a better performance for
all queries that have a join. Furthermore, the performance benefits from
our approaches are significant, sometimes several orders of magnitude.

Keywords: Provenance · Query result exploration · Query
optimization · Constraints

1 Introduction

Consider a user interacting with a database. Figure 1 shows a typical interaction.
Here the database is first assembled from various data sources (some databases
might have a much simpler process, or a much more complex process). A user
asks an *original query* and gets results. Now the user wants to *drill* deeper into
the results and find out explanations for the results. We refer to this drilling
deeper into the results as *query result exploration*.

For query result exploration, the user selects one or more interesting rows
from the results obtained for the original user query, and asks questions such
as: why are these rows in the result. The system responds by showing the rows
in the tables that combined to produce those results the user is interested in.
Different provenance semantics as described in [7,13] can be used for query result
exploration. In this paper, we use the *which*-provenance semantics (also referred
to as lineage) as in [9] and richer semantics is not needed. See Sect. 6 for a
discussion of different provenance semantics.

Partially supported by Office of Research, University of Michigan-Flint.

B. Glavic et al. (Eds.): IPAW 2020/IPAW 2021, LNCS 12839, pp. 127–144, 2021.
https://doi.org/10.1007/978-3-030-80960-7_8

Fig. 1. User asks original query and gets results. Now the user explores these results.

Table 1. Running Example: Tables (simplified) from TPC-H schema and sample data

Customers

c_key	c_name	c_address
c1	n1	a1

Orders

o_key	c_key	o_date
o1	c1	d1
o2	c1	d2

Lineitem

o_key	linenum	qty
o1	l1	200
o1	l2	150
o2	l1	100
o2	l2	160

Example 1. Consider three tables from TPC-H [1] simplified and with sample data as shown in Table 1. Consider $Q18$ from TPC-H modified as in [15] and simplified for our example. See that the query is defined in [15] in two steps: first a view $Q18\_tmp$ is defined, which is then used to define the original query as view R. The results of these two views are also shown.

(find total quantity for each order)
SQL: CREATE VIEW $Q18\_tmp$ AS
    SELECT $o\_key, sum(qty)$ as t_sum_qty
    FROM **Lineitem**
    GROUP BY o_key

$Q18\_tmp$

o_key	t_sum_qty
o1	350
o2	260

(for each order where total quantity is greater than 300, return the customer and order information, as well as the total quantity)
SQL: CREATE VIEW R AS
    SELECT $c\_name, c\_key, o\_key, o\_date,$
        $sum(qty)$ as tot_qty
    FROM **Customers** NATURAL JOIN **Orders**
        NATURAL JOIN **Lineitem**
        NATURAL JOIN $Q18\_tmp$
    WHERE $t\_sum\_qty > 300$
    GROUP BY $c\_name, c\_key, o\_key, o\_date$

R

c_name	c_key	o_key	o_date	tot_qty
n1	c1	o1	d1	350

☐

For this simplified example, there is one row in the result R. Suppose the user picks that row and wants to explore that row further. Suppose the user wants to find out what row(s) in the table **Customers** produced that row. We use R' to denote the table consisting of the rows picked by the user for query result exploration. We refer to the row(s) in the **Customers** table that produced the row(s) in R' as the provenance of R' for the **Customers** table, and denote it as $PCustomers$. In [9], the authors come up with a query for determining this provenance shown below. Note that we sometimes use SQL syntax that is not valid, but intuitive and easier.

SELECT **Customers.** *
FROM R' NATURAL JOIN **Customers**
  NATURAL JOIN **Orders** NATURAL JOIN
  Lineitem NATURAL JOIN $Q18\_tmp$
WHERE $t\_sum\_qty > 300$

$PCustomers$

c_key	c_name	c_address
c1	n1	a1

However, if we observe closely, we can note the following. Given that the row in R' appeared in the result of the original query with the value for c_key column as $c1$, and given that the key for **Customers** is c_key, the row from **Customers** table that produced that row in R must have $c\_key = c1$. Therefore the provenance retrieval query can be simplified as shown below. In this paper (Sect. 3), we study such optimization of provenance retrieval queries formally.

SELECT **Customers.** * FROM R' NATURAL JOIN **Customers**

As another example, consider the provenance of R' in the inner **LineItem** table (used for defining $Q18\_tmp$). This is computed in two steps. First we need to compute $PQ18\_tmp$. Below, we show the $PQ18\_tmp$ query as in [9], and then our optimized $PQ18\_tmp$ query (using the same reasoning as for $PCustomers$).

CREATE VIEW $PQ18\_tmp$ AS
SELECT $Q18\_tmp.$ *
FROM R' NATURAL JOIN **Customers**
  NATURAL JOIN **Orders** NATURAL JOIN
  Lineitem NATURAL JOIN $Q18\_tmp$
WHERE $t\_sum\_qty > 300$

$PQ18\_tmp$

o_key	t_sum_qty
o1	350

CREATE VIEW $PQ18\_tmp$ AS
SELECT $Q18\_tmp.$ * FROM R' NATURAL JOIN $Q18\_tmp$

Now, the provenance of R' in the inner **LineItem** table can be computed using the following provenance retrieval query.

SELECT LineItem. *
FROM **LineItem** NATURAL JOIN $PQ18\_tmp$

$PLineitem$

o_key	linenum	qty
o1	l1	200
o1	l2	150

It is possible to further improve the performance of the above provenance retrieval query if we materialize some additional data. Let us materialize the rows in R, along with the corresponding key value(s) from the inner **LineItem** table for each row in R. We denote this result table augmented with additional keys and materialized as **RK**. This will be done as follows.

$Q18\_tmpK$

| CREATE VIEW $Q18\_tmpK$ AS |
| SELECT $Q18\_tmp.*$, |
| **LineItem**.*linenum* AS linenum2 |
| FROM $Q18\_tmp$ NATURAL JOIN **LineItem** |

o_key	t_sum_qty	linenum2
o1	350	l1
o1	350	l2
o2	260	l1
o2	260	l2

RK

| CREATE TABLE **RK** AS |
| SELECT $R.*$, linenum2 |
| FROM R NATURAL JOIN |
| $Q18\_tmpK$ |

c_name	c_key	o_key	o_date	tot_qty	linenum2
n1	c1	o1	d1	350	l1
n1	c1	o1	d1	350	l2

For this example, only the *linenum* column needs to be added to the columns in R as part of this materialization, because *o_key* is already present in R (renamed as *linenum2* to prevent incorrect natural joins). Now the provenance retrieval query for the inner **LineItem** table can be defined as follows.

RK'

| CREATE VIEW RK' AS |
| SELECT * |
| FROM **R'** NATURAL JOIN |
| **RK** |

c_name	c_key	o_key	o_date	tot_qty	linenum2
n1	c1	o1	d1	350	l1
n1	c1	o1	d1	350	l2

| SELECT **LineItem**.* FROM RK' NATURAL JOIN **LineItem** |

See that the provenance retrieval query for the **LineItem** table in the inner block is now a join of 3 tables: **R'**, **RK** and **LineItem**. Without materialization, the provenance retrieval query involved three joins also: **R'**, $Q18\_tmp$ and **LineItem**; however, $Q18\_tmp$ was a view. Our experimental studies confirm the huge performance benefit from this materialization.

Our contributions in this paper include the following:

- We investigate constraints implied in our query result exploration scenario (Sect. 2.3).
- We investigate optimization of provenance retrieval queries using the constraints. We present our results as a Theorem and we develop an Algorithm based on our theorem (Sect. 3).
- We investigate materialization of select additional data, and investigate novel hybrid approaches for computing provenance that utilize the constraints and the materialized data (Sect. 4).
- We perform a detailed performance evaluation comparing our approaches and existing approaches using TPC-H benchmark [1] and report the results (Sect. 5).

2   Preliminaries

We use the following notations in this paper: a base table is in bold as $\mathbf{T_i}$, a materialized view is also in bold as $\mathbf{V_i}$, a virtual view is in italics as V_i. The set of attributes of table $\mathbf{T_i}$/materialized view $\mathbf{V_i}$/virtual view V_i is $A_{T_i}/A_{V_i}/A_{V_i}$; the key for table $\mathbf{T_i}$ is K_i. When the distinction between base table or virtual/materialized view is not important, we use X_i to denote the table/view; attributes of X_i are denoted A_{X_i}; the key (if defined) is denoted as K_i.

2.1 Query Language

For our work, we consider SQL queries restricted to ASPJ queries and use set semantics. We do not consider set operators, including union and negation, or outer joins. We believe that extension to bag semantics should be fairly straightforward. However, the optimizations that we consider in this paper are not immediately applicable to unions and outer joins. Extensions to bag semantics, and these additional operators will be investigated in future work. For convenience, we use a Datalog syntax (intuitively extended with group by similar to relational algebra) for representing queries. We consider two types of rules (referred to as SPJ Rule and ASPJ Rule that correspond to SPJ and ASPJ view definitions in [9]) that can appear in the original query as shown in Table 2. A query can consist of one or more rules. Every rule must be safe [20]. Note that Souffle[1] extends datalog with group by. In Souffle, our ASPJ rule will be written as two rules: an SPJ rule and a second rule with the group by. We chose our extension of Datalog (that mimics relational algebra) in this paper for convenience.

Table 2. The two types of rules that can appear in original queries and their Datalog representation. For the ASPJ rule, GL refers to the list of group by columns and AL refers to the list of aggregations.

SPJ Rule:	$R(A_R) :- X_1(A_{X_1}), X_2(A_{X_2}), \ldots, X_n(A_{X_n})$
ASPJ Rule:	$R(GL, AL) :- X_1(A_{X_1}), X_2(A_{X_2}), \ldots, X_n(A_{X_n})$

Example 2. Consider query $Q18$ from TPC-H (simplified) shown in Example 1 written in Datalog. See that the two rules in $Q18$ are ASPJ rules, where the second ASPJ rule uses the $Q18\_temp$ view defined in the first ASPJ rule. The second rule can be rewritten as an SPJ rule; however, we kept it as an ASPJ rule as the ASPJ rule reflects the TPC-H query faithfully as is also provided in [15].

$Q18\_tmp(o\_key, sum(qty)$ as $t\_sum\_qty) :-$**Lineitem.**
$R(c\_name, c\_key, o\_key, o\_date, sum(qty)$ as $tot\_qty) :-$**Customers, Orders,** **Lineitem,** $Q18\_tmp, t\_sum\_qty > 300.$

□

---

[1] https://souffle-lang.github.io/.

2.2   Provenance Definition

As said before, we use the *which*-provenance definition of [9]. In this section, we provide a simple algorithmic definition for provenance based on our rules.

The two types of rules in our program are both of the form: $R(A_R) :-RHS$. We will use A_{RHS} to indicate the union of all the attributes in the relations in RHS. For any rule, $R(A_R) :-RHS$, the provenance for $\mathbf{R}' \subseteq R$ in a table/view $X_i(A_{X_i}) \in RHS$ (that is, the rows in X_i that contribute to the results $\mathbf{R}'$) is given by the program shown in Table 3. See that $PView$ corresponds to the relational representation of *why*-provenance in [11].

Table 3. Algorithmic definition of provenance

Algorithmic definition of provenance for rule: $R(A_R)$ $:-RHS$. The rows in table/view $X_i(A_{X_i}) \in RHS$ that contribute to $\mathbf{R}' \subseteq R$ are represented as PX_i.
$PView(A_R \cup A_{RHS}) :-R(A_R), RHS.$ $PX_i(A_{X_i}) :-PView, \mathbf{R}'(A_R).$

Example 3. These examples are based on the schema and sample data in Table 1, and the $Q18\_tmp$ and R views in Example 2.

Consider the definition of view $Q18\_tmp$ in Example 2; rows in the view $Q18\_tmp = \{(o1, 350), (o2, 260)\}$. Let rows selected to determine provenance $Q18\_tmp' = \{(o2, 260)\}$.
First $PView$ (o_key, t_sum_qty, $linenum$, qty) is calculated as in Table 3. Here, $PView$ has four rows: { (o1, 350, l1, 200), (o1, 350, l2, 150), (o2, 260, l1, 100), (o2, 260, l2, 160)}   Now $PLineItem$ is calculated (according to Table 3) as: $PLineItem(o\_key, linenum, qty) :-PView, Q18\_tmp'.$ The resulting rows for $PLineItem = \{$ (o2, l1, 100), (o2, l2, 160)$\}$

$\square$

2.3   Dependencies

We will now examine some constraints for our query result exploration scenario that help optimize provenance retrieval queries. As in Sect. 2.2, the original query is of the form $R(A_R) :-RHS$; and A_{RHS} indicates the union of all the attributes in the relations in RHS. Furthermore, $\mathbf{R}' \subseteq R$. We express the constraints as tuple generating dependencies below. While these dependencies are quite straightforward, they lead to significant optimization of provenance computation as we will see in later sections.

Dependency 1. $\forall A_R, \mathbf{R}'(A_R) \rightarrow R(A_R)$

Dependency 1 is obvious as the rows for which we compute the provenance, $\mathbf{R}'$ is such that $\mathbf{R}' \subseteq R$. For the remaining dependencies, consider RHS as the join of the tables $X_1(A_{X_1}), X_2(A_{X_2}), \ldots, X_n(A_{X_n})$, as shown in Table 2.

Dependency 2. $\forall A_R, \quad R(A_R) \quad \rightarrow \quad \exists (A_{RHS} - A_R), \quad X_1(A_{X_1}),$ $X_2(A_{X_2}), \ldots, X_n(A_{X_n})$

Dependency 2 applies to both the rule types shown in Table 2. As any row in R is produced by the join of $X_1(A_{X_1}), X_2(A_{X_2}), \ldots, X_n(A_{X_n})$, Dependency 2 is also obvious. From Dependencies 1 and 2, we can infer the following dependency.

Dependency 3. $\forall A_R, \quad \mathbf{R}' \quad (A_R) \quad \rightarrow \quad \exists (A_{RHS} - A_R), \quad X_1(A_{X_1}),$ $X_2(A_{X_2}), \ldots, X_n(A_{X_n})$

3 Optimizing Provenance Queries Without Materialization

Consider the query for computing provenance given in Table 3 after composition: $PX_i(A_{X_i}) :- R(A_R), RHS, \mathbf{R}'(A_R)$. Using Dependency 1, one of the joins in the query for computing provenance can immediately be removed. The program for computing provenance of $\mathbf{R}' \subseteq R$ in table/view X_i is given by the following program. See that X_i can be a base table or a view.

Program 1. $PX_i(A_i) :- \mathbf{R}'(A_R), RHS.$

Program 1 is used by [9] for computing provenance. However, we will optimize Program 1 further using the dependencies in Sect. 2.3. Let P_1 below indicate the query in Program 1. Consider another query P_2 (which has potentially fewer joins than P_1). Theorem 1 states when P_1 is equivalent to P_2. The proof uses the dependencies in Sect. 2.3 and is omitted.

$P_1 : PX_i(A_{X_i}) :- \mathbf{R}'(A_R), X_1(A_{X_1}), X_2(A_{X_2}), \ldots, X_n(A_{X_n}).$
$P_2 : PX_i(A_{X_i}) :- \mathbf{R}', X_{j_1}(A_{X_{j_1}}), X_{j_2}(A_{X_{j_2}}), \ldots, X_{j_q}(A_{X_{j_q}}).,$
$$\text{where } \{j_1, j_2, \ldots, j_q\} \subseteq \{1, 2, \ldots, n\}$$

Notation. For convenience, we introduce two notations below. $A'_{RHS} = A_{X_{j_1}} \cup A_{X_{j_2}} \cup \ldots \cup A_{X_{j_q}}$. Consider the tables that are present in the RHS of P_1, but not in the RHS of P_2. A''_{RHS} denotes all the attributes in these tables.

Theorem 1. *Queries P_1 and P_2 are equivalent, if for every column $C \in A'_{RHS}$, at least one of the following is true:*

- $A_R \rightarrow C$ *(that is, A_R functionally determines C) is true for the tables in P_2*
- $C \notin A''_{RHS}$

Based on Theorem 1, we can infer the following corollaries. Corollary 1 says that if all the columns of X_i are present in the result, no join is needed to compute the provenance of X_i. Corollary 2 says that if a key of X_i is present in the result, then the provenance of X_i can be computed by joining $\mathbf{R}'$ and X_i.

Corollary 1. *If $A_{X_i} \subseteq A_R$, then $PX_i(A_{X_i}) :- \mathbf{R}'(AR)$.*

Corollary 2. *If $K_i \subseteq A_R$, then $PX_i(A_{X_i}) :- \mathbf{R}'(AR), X_i(A_{X_i})$.*

3.1   Provenence Query Optimization Algorithm

In this section, we will come with an algorithm based on Theorem 1 that starts with the original provenance retrieval query and comes up with a new optimized provenance retrieval query with fewer joins. Suppose the original user query is: $R(A_R) :- X_1(A_{X_1}), X_2(A_{X_2}), \ldots, X_n(A_{X_n})$. The user wants to determine the rows in X_i that contributed to the results $\mathbf{R}'(A_R) \subseteq R(A_R)$. Note that X_i can either be a base table or a view.

Algorithm 1. Efficient Provenance Retrieval Query

1: start with $CurRHS = \mathbf{R}'(A_R)$
2: **if** $A_{X_i} \subseteq A_R$ **then return** $CurRHS$
3: add X_i to $CurRHS$
4: let $CurRHSTables = X_i$; $A'_{RHS} = \bigcup A_{X_j}$, where $X_j \in CurRHSTables$
5: let $RemTables = \{X_1, X_2, \ldots, X_n\}$ -X_i; $A''_{RHS} = \bigcup A_{X_j}$, where $X_j \in RemTables$
6: **while** there is a column $C \in A'_{RHS} \cap A''_{RHS}$, and there is no functional dependency $A_R \to C$ in $CurRHSTables$ **do**
7:    Add all tables in $RemTables$ that have the column C to $CurRHS$, and to $CurRHSTables$. Adjust A'_{RHS}, $RemTables$, A''_{RHS} appropriately.
8: **return** $CurRHS$

Illustration of Algorithm 1

Consider the SPJA rule for R for Q18 in TPC-H from Example 2.
$R(c\_name, c\_key, o\_key, o\_date, sum(qty)$ as $total\_qty) :-$
   Customers, Orders, Lineitem, $Q18\_tmp, t\_sum\_qty > 300$.
Algorithm 1 produces the provenance retrieval query for **Customers** as follows. After line 3, $CurRHS = \mathbf{R}'$, **Customers**. At line 6, $A'_{RHS} \cap A''_{RHS} = \{c\_key\}$. As $c\_key \in A_R$, and $A_R \to c\_key$, no more tables are added to $CurRHS$. Thus, the final provenance retrieval query is: $PCustomers :- \mathbf{R}'$, **Customers**.

4   Optimizing Provenance Queries with Materialization

In Sect. 3, we studied optimizing the provenance retrieval queries for the lazy approach, where no additional data is materialized. Eager and hybrid approaches materialize additional data. An eager approach could be to materialize $PView$ (defined in Table 3). However, $PView$ could be a very large table with several columns and rows of data. In this section, we investigate novel hybrid approaches that materialize much less additional data, and perform comparable to (and often times, even better than) the eager approach that materializes $PView$. The constraints identified in Sect. 2.3 are still applicable, and are used to decrease the joins in the provenance retrieval queries.

A user query can have multiple rules that form multiple steps (for instance, Q18 in TPC-H has two steps). While our results apply for queries with any number of steps, for simplicity of illustration, we consider only queries with two steps (the results extend in a straightforward manner to any number of steps). A query with two steps is shown in Fig. 2. The Datalog program corresponding to Fig. 2 is shown in Program 2. R is the result of the query. R is defined using the base tables $\mathbf{T_1}$, $\mathbf{T_2}$, ..., $\mathbf{T_n}$, and the views V_1, V_2, ..., V_m. Remember that from Sect. 2, $\mathbf{T_1}$ has attributes A_{T_1} and key attributes K_1; $\mathbf{T_{1n_1}}$ has attributes $A_{T_{1n_1}}$ and key attributes K_{1n_1}; V_1 has attributes A_{V_1}.

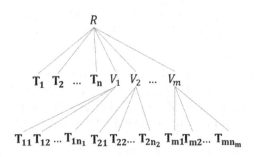

Fig. 2. Query with two steps

Program 2.
$$V_i(A_{V_i}) :\!-\mathbf{T_{i1}}, \mathbf{T_{i2}}, \ldots, \mathbf{T_{in_i}}. \qquad \forall\, i \in 1, 2, ..., m$$
$$R(A_R) :\!-\mathbf{T_1}, \mathbf{T_2}, \ldots, \mathbf{T_n}, V_1, V_2, \ldots, V_m.$$

Given a query R as in Program 2, we materialize a view $\mathbf{RK}$ with columns A_{RK}. A_{RK} consists of the columns A_R in R and the keys of zero or more of the base tables used in R (how A_{RK} is determined is discussed later). $\mathbf{RK}$ is defined using R, the base tables that define R and the VK_i views corresponding to each of the V_i that define R. See Program 3. VK_i is a virtual view defined using V_i and the tables that define V_i. If no keys are added to V_i to form VK_i (i.e., $A_{VK_i} = A_{V_i}$), then VK_i can be optimized to be just V_i. Algorithm 1 can be used to optimize VK_i and $\mathbf{RK}$ as well; details are omitted.

Program 3.
$$V_i(A_{V_i}) :\!-\mathbf{T_{i1}}, \mathbf{T_{i2}}, \ldots, \mathbf{T_{in_i}}. \qquad \forall\, i \in 1, 2, ..., m$$
$$R(A_R) :\!-\mathbf{T_1}, \mathbf{T_2}, \ldots, \mathbf{T_n}, V_1, V_2, \ldots, V_m.$$
$$VK_i(A_{VK_i}) :\!-V_i, \mathbf{T_{i1}}, \mathbf{T_{i2}}, \ldots, \mathbf{T_{in_i}}. \; \forall\, i \in 1, 2, ..., m$$
$$\mathbf{RK}(A_{RK}) :\!-R, \mathbf{T_1}, \mathbf{T_2}, \ldots, \mathbf{T_n}, VK_1, VK_2, \ldots, VK_m.$$
$$OQ(A_R) :\!-\mathbf{RK}.$$

The original user query results (computed as R in Program 2) are computed by OQ in Program 3. This is because we assume that $\mathbf{RK}$ is materialized during the original user query execution and we expect that computing OQ from $\mathbf{RK}$ will be faster than computing the results of R.

For query result exploration, suppose that the user selects $\mathbf{R'} \subseteq R$ and wants to find the provenance of $\mathbf{R'}$ in the table $\mathbf{T_i}$. We will assume that $\mathbf{T_i}$ is a base table that defines V_j. For this, we first define $RK' \subseteq \mathbf{RK}$ as shown below.
$RK' :- \mathbf{R'}, \mathbf{RK}.$

RK' denotes the rows in $\mathbf{RK}$ corresponding to the rows in $\mathbf{R'}$. Now to compute the provenance of $\mathbf{R'}$ in the table $\mathbf{T_i}$, we compute the provenance of RK' in the table $\mathbf{T_i}$. There are two cases:

$$\text{Case 1:} \quad K_i \subseteq A_{RK}: \qquad PT_i :- RK', \mathbf{T_i}.$$
Program 4. $\quad$ Case 2: $\quad K_i \not\subseteq A_{RK}: \qquad PT_i :- PV_j, V_{jRHS}.$
$\qquad (V_{jRHS}$ is the RHS of the rule that defines V_j.)

Case 1 is similar to Corollary 2 except that R may not be defined using $\mathbf{T_i}$ directly. For Case 2, V_j is defined using $\mathbf{T_i}$ directly. PV_j is the provenance of RK' in the view V_j, computed recursively using Program 4. Given PV_j, the rule for computing the provenance of PV_j in the table $\mathbf{T_i}$ is given by Program 1. Both the rules in Program 4 can be optimized using Algorithm 1.

Example 4. Consider $Q18$ from Example 2. There are 4 base tables used in $Q18$ – **Customers, Orders, Lineitem1** and **Lineitem2**. We distinguish the two **Lineitem** tables; **Lineitem2** denotes the table used in $Q18\_tmp$ definition.

The materialized **RK** view contains the columns in R and additionally the key for **Lineitem2** table. The key for the **Lineitem2** table is $(o\_key, linenum)$; however o_key is already present in R. Therefore only the $linenum$ column from **Lineitem2** is added in A_{RK}. The revised program (as in Program 3) that materializes **RK** and computes OQ is shown below. Note that optimizations as in Algorithm 1 are applicable (for example, definition of **RK**); details are omitted.

$Q18\_tmp(o\_key, sum(qty)$ as $t\_sum\_qty) :- \mathbf{Lineitem}.$
$R(c\_name, c\_key, o\_key, o\_date, o\_totalprice, sum(qty)$ as $total\_qty)$
$\quad :- \mathbf{Customers, Orders, Lineitem}, Q18\_tmp, t\_sum\_qty > 300.$

$Q18\_tmpK(o\_key, linenum$ as $linenum2, t\_sum\_qty) :- Q18\_tmp, \mathbf{Lineitem}.$
$\mathbf{RK}(c\_name, c\_key, o\_key, o\_date, o\_totalprice, linenum2, total\_qty)$
$\quad :- R, Q18\_tmpK.$
$OQ(c\_name, c\_key, o\_key, o\_date, o\_totalprice, total\_qty) :- \mathbf{RK}.$

Let $\mathbf{R'}$ denote the selected rows in R whose provenance we want to explore. To compute their provenance, we first need to determine which rows in **RK** correspond to the rows in $\mathbf{R'}$. This is done as:

$RK'(A_{RK}) :- \mathbf{R'}, \mathbf{RK}.$
Now, we need to compute the provenance of the rows in RK' from the different tables, which is computed as follows. See that all the rules have been optimized using Algorithm 1, and involve a join of RK' and one base table.

$PCustomers(c\_key, c\_name, c\_address) :- RK'$, **Customers**.
$POrders(o\_key, c\_key, o\_date, o\_totalprice) :- RK'$, **Orders**.
$PLineitem1(o\_key, linenum, qty) :- RK'$, **Lineitem**.
$PLineitem2(o\_key, linenum, qty) :- RK'$ $(c\_name, c\_key, o\_key,$
  $o\_date, o\_totalprice, linenum2$ as $linenum, total\_qty)$, **Lineitem**.

$\square$

4.1   Determining the Keys to Be Added to the Materialized View

When we materialize **RK**, computing the results of the original user query is expected to take longer because we consider that materialization of **RK** is done during original query execution, and because **RK** is expected to be larger than the size of R: the number of rows (and the number of columns) in **RK** will not be fewer than the number of rows (and the number of columns) in R. However, materialization typically benefits result exploration because the number of joins to compute the provenance for some of the base tables is expected to be smaller (although it is possible that the size of **RK** might be large and this may slow down the provenance computation).

For the materialized view **RK**, we consider adding keys of the different base tables and compute the cost vs. benefit. The ratio of the estimated number of rows of **RK** and the estimated number of rows in R forms the cost. The ratio of the number of joins across all provenance computations of base tables with and without materialization give the benefit. We use a simple cost model that combines the cost and the benefit to determine the set of keys to be added to **RK**. For the example query $Q18$, the provenance retrieval queries for **Customers**, **Orders** and **Lineitem** tables in the outer block already involve only one join. Therefore no keys need to be added to improve the performance of these three provenance retrieval queries. However, we can improve the performance of the provenance retrieval query for the **Lineitem** table in the inner block by adding the keys for the inner **Lineitem** table to **RK** as shown in Example 4.

For **RK**, we currently consider adding the key for every base table as part of the cost-benefit analysis. In other words, the number of different hybrid options we consider is exponential in the number of tables in the original user query. For each option, the cost vs. benefit is estimated and one of the options is selected. As part of future work, we are investigating effective ways of searching this space. Other factors may be included in our cost model to determine which keys to be added to **RK**, including the workload of provenance queries.

5   Evaluation

For our evaluation, we used the TPC-H [1] benchmark. We generated data at 1GB scale. Our experiments were conducted on a PostgreSQL 10 database server running on Windows 7 Enterprise operating system. The hardware included a 4-core Intel Xeon 2.5 GHz Processor with 128 GB of RAM. For our queries, we again used the TPC-H benchmark. The queries provided in the benchmark were considered the original user queries. Actually, we considered the version of the TPC-H queries provided by [15], which specifies values for the parameters for the TPC-H benchmark and also rewrites nested queries. For the result exploration part, we considered that the user would pick one row in the result of the original query (our solutions apply even if multiple rows were picked) and ask for the rows in the base tables that produce that resulting row.

We compare the following approaches:

- The approach in [9] that we refer to as: W (lazy approach). No additional data is materialized; the materialization studied in [8] is not considered.
- The approach in [11] that we refer to as: G. Here we assume that the relational representation of provenance is materialized while computing the original user query (eager approach). Provenance computation is then translated into mere look-ups in this materialized data.
- Algorithm 1 without materialization that we refer to as: O1 (lazy approach).
- Our approach with materialization from Sect. 4 that we refer to as: O2 (hybrid approach).

5.1   Usefulness of Our Optimization Rules

Algorithm 1 results in queries with much fewer joins. We tested the provenance retrieval queries for $Q18$ from TPC-H as given in [15] (for our experiments, the schema and the queries were not simplified as in our running example). The times observed are listed in Table 4. See that the provenance retrieval queries generated by Algorithm 1 (O1) run much faster than the ones used in [9] (W).

Table 4. O1 compared to W for $Q18$ in [15]. All times are reported in milliseconds.

	PCustomers	POrders	PLineItem
O1	0.07	0.06	0.30
W	1522.44	1533.88	1532.74

We considered all the TPC-H queries as given in [15] except for the ones with outer joins (as we do not consider outer joins in this paper). Of the 22 TPC-H queries, the queries with outer joins are Q13, Q21, Q22, and these were not considered. $Q19$ has *or* in its predicate, which can be rewritten as a union. However, we considered the *or* predicate as a single predicate without breaking it into a union of multiple rules. For 7 out of these 19 queries, O1 results in provenance retrieval queries with fewer joins than the ones in W. They were Q2, Q3, Q7, Q10, Q11, Q15 and Q18. In other words, Algorithm 1 was useful for around 36.84% of the TPC-H queries.

5.2 Usefulness of Materialization

For $Q18$ [15], we compared the time to compute the original query results (OQ) and the time to compute the provenance of the four tables for the four approaches: O1, W, G and O2. The materialized view **RK** in O2 included the key for the **LineItem** table in the inner block. The results are shown in Table 5.

Table 5. Performance Benefits of materialization proposed in Sect. 4 for Q18 in [15]. All times are reported in milliseconds.

	O1	W	G	O2
OQ	5095.67	5095.67	5735446.19	13794.26
PCustomers	0.07	1522.44	3.86	0.96
POrders	0.06	1533.88	3.73	0.43
PLineItem1	0.30	1532.74	5.77	0.59
PLineItem2	1641.52	1535.22	6.16	0.43

There are several points worth observing in Table 5. We typically expect O2 to outperform G in computing the results of the original user query. This is because G maintains all the columns of every base table in the materialized view, whereas O2 maintains only some key columns in the materialized view - in this case, the materialized view consists of the columns in R and only one addition column $linenum2$. The performance impact of this is significant as G takes about 420 times the time taken by O2 to compute the results of the original user query. Actually the time taken by G is about 5700 s, which is likely to be unacceptable. On the other hand, O2 takes about 2.7 times the time taken by O1 for computing the results of the original user query. Drilling down further, we found that computing the results from the materialized view **RK** took about 0.39 ms for O2 and about 3.07 ms for G (Table 6(**b**)).

Table 6. (a) Comparing the size of the tables: R (result of the original user query), **RK_G** (materialized view **RK** used by G) and **RK_O2** (materialized view **RK** used by O2). (b) Comparing time for computing materialized view **RK** and time for computing original query results from **RK** for Q18 [15]. All times are reported in milliseconds.

	R	RK_G	RK_O2
# Columns	6	51	7
# Rows	57	2793	399

(a)

	G	O2
Computing **RK**	5735443.12	13793.88
Computing OQ from **RK**	3.07	0.39

(b)

We expect G to outperform O2 in computing the provenance. This is because the provenance retrieval in G requires a join of R' with **RK**. O2 requires a join of

3 tables (if the key is included in **RK**). For Q18, the provenance retrieval query for *LineItem*2 requires a join of **R′** with **RK** to produce *RK′*, which is then joined with **LineItem** table. However the larger size of **RK** in G (Table 6(a)) results in O2 outperforming G for provenance retrieval (Table 5).

In practice, O2 will never perform worse than O1 for provenance retrieval. This is because for any table, the provenance retrieval query for O1 (that does not use *RK′*, but instead uses **R′**) may be used instead of the provenance retrieval query for O2 (that uses *RK′* as in Program 4) if we expect the performance of the provenance retrieval query for O1 to be better. However, we have not considered this optimization in this paper.

Other things to note are that computing the results of the original query for O1 and W is done exactly the same way. Moreover, for Q18, O1 outperforms all approaches even in provenance retrieval except for *PLineItem*2. This is because Algorithm 1 is able to optimize the provenance retrieval queries significantly for *PCustomers*, *POrders*, *PLineItem*1. However, for *PLineItem*2, the provenance retrieval required computing *PQ18_tmp* and then using it to compute *PLineItem*2, which needed more joins. Usually, we expect every provenance retrieval query from O1 to outperform W, but in this case W did outperform O1 for *PLineItem*2 (by a small amount); we believe the reason for this is the extra joins in W ended up being helpful for performance (which is not typical).

We report on the 19 TPC-H queries without outer joins in Table 7. In this table, OQ refers to the time taken for computing the results of the original user query, AP (average provenance) refers to the time taken to compute the provenance averaged over all the base tables used in the query, and MP (minimum provenance) refers to the minimum time to compute provenance over all the base tables used in the query. For W, we typically expect AP and MP to be almost the same (unless for nested queries); this is because in W, every provenance retrieval query (for non-nested original user queries) performs the same joins. Similarly for G, we typically expect AP and MP to be almost the same (because every provenance computation is just a look-up in the materialized data), except for the difference in the size of the results. For O1 and O2, MP might be significantly smaller than AP because some provenance computation might have been optimized extensively (example: Q2, Q10, Q11, Q15, Q18).

We find that except for one single table query Q1, where W performs same as O1, our approaches improve performance for provenance computation, and hence for result exploration. Furthermore, the eager materialization approach (G) could result in prohibitively high times for original result computation.

6   Related Work

Different provenance semantics as described in [7,13] can be used for query result exploration. Lineage, or *which*-provenance [9] specifies which rows from the different input tables produced the selected rows in the result. *why*-provenance [5] provides more detailed explanation than *which*-provenance and collects the input tuples separately for different derivations of an output tuple.

Table 7. Summary of experiments. The times are reported in milliseconds to two decimal places accuracy. However, considering the width of the table, if the time is 100 ms or greater, we report in scientific notation with two significant numbers.

	O1			W			G			O2		
	OQ	AP	MP	OQ	AP	MP	OQ	AP	MP	OQ	AP	MP
Q1	3.4e3	3.2e3	3.2e3	3.4e3	3.2e3	3.2e3	1.5e5	3.7e4	3.7e4	1.1e5	2.7e4	2.7e4
Q2	55.88	37.41	0.21	55.88	55.59	43.03	1.3e4	1.25	0.98	7.7e3	0.61	0.52
Q3	8.7e2	0.06	0.04	8.7e2	0.09	0.08	2.9e3	45.57	43.11	2.5e3	4.28	3.47
Q4	4.1e3	5.3e3	4.3e3	4.1e3	5.3e3	4.3e3	3.3e4	1.6e2	1.4e2	7.7e3	4.5e2	3.5e2
Q5	6.3e2	6.7e2	6.5e2	6.3e2	6.7e2	6.5e2	2.9e3	13.01	10.71	2.5e3	11.45	4.73
Q6	6.2e2	6.7e2	6.7e2	6.3e2	6.7e2	6.7e2	3.2e3	90.28	90.28	2.9e3	9.0e2	9.0e2
Q7	8.7e2	6.7e2	6.6e2	8.7e2	6.7e2	6.6e2	4.9e3	13.22	11.12	4.5e3	12.26	6.88
Q8	8.3e2	1.7e3	1.6e3	8.3e2	1.7e3	1.6e3	4.1e3	5.05	2.17	3.3e3	7.92	3.74
Q9	3.7e3	2.3e6	2.2e6	3.7e3	2.3e6	2.2e6	2.2e5	1.7e2	1.7e2	1.9e5	7.2e2	1.0e2
Q10	1.5e3	99.69	0.06	1.5e3	1.3e2	1.3e2	9.6e6	1.1e2	1.1e2	3.1e3	1.0e2	30.27
Q11	4.3e2	2.6e2	4.06	4.3e2	6.0e2	3.9e2	1.9e6	8.2e4	7.4e4	1.3e3	3.1e2	0.58
Q12	8.9e2	7.9e2	7.8e2	8.9e2	7.9e2	7.8e2	4.0e3	9.15	8.60	3.9e3	30.00	21.31
Q14	7.7e2	9.8e2	9.2e2	7.7e2	9.8e2	9.2e2	4.3e3	1.8e2	1.7e2	3.3e3	5.8e2	2.8e2
Q15	1.43e3	1.0e3	4.62	1.4e3	2.2e3	1.4e3	2.0e5	6.0e4	3.0e4	1.7e5	9.7e4	5.5e4
Q16	1.2e3	1.3e2	1.1e2	1.2e3	1.3e2	1.1e2	4.9e3	55.37	54.03	2.6e3	2.2e2	2.2e2
Q17	4.2e3	5.9e3	4.3e3	4.2e3	5.9e3	4.3e3	2.2e4	41.79	37.96	2.2e4	4.3e3	4.3e3
Q18	5.1e3	4.1e2	0.06	5.1e3	1.5e5	1.5e5	5.7e6	4.88	3.73	1.4e4	0.60	0.43
Q19	2.4e3	2.4e3	2.4e3	2.4e3	2.4e3	2.4e3	1.3e4	13.35	12.62	1.3e4	86.23	83.44
Q20	2.0e3	2.3e3	1.9e3	2.0e3	2.3e3	1.9e3	6.9e4	0.34	0.28	4.0e3	5.6e2	0.21

how-provenance [7,12,13] provides even more detailed information than *why*-provenance and specifies how the different input table rows combined to produce the result rows. Trio [3] provides a provenance semantics similar to *how*-provenance as studied in [7]. Deriving different provenance semantics from other provenance semantics is studied in [7,13]: *how*-provenance provides the most general semantics and can be used to compute other provenance semantics [7]. A hierarchy of provenance semirings that shows how to compute different provenance semantics is explained in [13]. Another provenance semantics in literature is *where*-provenance [5], which only says where the result data is copied from. Provenance of non-answers studies why expected rows are not present in the result and is studied in [6,14,16]. Explaining results using properties of the data are studied in [18,19].

For our work, we choose *which*-provenance even though it provides less details than *why* and *how* provenance because: (a) *which*-provenance is defined for queries with aggregate and group by operators [13] that we study in this paper, (b) *which*-provenance is complete [7], in that all the other provenance semantics provide explanations that only include the input table rows selected by *which*-provenance. As part of our future work, we are investigating computing other provenance semantics starting from *which*-provenance and the original user query, (c) *which*-provenance is invariant under equivalent queries (provided tables in self-joins have different and "consistent" names), thus supporting correlated queries (d) results of *which*-provenance is a set of tables that can be represented in the relational model without using additional features as needed by *how*-provenance, or a large number of rows as needed by *why*-provenance.

When we materialize data for query result exploration, the size of the materialized data can be an issue as identified by [13]. Eager approaches record annotations (materialized data) which are propagated as part of provenance computation [4]. A hybrid approach that uses materialized data for computing provenance in data warehouse scenario as in [9] is studied in [8]. In our work, we materialize the results of some of the intermediate steps (views). While materializing the results of an intermediate step, we augment the result with the keys of some of the base tables used in that step. Note that the non-key columns are not stored, and the keys for all the tables may not need to be stored; instead, we selectively choose the base tables whose keys are stored based on the expected benefit and cost, and based on other factors such as workload.

Other scenarios have been considered. For instance, provenance of non-answers are considered in [6,14]. In [16], the authors study a unified approach for provenance of answers and non-answers. However, as noted in [13], research on negation in provenance has so far resulted in divergent approaches. Another scenario considered is explaining results using properties of the data [18,19].

Optimizing queries in the presence of constraints has long been studied in database literature, including chase algorithm for minimizing joins [2]. Join minimization in SQL systems has typically considered key-foreign key joins [10]. Optimization specific to provenance queries is studied in [17]. Here the authors study heuristic and cost based optimization for provenance computation. The constraints we study in this paper are tuple generating dependencies as will occur in scenario of query result exploration; these are more general than key-foreign key constraints. We develop practical polynomial time algorithms for join minimization in the presence of these constraints.

7 Conclusions and Future Work

In this paper, we studied dependencies that are applicable to query result exploration. These dependencies can be used to optimize query performance during query result exploration. For the TPC-H benchmark, we could optimize the performance of 36.84% (7 out of 19) of the queries that we considered. Furthermore, we investigated how additional data can be materialized and then be used for optimizing the performance during query result exploration. Such materialization of data can optimize the performance of query result exploration for almost all the queries.

One of the main avenues worth exploring is extensions to the query language that we considered. The dependencies we considered can be used when the body of a rule is a conjunction of predicates. We did not consider union queries, negation or outer joins. These will be interesting to explore as the dependencies do not extend in a straightforward manner. Another interesting future direction is studying effective ways of navigating the search space of possible materializations. Also, it will be worthwhile investigating how to start from provenance tables and define other provenance semantics (such as *how*-provenance) in terms of the provenance tables.

References

1. TPC-H, a decision support benchmark (2018). http://www.tpc.org/tpch/
2. Abiteboul, S., Hull, R., Vianu, V.: Foundations of Databases. Addison-Wesley (1995). http://webdam.inria.fr/Alice/
3. Benjelloun, O., Sarma, A.D., Halevy, A.Y., Theobald, M., Widom, J.: Databases with uncertainty and lineage. VLDB J. **17**(2), 243–264 (2008)
4. Bhagwat, D., Chiticariu, L., Tan, W.C., Vijayvargiya, G.: An annotation management system for relational databases. VLDB J. **14**(4), 373–396 (2005)
5. Buneman, P., Khanna, S., Wang-Chiew, T.: Why and where: a characterization of data provenance. In: Van den Bussche, J., Vianu, V. (eds.) ICDT 2001. LNCS, vol. 1973, pp. 316–330. Springer, Heidelberg (2001). https://doi.org/10.1007/3-540-44503-X_20
6. Chapman, A., Jagadish, H.V.: Why not? In: Proceedings of the ACM SIGMOD International Conference on Management of Data, SIGMOD 2009, Providence, Rhode Island, USA, 29 June–2 July 2009, pp. 523–534 (2009). https://doi.org/10.1145/1559845.1559901
7. Cheney, J., Chiticariu, L., Tan, W.C.: Provenance in databases: why, how, and where. Found. Trends Databases **1**(4), 379–474 (2009)
8. Cui, Y., Widom, J.: Storing auxiliary data for efficient maintenance and lineage tracing of complex views. In: Proceedings of the Second Intl. Workshop on Design and Management of Data Warehouses, DMDW 2000, Stockholm, Sweden, 5–6 June 2000, p. 11 (2000). http://ceur-ws.org/Vol-28/paper11.pdf
9. Cui, Y., Widom, J., Wiener, J.L.: Tracing the lineage of view data in a warehousing environment. ACM Trans. Database Syst. **25**(2), 179–227 (2000)
10. Eder, L.: Join elimination: an essential optimizer feature for advanced SQL usage. DZone (2017). https://dzone.com/articles/join-elimination-an-essential-optimizer-feature-fo
11. Glavic, B., Miller, R.J., Alonso, G.: Using SQL for efficient generation and querying of provenance information. In: Tannen, V., Wong, L., Libkin, L., Fan, W., Tan, W.-C., Fourman, M. (eds.) In Search of Elegance in the Theory and Practice of Computation. LNCS, vol. 8000, pp. 291–320. Springer, Heidelberg (2013). https://doi.org/10.1007/978-3-642-41660-6_16
12. Green, T.J., Karvounarakis, G., Tannen, V.: Provenance semirings. In: Proceedings of the Twenty-Sixth ACM SIGACT-SIGMOD-SIGART Symposium on Principles of Database Systems, Beijing, China, 11–13 June 2007, pp. 31–40 (2007). https://doi.org/10.1145/1265530.1265535
13. Green, T.J., Tannen, V.: The semiring framework for database provenance. In: Proceedings of the 36th ACM SIGMOD-SIGACT-SIGAI Symposium on Principles of Database Systems, PODS 2017, Chicago, IL, USA, 14–19 May 2017, pp. 93–99 (2017). https://doi.org/10.1145/3034786.3056125
14. Huang, J., Chen, T., Doan, A., Naughton, J.F.: On the provenance of non-answers to queries over extracted data. PVLDB **1**(1), 736–747 (2008). https://doi.org/10.14778/1453856.1453936. http://www.vldb.org/pvldb/1/1453936.pdf
15. Jia, Y.: Running the TPC-H benchmark on Hive (2009). https://issues.apache.org/jira/browse/HIVE-600

16. Lee, S., Ludäscher, B., Glavic, B.: PUG: a framework and practical implementation for why and why-not provenance. VLDB J. **28**(1), 47–71 (2019)
17. Niu, X., Kapoor, R., Glavic, B., Gawlick, D., Liu, Z.H., Krishnaswamy, V., Radhakrishnan, V.: Heuristic and cost-based optimization for diverse provenance tasks. CoRR abs/1804.07156 (2018). http://arxiv.org/abs/1804.07156
18. Roy, S., Orr, L., Suciu, D.: Explaining query answers with explanation-ready databases. PVLDB **9**(4), 348–359 (2015). https://doi.org/10.14778/2856318.2856329. http://www.vldb.org/pvldb/vol9/p348-roy.pdf
19. Wu, E., Madden, S.: Scorpion: explaining away outliers in aggregate queries. PVLDB **6**(8), 553–564 (2013). https://doi.org/10.14778/2536354.2536356. http://www.vldb.org/pvldb/vol6/p553-wu.pdf
20. Zaniolo, C., Ceri, S., Faloutsos, C., Snodgrass, R.T., Subrahmanian, V.S., Zicari, R.: Advanced Database Systems. Morgan Kaufmann, Burlington (1997)

Incremental Inference of Provenance Types

David Kohan Marzagão[✉] , Trung Dong Huynh , and Luc Moreau

King's College London, London WC2B 4BG, UK
{david.kohan,dong.huynh,luc.moreau}@kcl.ac.uk

Abstract. Long-running applications nowadays are increasingly instrumented to continuously log provenance. In that context, we observe an emerging need for processing fragments of provenance continuously produced by applications. Thus, there is an increasing requirement for processing of provenance incrementally, while the application is still running, to replace batch processing of a complete provenance dataset available only after the application has completed. A type of processing of particular interest is summarising provenance graphs, which has been proposed as an effective way of extracting key features of provenance and storing them in an efficient manner. To that goal, summarisation makes use of provenance types, which, in loose terms, are an encoding of the neighbourhood of nodes.

This paper shows that the process of creating provenance summaries of continuously provided data can benefit from a mode of incremental processing of provenance types. We also introduce the concept of a library of types to reduce the need for storing copies of the same string representations for types multiple times. Further, we show that the computational complexity associated with the task of inferring types is, in most common cases, the best possible: only new nodes have to be processed. We also identify and analyse the exception scenarios. Finally, although our library of types, in theory, can be exponentially large, we present empirical results that show it is quite compact in practice.

Keywords: Provenance summaries · Provenance types · Incremental processing of provenance

1 Introduction

Let us imagine an application continuously monitoring a system that records all sorts of hospital data. Patient flows, chains of procedures, and staff rotation are examples of such data. The application monitoring this system aims to help identify issues, such as bottlenecks, helping hospital administration to channel resources where needed the most. For that, however, this application needs to

This work is supported by a Department of Navy award (Award No. N62909-18-1-2079) issued by the Office of Naval Research. The United States Government has a royalty-free license throughout the world in all copyrightable material contained herein.

© Springer Nature Switzerland AG 2021
B. Glavic et al. (Eds.): IPAW 2020/IPAW 2021, LNCS 12839, pp. 145–162, 2021.
https://doi.org/10.1007/978-3-030-80960-7_9

process and present the data in a meaningful way, given its potentially very large size and complexity. That is a domain in which provenance can offer analysing tools and techniques, thanks to its capability of recording what influenced the generation of data or information. In particular, summarisation of provenance graphs can then be of use to extract information from large quantities of data.

More specifically, the World Wide Web Consortium (W3C) has defined provenance as "the record about entities, activities, and people involved in producing a piece of data or thing, which can be used to form assessments about its quality, reliability or trustworthiness" [7]. It has been widely adopted in various domains, including climate science [10], computational reproducibility [1], and emergency responses [15].

Like in our hospital data example, increasingly, applications are generating provenance information continuously [8], and there is an emerging need for processing incoming data in a similar fashion, i.e., without having to wait for the application to terminate for data to be processed altogether. The need for reprocessing data is costly, as well as the need to store large quantities of provenance information [12].

A type of processing of particular interest is summarising provenance graphs [13]. It has been proposed as a way to extract features of the original graphs and store them efficiently. Summaries can be easily compared to one another, and be used to identify common patterns or find outliers. The process of provenance summarisation makes use of provenance types, which can be described as an abstraction of the shapes of the neighbourhood of nodes. The idea is that nodes that have similar neighbourhoods will be given the same type and thus will be treated similarly when a summary is created. More specifically, we consider a summary as a graph in which nodes represent the collection of nodes in the original graph that are assigned the same provenance type. Similarly, edges in a summary graph connecting two types represent that there is at least one edge connecting nodes of such provenance types in the original graph.

Provenance summaries, therefore, could be an important tool to analyse data from a domain such as the hospital scenario described above. For example, we might want to investigate 'how do patient flows compare week after week?', or 'what are the differences and similarities of hospital procedures day after day?'. For these particular examples, we need to compare summaries generated over dynamic sliding windows over time. The existing summarisation techniques (e.g. [13]), however, are currently not designed to process data incrementally. In this paper, we will propose an efficient way to infer provenance types, the main ingredients for the creation of provenance summaries. We are interested in addressing the following questions:

Q1 Considering our goal of inferring provenance types over continuously provided provenance, is it necessary to store all provenance information from the beginning of our application?

Q2 Is there a need to reprocess the provenance types of any previously seen provenance expressions with the addition of new provenance data?

Q3 How can we optimise the need for storage space in case multiple copies of the same provenance types appear as the application runs?

With regards to Questions **Q1** and **Q2**, we show that in the most common cases, there is no need to store all provenance information, nor to reprocess previously seen nodes. We then identify the exception conditions and provide an algorithm to address these scenarios. Regarding Question **Q3**, we propose the creation of a library of types that enumerate all provenance types encountered from the start and that can be updated, if needed, with the incoming of new data. Finally, we will provide empirical results that support the claim that the use of such a library can indeed optimise storage space.

2   Background and Definitions

We will consider $G = (V, E, T, L)$ a **provenance graph** in which $G(V)$, or simply V, corresponds to the set of nodes of G, $E(G)$, or E, its set of its edges, and T and L correspond, respectively, to the sets of labels of nodes and edges in G. An edge $e \in E$ is a triplet $e = (v, u, l)$, where $v \in V$ is its **starting point**, $u \in V$ is its **ending point**, and $l \in L$, also denoted $lab(e)$, is the edge's **label**. Each node $v \in V$ can have more than one label, and thus $lab(v) \in \mathbb{P}(S)$, where $\mathbb{P}(S)$ denotes the power-set of S, i.e., the set of subsets of S.[1] Note that provenance graphs are **finite**, **directed**, and **multi-graphs** (as more than one edge can exist between the same pair of nodes). We do not make the assumption that provenance graphs are acyclic.

In provenance, we typically have $T = \{ag, act, ent, \dots\}$, where 'ag' denotes an agent, 'act' denotes an activity, and 'ent' denotes an entity. There are also application specific labels (e.g. 'hospital:Nurse' to denote a specific label for agents in our hospital example) that also belong to set T. On the other hand, typically $L = \{abo, used, waw, wro, \dots\}$, where the edge (v, u, abo), for example, indicates that agent v acted on behalf of agent u. We assume sets T and L are totally ordered, which implies that for any two elements $l_1, l_2 \in L$, either $l_1 < l_2$, $l_2 < l_1$, or $l_1 = l_2$ (analogously for T). In this paper, we will choose the alphabetical ordering for node and edge labels. Finally, we denote $\mathcal{G} = (\mathcal{V}, \mathcal{E}, \mathcal{S}, \mathcal{L})$ as a (finite) family of graphs, where $\mathcal{V}$, $\mathcal{E}$, $\mathcal{T}$, and $\mathcal{L}$, are the union of the sets of, respectively, nodes, edges, node labels, and edge labels of graphs in $\mathcal{G}$. For a node $v \in \mathcal{V}$, we will refer to the **forward-neighbourhood** of v as v^+, where $v^+ = \{u \mid (v, u, l) \in \mathcal{E}\}$. Analogously, the **backward-neighbourhood** of v is denote by $v^- = \{u \mid (u, v, l) \in \mathcal{E}\}$. We say a node u is **distant from** v by x if there is a sequence of x concatenated edges (repetitions allowed) starting at v and ending at u. Finally, we extend the notion of forward-neighbourhood (resp. backward-neighbourhood) for **sets of nodes** $W \subset \mathcal{V}$, i.e., $W^+ = \{u \mid u \in v^+ \text{ for some } v \in W\}$ (resp. $W^- = \{u \mid u \in v^- \text{ for some } v \in W\}$).

---

[1] Note that when application types are included, a provenance expression may have more than one label, for e.g. $lab(v) = \{ag, Prov:Operator\}$. When $lab(v)$ is a singleton set, we will abuse notation and omit the set-brackets.

Fig. 1. An abstract graph (left) processed before window slides (right). Formally, $\mu_\mathcal{V} = \{1,2\}$, $\mu_\mathcal{E} = \{e_1, e_2, e_3, e_5\}$, $\delta_\mathcal{V} = \{6,7\}$, $\delta_\mathcal{E} = \{e_6, e_7, e_8, e_9\}$, $\lambda_\mathcal{V} = \{3,4\}$.

When there is the addition of unprocessed (new) data to a database of already processed provenance information, we define $\delta_\mathcal{V}$ as the **set of new nodes**, i.e., that have not been processed yet, and $\delta_\mathcal{E}$ the **set of new edges**. We now introduce the notation for removal of provenance information. This will be particularly necessary to study provenance types over dynamic sliding windows over time. When there is removal of already processed provenance, we define $\mu_\mathcal{V}$ as the **set of removed nodes**, $\mu_\mathcal{E}$ as the **set of removed edges**.[2] Finally, we define $\lambda_\mathcal{V}$ as the set of **previously processed (and non removed) nodes v that either received a new edge starting at v or had an edge starting at v removed**, i.e., $\lambda_\mathcal{V} = \{v \mid v \notin \mu_\mathcal{V} \cup \delta_\mathcal{V} \text{ and } \exists e \in \mu_\mathcal{E} \cup \delta_\mathcal{E} \text{ s.t. } e = (v, u, l) \text{ for some } u \text{ and } l\}$. Figure 1 shows an abstract example with $\lambda_\mathcal{V}$ highlighted in red and $\delta_\mathcal{V}$ in blue.

3 Provenance Types

In this section, we will first present a similar definition of provenance types to the one introduced in [13]. Subsequently, we will provide an algorithm that infers provenance types for nodes in a family of graphs. As we will demonstrate, this alternative definition allows us to improve the computational complexity of inferring nodes' types from an exponential to a polynomial function on the number of edges in our family of graphs. Lastly, we define the notion of a library of types, that records all different provenance types seen up to a given point in time, as well as allowing a more efficient way to store types of all nodes in a family of graphs.

As a motivation for the main definition presented in this section, consider the provenance graph in Fig. 2 extracted from [3]. It depicts a scenario in which a blogger is analysing the provenance of an online newspaper article, including a chart produced from a government agency dataset. The blogger, the newspaper, the chart generator company, and the government agency are the different sources from which the provenance information was obtained.

Consider nodes *composer*1 and *illustrate*1. We can say that they share some similarity as both represent activities in this provenance graph. Further, we can say that they share even more similarities as they related to entities (via the *used* relation) and to some agent (via the *waw* edge label). Note that here we are ignoring the number of times a given pattern appears, since *composer*1 *used*

---

[2] Note that removing a node automatically removes all edges connected to it.

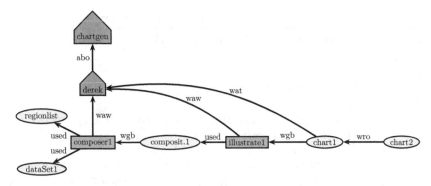

Fig. 2. Example of provenance graph from [3]

two entity nodes, whereas *illustrate*1, only one. Going one step further, however, these nodes no longer have the same 'history': *illustrate*1 used an entity that was generated by some other activity, whereas *composer*1 did not. Later, we formally define these patterns that we denote the **provenance types** of a node.

We will be looking into a variant of the provenance types defined in [13]. In loose terms, a provenance type of depth k describes the neighbourhood of a node v up to distance k from v. Another way of viewing such structures is to think of a subtree rooted at v, in which all branches have exactly depth k and no branch is repeated. A more precise (recursive) definition of k-types is given as follows.

Definition 1 (Provenance k-type of a node). *Let G be a provenance graph and $v \in V$ a node. Firstly we define, according to definition in Sect. 2,*

$$0\text{-}type(v) = lab(v) \qquad (1)$$

Further, we define k-type(v) recursively. Consider v^+, the forward-neighbourhood of v. We will make use of pairs that combine the label of an edge e starting at v with the $(k-1)$-type of the destination node of e. We define

$$k\text{-}type(v) = \{(l, (k\text{-}1)\text{-}type(u)) \mid e = (v, u, l) \in E \text{ and } (k\text{-}1)\text{-}type(u) \neq \emptyset\} \qquad (2)$$

Example 1. We will now formally present what we discussed at the begining of this section. Consider nodes *composer*1 and *illustrate*1 in Fig. 2 and note that they have the same k-type: for $k = 0$ and $k = 1$:

$$0\text{-}type(composer1) = 0\text{-}type(illustrate1) = \{act\}$$
$$1\text{-}type(composer1) = 1\text{-}type(illustrate1) = \{(used, \{ent\}), (waw, \{ag\})\}$$

However, they differ with regards to their 2-*type*:

$$2\text{-}type(composer1) = \{(waw, \{(abo, \{ag\})\})\}$$
$$2\text{-}type(illustrate1) = \{(used, \{(wgb, \{act\})\}), (waw, \{(abo, \{ag\})\})\}$$

In this case, this difference is a result of the fact that the nodes *regionlist* and *dataSet*1, part of the out-neighbourhood of *composer*1, have an empty 1-type.

Algorithm 1.1: Non Incremental Inferring of types$(\mathcal{V}, \mathcal{E}, k)$

```
1  initialise for all v ∈ V and for all i ≤ k
2        i-type(v) ← ∅
3  for v ∈ V
4        0-type(v) ← lab(v)
5  for 1 ≤ i ≤ k
6        for each edge e = (v, u, l) ∈ E such that (i − 1)-type(u) ≠ ∅
7              add (l, (i − 1)-type(u)) to set i-type(v)
8  return i-type(v) for all v ∈ V and 0 ≤ i ≤ k
```

Note that if v is a leaf node in a provenance graph, then k-$type(v) = \emptyset$ for all $k \geq 1$. Also, note that nodes might coincide with regards to i-$types$ but differ with regards to j-$types$, for some $j < i$. Clearly, they can also differ for some $j > i$. The parameter k may be referred to as the depth of a provenance type.

The choice of looking into edge labels comes from the fact that, in the context of provenance, a sequence of edges culminating at a given node provides a good description of the transformation that occurred to this particular node, or the information that it contained. And thus the k-type of a node v provides the set of transformations acting on different provenance elements of the graph leading to the existence of v.

Note that in the definition of a k-type, repetitions of pairs $(l, (k$-$1)$-$type(u))$ are discarded. For example, both *composer*1 and *illustrate*1, in Fig. 2, have the same 1-*type*, regardless of the fact that *composer*1 is related to two entities (in the same way). The intuition behind that is that the nature of the transformations that generated v are more important than the number of occurrences of a particular transformation.

Algorithm 1.1 infers types according to Definition 1. It takes as input a set of nodes $\mathcal{V}$, a set of edges $\mathcal{E}$, and a parameter k. It infers all i-$type(v)$, for all $v \in \mathcal{V}$ and $0 \leq i \leq k$. This is a non-incremental algorithm, as it is batch-processing all nodes in $\mathcal{V}$. We first initialise our sets i-$type(v) = \emptyset$ for all nodes. Lines 3-4 infer the 0-*types* according to Definition 1. The loop starting at line 5, for each i, visits all the edges (v, u, l) that terminate at a node u which has been assigned a non-empty $(i$-$1)$-$type(u)$ and add the pair $(l, (i$-$1)$-$type(u))$ to i-$type(v)$. Note that this is a sequential loop, and thus cannot be run in parallel. This restriction comes from the recursive definition of types. It is, however, possible to run this loop (or the entire algorithm) in parallel for different graphs G of $\mathcal{G}$.

3.1 Library of Types

In the previous section, we have shown how to infer k-*types* of nodes in a graph or family of graphs. Note, however, that for large sizes of $\mathcal{G}$, we expect a significant recurrence rate with respect to nodes' types. With that in mind, we propose the creation of library that records all types seen up to a given point, as well as a function that maps each node to the library index of its type.

Table 1. Libraries of types generated from graph in Fig. 2

$\mathcal{T}_0$	$\mathcal{T}_1$	$\mathcal{T}_2$	$\mathcal{T}_3$
$1_0 \to (ag)$	$1_1 \to ((used, 3_0), (waw, 1_0))$	$1_2 \to ((wgb, 1_1))$	$1_3 \to ((wgb, 3_2))$
$2_0 \to (act)$	$2_1 \to ((wgb, 2_0))$	$2_2 \to ((used, 2_1), (waw, 5_1))$	$2_3 \to ((used, 1_2))$
$3_0 \to (ent)$	$3_1 \to ((wat, 1_0), (wgb, 2_0))$	$3_2 \to ((waw, 5_1))$	$3_3 \to ((wgb, 2_2))$
	$4_1 \to ((wro, 3_0))$	$4_2 \to ((wro, 3_1))$	$4_3 \to ((wro, 5_2))$
	$5_1 \to ((abo, 1_0))$	$5_2 \to ((wat, 5_1), (wgb, 1_1))$	

Example 2. Consider once more graph G in Fig. 2. Table 1 presents four library of types of nodes in G. Note that elements from list $\mathcal{T}_k$ will make reference to elements in map $\mathcal{T}_{(k-1)}$.[3] Also, although libraries may not be sorted in any particular way, each entry is. The reason is that we need to be able to uniquely identify each type. In this particular example, the ordering of edge-labels is the alphabetical one. As before, if more than one pair has the same edge label, the second coordinate is compared.

Note for example that none of the 3-*types* have two branches. That is a result of node *derek* having an empty 2-*type*.

Like in Example 2, libraries make use of the recursive definition of types to further simplify their representation. A key characteristic is that entries in our libraries in Table 1 are not exactly provenance k-types, but a compact representation of them. For example, entry $2_2 \to ((used, 2_1), (waw, 5_1))$ corresponds to the k-*type* defined by $\{(used, \{(wgb, \{act\})\}), (waw, \{(abo, \{ag\})\})\}$. The definitions of library of types and compact types are somehow intertwined. We now formally define a library of types that would give us the table above.

Definition 2 (Library of Types and Compact Types). *Given a family of graphs $\mathcal{G} = (\mathcal{V}, \mathcal{E}, \mathcal{S}, \mathcal{L})$, and given $k \geq 0$, we create $k+1$ libraries $\mathcal{T}_i$, $0 \leq i \leq k$, which are one-to-one mappings from integers to compact type expressions encountered in nodes of $\mathcal{G}$. We provide the definition recursively.*

Regarding the compact representation of 0-types, note that there is nothing to further simplify, so the set of compact 0-types is defined by $\mathcal{C}_0 = \mathbb{P}(\mathcal{S})$, i.e., set of possible values for $lab(v)$.[4] For $i = 0$, $\mathcal{T}_0 : \mathcal{N}_0 \to \mathcal{C}_0$ is a mapping from integers ($\mathcal{N}_0 \subset \mathbb{N}$) to compact 0-types.

For $1 \leq i \leq k$, $\mathcal{T}_i : \mathcal{N}_i \to \mathcal{C}_i$, where $\mathcal{C}_i$ is the set of compact type-expressions of depth i, i.e. $t_i \in \mathcal{C}_i$ if t_i is an ordered sequence of the form

$$t_i = \left(\left(l_1, \mathcal{T}_{i-1}^{-1}(t_{i-1}^1) \right), \ldots, \left(l_x, \mathcal{T}_{i-1}^{-1}(t_{i-1}^x) \right) \right) \tag{3}$$

where $l_1 \leq \cdots \leq l_x \in \mathcal{L}$, and $t_{i-1}^1, \ldots, t_{i-1}^x \in \mathcal{C}_{i-1}$. Also, $\mathcal{T}^{-1}$ denotes the inverse mapping that takes a compact type to its index. If $l_j = l_{j'}$ for two different pairs in t_i, their order is defined by their respective library index.

---

[3] For readability, we index elements of map $\mathcal{T}_k$ with k.

[4] Recall that nodes may have more than one label.

Remark 1. Note that in order to transform a compact *k-type* into its full form, a serialiser would need to make use of libraries $T_0, \ldots, T_{k-1}$. The total number of calls to libraries is bounded by $O(\Delta^k)$, where Δ is the maximum forward-degree of nodes in V.

Note that, although a library is created from actual data (as opposed to including all possible theoretical *k-types*), its definition does not include any mapping from nodes to their types. It is useful, therefore, to create and maintain such a mapping from nodes to the indexes of their types in T_i.

Definition 3. *Let G be a family of graphs and T_k a library of types that cover types in G. For each $v \in V$, $t_k(v) \in C_k$ the compact representation of its k-type. We define $\theta_k : V \to \mathbb{N}$ the function that takes a node v and outputs the library index associated with its k-type, i.e., for all $v \in V$,*

$$T_k(\theta_k(v)) = t_k(v) \tag{4}$$

When considering node increments δ_V, we denote $\theta_{V,k}$ as the function associated with the set of previously processed nodes only, whereas $\theta_{\delta_V,k}$ is the function related to new nodes only.

Example 3. Consider once more the provenance graph in Fig. 2 and the library in Example 2. We have $t_2(illustrate1) = ((used, 2_1), (waw, 5_1))$, we have $\theta_2(illustrate1) = 2_2$, and, finally,

$$T_2(\theta_2(illustrate1)) = T_2(2_2) = ((used, 2_1), (waw, 5_1)) = t_2(illustrate1) \tag{5}$$

The definition of a library partially addresses Question **Q3**. In the the following section, we show how to construct such a library, and in Sect. 4 how to maintain it in the context of an incremental mode of processing provenance types.

3.2   Creating a Provenance Types Library

In this section we will present an efficient algorithm for creating libraries of types as defined Sect. 3.1, as well as maintaining functions θ_k that map nodes to the library index associated with their (compact) *k-type*. We use an auxiliary Algorithm 1.2 receiving a set of nodes V and edges $\mathcal{E}$ as input, as well as the depth i. This algorithm first infers the compact representations of v, $t_i(v)$, for $v \in V$, and then check if this type is already part of the current library T_i. If yes, mapping θ_i is updated for v. If not, a new entry is added to the library and θ_i is also updated accordingly.

With that, we are able to present Algorithm 1.3, that creates all libraries of types up to k from V and $\mathcal{E}$. It calls our auxiliary Algorithm 1.2 $k + 1$ times, creating overall libraries $T_0, \ldots, T_k$ and functions that assign a node's (compact) type-index $\theta_0, \ldots, \theta_k$.

Algorithm 1.2: TYPE LIBRARY $(\mathcal{V}, \mathcal{E}, i, \theta_{i-1}, \mathcal{T}_i, \theta_i)$

```
1   if  i == 0
2       for  all  v ∈ V
3             t₀(v) ← lab(v)
4   else
5           for  each  edge  e = (v, u, l) ∈ E  such  that  θᵢ₋₁(u) ≠ 0
6                 add  (l, θᵢ₋₁(u))  to  ordered  sequence  tᵢ(v)
7   for  all  v ∈ V
8         if  tᵢ(v) == Tᵢ(x)  for  some  x
9               add  (v → x)  to  θᵢ
10        else
11              add  (y → tᵢ(v))  to  Tᵢ  for  new  index  y
12              add  (v → y)  to  θᵢ
13  return  Tᵢ, θᵢ
```

Algorithm 1.3: CREATING LIBRARIES AND MAPPINGS$(\mathcal{V}, \mathcal{E}, k)$

```
1   initialise  for  all  v ∈ V  and  for  all  i ≤ k
2       tᵢ(v) ← ∅
3       Tᵢ ← ∅
4       θᵢ ← ∅
5   for  0 ≤ i ≤ k
6         TYPE LIBRARY  (V, E, i, θᵢ₋₁, Tᵢ, θᵢ)
7   return  T₀, . . . , Tₖ, θ₀, . . . , θₖ
```

Running Time of Algorithm 1.3. We are now showing that we need $O(k\,|\mathcal{E}|)$ operations (amortised time) to create all $k+1$ libraries and functions $\theta_0, \ldots, \theta_k$, i.e., to infer all (compact) i-types for all $v \in \mathcal{V}$, and all $0 \le i \le k$. Note that we can infer the i-types on each graph in parallel.

The first iteration ($i = 0$) of auxiliary Algorithm 1.2 can be run in $O(|\mathcal{V}|)$ amortised time. Lines 2-3 take $O(|\mathcal{V}|)$. In loop starting at line 7, for each node, we can check whether its type has been recorded in the library (line 8) in amortised constant time using a suitable hash map. Lines 9-12 run in constant time, so overall complexity is amortised $(\mathcal{V})$ as we enter the loop $|\mathcal{V}|$ times. The other k iterations ($1 \le i \le k$) of auxiliary Algorithm 1.2 takes (amortised) $O(|\mathcal{E}|)$ time. It visits each edge at most once (line 5). To order each set $t_i(v)$ for all $v \in \mathcal{V}$, we execute bucket sorting twice (i.e., a version of radix sort) in all lists at the same time, recording from which vertex each pair $(l, \theta_{i-1}(u))$ came from. We perform the first bucket sort in which buckets represent values $\theta_{i-1}(u)$ for some $u \in \mathcal{V}$ (takes $O(|\mathcal{E}|)$). Note that the size of each library, and therefore the image of θ_{i-1} is bounded by the number of nodes $|\mathcal{V}|$. The second iteration of this sort orders the partially ordered set into buckets representing the edge-labels $l \in \mathcal{L}$ (again takes $O(|\mathcal{E}|)$). Recall that we record the vertex from which each pair comes from. Then, as in its first iteration, looking up whether a compact type is already part of the library (line 8) takes amortised constant time. Then, iterations for $1 \leq i \leq k$, Algorithm 1.2 runs on average in $O(|\mathcal{E}|)$.

Finally, assuming $\mathcal{V} = O(|\mathcal{E}|)$, Algorithm 1.3 can then be run in amortised $O(k\,|\mathcal{E}|)$, because auxiliary Algorithm 1.2 is called k times for $i > 0$.

4 Incremental Inference of Provenance Types

In this section, we look into the main motivation of this paper: how to process provenance types incrementally. We have proposed three research avenues: The need for storing all provenance data from the beginning (**Q1**), the need for reprocessing previously seen nodes (**Q2**), and how to efficiently deal with the possibly multiple occurrence of provenance types among all nodes (**Q3**).

At this point, we need to clarify what we define as increments of provenance data. We can have either a stream of provenance graphs, or a stream of nodes and edges of a provenance graph. We will show that the main difference, however, is whether previously seen nodes have any deleted edges or added edges that start at v (recall definition of $\lambda_{\mathcal{V}}$ from Sect. 2). We thus propose the study of the following cases:

Monotonically Increasing Stream (case $\lambda_{\mathcal{V}} = \emptyset$)): As there is new provenance being received, there are no new edges starting at a previously processed node. There is also no deletion of previously seen edges.

Non-monotonically Increasing Stream (case $\lambda_{\mathcal{V}} \neq \emptyset$): As new provenance is received, there is at least one new edge starting at a previously processed node, or at least one edge removed that started at a previously processed node.

In the next sections, we will show that the answer to Question **Q1** is negative for monotonically increasing streams. For, non-monotonically increasing ones, however, we might need to revisit all previously processed provenance. Similarly, we will show that Question **Q2** is negative for monotonically increasing streams, as there no need to reprocess previously seen nodes. However, when $\lambda_{\mathcal{V}} \neq \emptyset$, there might be the need to reprocess nodes.

4.1 Monotonically Increasing Streams

In this section, we are studying the cases in which we have monotonically increasing streams of provenance data. This includes the introduction of entirely new provenance graphs, but also the addition of new nodes to existing graphs as long as $\lambda_{\mathcal{V}} = \emptyset$. This definition is broad and includes situations in which a single node (or edge) is added, or situations in which entire new graphs together with nodes in previously seen graphs are added. We first show that, when $\lambda_{\mathcal{V}} = \emptyset$, there is no need to reprocess previously seen nodes.

Algorithm 1.4: INCREMENTAL INFERENCE UNDER MONOT. CASE$(\mathcal{V}, \mathcal{E}, \delta_{\mathcal{V}}, \delta_{\mathcal{E}}, k)$

1	initialise **for** all $v \in \delta_{\mathcal{V}}$ and **for** all $i \leq k$
2	$\quad t_i(v) \leftarrow \emptyset$
3	**for** $0 \leq i \leq k$
4	$\quad$ define $\mathcal{T}_i = \mathcal{T}_i(\mathcal{V})$ and $\theta_i = \theta_{(\mathcal{V}, i)}$
5	$\quad$ TYPE LIBRARY $(\delta_{\mathcal{V}}, \delta_{\mathcal{E}}, i, \theta_{i-1}, \mathcal{T}_i, \theta_i)$
6	**return** $\mathcal{T}_0, \ldots, \mathcal{T}_k, \theta_0, \ldots, \theta_k$

Lemma 1 (Addressing Q2). *No previously processed node will have their k-types altered in a monotonically increasing increment. Thus, they do not need to be reprocessed.*

Proof. We prove by induction on k. For $k = 0$, the result follows since all nodes' provenance types remain the same. Assume the result holds for $k = i$, we shall prove it also holds for $i + 1$. From the recursiveness of the definition of k-types (Definition 1), for any v, $(i + 1)$-$type(v)$ rely only on (1) the label on edges starting at v, and (2) the i-$type(u)$, for $u \in v^+$. Since there is no new edge starting on v, all $u \in v^+$ have all previously processed. That fact, together with the induction hypothesis (i-$type(u)$ unchanged) we conclude that $(i + 1)$-$type(u)$ will not been altered. The result follows by induction. $\square$

Lemma 1 suggests that not much information needs to be stored to deal with incremental processing of monotonically increasing streams. The following lemma formalises this idea.

Lemma 2 (Addressing Q1). *In order to infer i-types, $0 \leq i \leq k$, of newly added nodes (equivalent to constructing $\theta_{\delta_{\mathcal{V}}, i}$) there is no need to store previously seen edges, but only the set of maps $\theta_{\mathcal{V}, i}$, $0 \leq i \leq k$.*

Proof. From Lemma 1, no previously processed node needs reprocessing, therefore no edge starting at them will be visited. Therefore there is no need to store previously seen edges. $\square$

Algorithm for Incremental Inference of Types and Libraries. Given the results of the lemmas above, the algorithm for incrementally referring types of monotonically increasing streams is simple if we have maintained libraries of types (and mapping functions) from the already processed data.

Consider Algorithm 1.4. It takes as input the set of already processed nodes $\mathcal{V}$ and edges $\mathcal{E}$, as well as the new ones ($\delta_{\mathcal{V}}$ and $\delta_{\mathcal{E}}$). It also takes depth k as input. We consider $\mathcal{T}_i(\mathcal{V})$, library over nodes in $\mathcal{V}$, and $\theta_{(\mathcal{V}, i)}$, mapping from nodes of $\mathcal{V}$ to library indexes, as global variables, for all $0 \leq i \leq k$. The algorithm calls auxiliary Algorithm 1.2 only with the new sets of nodes and edges as inputs. Note that the algorithm deals with the introduction of new node labels by updating $\mathcal{T}_0$ and θ_0 accordingly.

Complexity of Algorithm 1.4. As expected from the lemmas above, the complexity of inferring types of incoming data (and updating libraries and mappings, when needed) is given by $O(k|\delta_{\mathcal{E}}|)$ amortised time.

Remark 2. Note that the only entries of θ_i that will be accessed in Algorithm 1.4 are the ones for nodes in set δ_V^+. Therefore, further storage optimisations can be achieved when there is previous knowledge with regards to δ_V.

4.2   Non-monotonically Increasing Streams

In this section, we analyse the case of non-monotonically increasing increments, i.e., $\lambda_V \neq \emptyset$. A particular example of such a scenario is the consideration of dynamic sliding windows of time, in which 'old' provenance is deleted as new provenance is added. We will then show that the answer for Question **Q2**, in this case, is positive: we might need to revisit (in the worst case, all) provenance expressions and possibly update their types. This implies that, because previously seen nodes may need reprocessing, it is required that all provenance data, including edges, is kept accessible (Question **Q1**).

Under non-monotonically increasing streams, Algorithm 1.5 infers the provenance types of new nodes as well as reprocess previously seen provenance expressions that may have had their types altered. In line 4, it infers all 0-*types* of newly added nodes. Line 5 flags such nodes since all nodes in their backward-neighbourhood will need their 1-*type* to be (re)processed. The loop in line 6 start by marking all nodes in the backward-neighbourhood of previously marked nodes, making sure to add all provenance expressions from set λ_V. That last part is needed because such nodes need reprocessing regardless of the types of their forward-neighbours. Notation in line 11 refers to whether the updated value $\theta_i'(v)$ has changed or not compared to its value before the auxiliary function in line 9. If is has not changed, then it will not contribute for a change in $(i+1)$-types of nodes in its backwards neighbourhood. Although nothing prevents the same node v to be added back to M in line 7 of the next iteration of the loop.

Correctness of Algorithm 1.5. We show that the algorithm will correctly reprocess the k-types of all nodes that were directly or indirectly affected by the addition or removal of edges. The bottom line of the algorithm is to take in account that not only nodes that were immediately affected will need to have their k-types updated, but that the effect may cascade down along the graph to a distance up to k.

We first consider $v \in \lambda_V$. Even though we may have no change in, for example, 1-*type*(v), that does not imply that 2-*type*(v) will be also unchanged (the added or removed edge might connect or have connected v to different branches), and thus we need to reprocess this node for all $0 \leq i \leq k$. Line 7 guarantees that by adding λ_V to all M_i. Now consider all other nodes, including the ones previously processed. We are going to show, by induction, that Algorithm 1.5 correctly identifies the need for reprocessing. For $i = 0$, all new nodes (and only those) need 0-*type*(v) inferred (line 4). Note that, for $i > 1$, a node v's k-*type*(v) needs to be reprocessed if and only if at least one of its forward-neighbours $u \in v^+$ had their $(k-1)$-*type*(u) updated, i.e., reprocessed and changed. For $i > 1$, assume

Algorithm 1.5: INCREMENTAL INFERENCE UNDER NON-MONOT. CASE($\mathcal{V}, \mathcal{E}, \delta_\mathcal{V}, \delta_\mathcal{E}, k$)

```
1    initialise for all v ∈ δᵥ and for all 0 ≤ i ≤ k
2        tᵢ(v) ← ∅
3    define 𝒯ᵢ = 𝒯ᵢ(𝒱) and θᵢ = θ₍ᵥ,ᵢ₎ , for 0 ≤ i ≤ k
4    TYPE LIBRARY (δᵥ, δₑ, 0, ∅, 𝒯₀, θ₀)
5    define set M₀ = δᵥ                          [these are marked nodes]
6    for i = 1 until k
7        define Mᵢ = Mᵢ₋₁⁻ ∪ λᵥ
8        define Lᵢ set of edges starting at nodes in Mᵢ
9        TYPE LIBRARY (Mᵢ, Lᵢ, i, θᵢ₋₁, 𝒯ᵢ, θᵢ)
10       for v ∈ Mᵢ                     [compare types for v before and after line 9]
11           if (θᵢ′(v) == θᵢ(v))
12               remove v from Mᵢ
13   return 𝒯₀, . . . , 𝒯ₖ, θ₀, . . . , θₖ
```

that all nodes that required processing were reprocessed. We show that this is also true for $i + 1$. Indeed, no node that had their i-type modified was removed from M_i (lines 11-12), and thus, v will be in set M_{i+1} if and only if at least one of its neighbours was not removed from M_i (or, of course, if $v \in \lambda_\mathcal{V}$).

Complexity of Algorithm 1.5. In the worst case, this algorithm may need to reprocess all nodes that have been previously seen. Line 4 takes $O(|\delta_\mathcal{V}|)$ operations on average. Let L_i be the set of edges starting at nodes in M_i, i.e., $|L_i| = \sum_{v \in M_i} \deg^+(v)$. Then, each iteration of the loop starting in line 6 takes $O(|L_i|)$, similarly to Algorithm 1.3. Finally, denoting $|L| = \sum_{i=1}^{k} |L_i|$, we conclude that Algorithm 1.5's running time complexity is $O(|\delta_\mathcal{V}| + |L|)$ amortised time. Note that visiting all nodes in M_i (line 10) does not increase the complexity as $|L_i| > |M_i|$.

In Sect. 4, we investigated the different modes of incremental processing of provenance types, showing that, in the context of monotonically increasing streams, provenance types of new nodes can be inferred fast and without the need to reprocess previously seen nodes or access all past provenance data. In non-monotonically increasing streams, however, reprocessing of old nodes might be necessary, as well as access to edges of previously seen graphs.

5   Empirical Evaluation

In this section, we show that the size of a library is indeed much smaller than $|\mathcal{V}|$. We present empirical results of the processing of more than 36,000 graphs, that show that the number of distinct i-types, for each $i \leq 5$, is approximately 5,000. The challenge of choosing i to best analyse and compare summary graphs left for future work. We analysed datasets from 3 different domains. CollabMap [14] (CM) is a database of provenance graphs for evacuation planning generated in a crowd-sourcing platform. We separate CollabMap graphs into buildings, routes, and route sets. MIMIC [9] is a database of information of patients in critical

Table 2. Number of graphs in each dataset, as well as the number of nodes with a non-empty *i-type* for each $i = 0, \ldots, 5$

Datasets	Number of graphs	Nodes with non-empty *i-type* for $i =$					
		0	1	2	3	4	5
CM-buidings	5175	94k	89k	71k	58k	51k	38k
CM-routes	4997	105k	100k	90k	70k	44k	40k
CM-Routeset:	4710	101k	97k	76k	49k	45k	37k
MIMIC:	21892	1208k	865k	843k	821k	788k	753k
PG:	80	18k	14k	14k	14k	14k	14k
Total	36854	1526k	1165k	1094k	1012k	943k	883k

hospital care. Finally, our last dataset of graphs describes actions of players on Pokemón Go (PG) simulations.

We first provide an overview of the size of our datasets in Table 2. We have a total of $36,854$ different provenance graphs, with an average of 41.4 nodes each. Note that, although all nodes have a non-empty 0-*type* associated with them, the same is not valid for deeper types. For example, leaf nodes have an empty 1-*type* (and thus an empty *i-type* for $i \geq 1$). The quantity of nodes with a non-empty *i-type* for each $i = 0, \ldots, 5$ is given rounded up to the nearest thousand. Observe, for example, that of the nodes in graphs of the MIMIC dataset, approximately $343,000$ ($\approx 28\%$) are leaf nodes, as they have an empty 1-*type*.

Table 3 shows the sizes of libraries of types $\mathcal{T}_i$, for $0 \leq i \leq 5$, for each dataset separately, as well as them combined, using one common library of types. In these experiments, we ignore application-specific labels of provenance expressions, and thus $\mathcal{T}_0 = \{\mathrm{ag}, \mathrm{act}, \mathrm{ent}\}$ for the combined dataset, although there are no agents in neither CollabMap nor PokemonGo datasets. The 6th row gives us the size of libraries generated from all datasets, which implies that if the same type appears in more than one dataset, it will be counted only once in our joint library.

Table 3. Number of entries in libraries of types for different datasets, as well as for a common one.

Datasets	$|\mathcal{T}_0|$	$|\mathcal{T}_1|$	$|\mathcal{T}_2|$	$|\mathcal{T}_3|$	$|\mathcal{T}_4|$	$|\mathcal{T}_5|$
CM-buidings	2	3	3	5	14	102
CM-routes	2	4	10	35	155	577
CM-Routeset:	2	4	8	23	58	262
MIMIC:	3	5	11	39	405	4328
PG:	2	3	5	10	23	54
Sum of individual library sizes	11	19	37	112	655	5323
Sizes of common libraries for all domains	3	9	23	84	601	5197

In contrast, the last row gives the sum of sizes of the 5 individual libraries. We can see that, especially for low-depth types, there is a significant overlap of types across datasets.

This experiment shows that maintaining a library of types is an efficient way of avoiding the need to store multiple copies of the same types. As the depth increases, so does the number of different patterns to be stored and, although this is expected due to increased complexity of neighbourhoods of greater radius, the final library sizes continue to be much more compact than the size of original data. Note also that there is a significant overlap of types between different domains, which indicates that keeping a library of types across different domains can contribute to further storage optimisation. The full library of types for each of the datasets can be found at https://openprovenance.org/typelibrary/.

6   Related Work

To the best of our knowledge, this is the first work that proposes the study of incremental processing of provenance types, which contributes to the study of incremental provenance sumaries. There is, however, literature on dynamic analysis of provenance, such as [8], which proposes the analysis of dynamic sliding windows to identify behaviour anomalies. Also, MaMaDroid [11] builds a Markov chain over continuously provided data for malware detection. Provenance data streams without the focus on data incremental processes for constructing summaries were also studied in [4] and [18].

Beyond the domain of provenance, there is also work on incremental inferences of summaries. In particular, a DataGuide [5] provides summaries of databases, in both incremental and non-incremental modes, although their model may take exponential time and space complexity on the number of nodes and edges of input graphs. Also, [2] studies pattern matching in incremental scenarios. The main difference with our work is that they focus on finding a specific pattern within a large (and changing) graph, rather than inferring each node's type. On a similar domain, [6] proposes the incremental processing of a summary graph in which nodes are associated to a hash value, although they do not consider edge labels in their work. Song and Ge [17], on the other hand, do consider edge labels and construct graph sketches over sliding windows. The main difference compared to provenance types is that they do not consider patterns within graphs, but only information encoded in edges such as their label and endpoints. In the context of machine learning and Weisfeiler-Lehman graph kernels, [20] provides graph classification with continuously provided data. Unlike in our work, they discard nodes with less discriminatory power to facilitate the classification process.

The concept of provenance types was introduced in [13] as the main step to construct summary graphs, which are, in turn, a way to extract the essence of provenance graphs. Based on their definition of provenance types, however, the algorithm presented in [13] to infer types has an exponential time complexity in function of the parameter k. This drawback comes from the fact that all walks of lengh k from a given node may need to be inspected. In this paper, we offer similar but recursive definition of provenance types which allows us infer them in polynomial time. This recursive definition is similar to the one used in the context of Weisfeiler-Lehman Graph Kernels [16], with the differences that our sets $\theta_k(v)$ consist of pairs instead of single values, and that we discard repetitions in such sets. Another difference, also explored in [19], is that we work on graphs with labelled edges, thus edge labels are taken into account when processing nodes' types.

7   Conclusions and Future Work

In this paper, we studied incremental processing of provenance in the context of summarisation of provenance graphs. Our contribution focused on the inference of provenance types, as we leave incremental computation of summary graphs for future work.

First, we suggested an alternative definition of provenance types (Definition 1), which, in loose terms, consist of an abstraction of the forward-neighbourhood of nodes in a provenance graph. This definition allows provenance types to be inferred in polynomial time taking into account the size of the input data (Algorithm 1.3). To avoid storing the same provenance types multiple times, we suggest the creation of a library of types for each parameter k (Definition 2). Such libraries record all seen (compact) provenance types. We also define, for each parameter k, a function that maps each node to the library entry associated with the node's compact type (Definition 3).

In order to study the different modes of data increments, we considered two broad scenarios: when previously processed edges are removed from - or when new edges start at - previously seen nodes (non-monotonically increasing streams), and when that is not the case (monotonically increasing streams). For the former case, we provide Algorithm 1.5 that reprocess nodes when needed. The latter scenario, on the other hand, was shown to allow the processing of incoming data without the need to reprocessing previous provenance information (Question **Q2**). In that case, there is also no need to keep stored previously seen provenance relations (Question **Q1**).

Subsequently, we presented an analysis of more than 36.000 provenance files and showed that the size of libraries of types is small compared to the size of our datasets (Question **Q3**).

As future work, it would be useful to develop an empirical analysis of the time it takes to run Algorithm 1.5 in practice, i.e., to understand what proportion of the graph needs to be reprocessed. Another important further step is to extend the incremental inference to constructing summary graphs over continuously provided provenance.

References

1. Chirigati, F., Shasha, D., Freire, J.: Reprozip: using provenance to support computational reproducibility. In: Presented as part of the 5th USENIX Workshop on the Theory and Practice of Provenance (2013)
2. Fan, W., Wang, X., Wu, Y.: Incremental graph pattern matching. ACM Trans. Database Syst. **38**(3) (2013). https://doi.org/10.1145/2489791
3. Gil, Y., et al.: PROV model primer. W3C Working Group Note (2013)
4. Glavic, B., Sheykh Esmaili, K., Fischer, P.M., Tatbul, N.: Ariadne: managing fine-grained provenance on data streams. In: Proceedings of the 7th ACM International Conference on Distributed Event-Based Systems, DEBS 2013, pp. 39–50. Association for Computing Machinery, New York (2013). https://doi.org/10.1145/2488222.2488256
5. Goldman, R., Widom, J.: Dataguides: enabling query formulation and optimization in semistructured databases. In: 23rd International Conference on Very Large Data Bases (VLDB 1997) (1997). http://ilpubs.stanford.edu:8090/232/
6. Gou, X., Zou, L., Zhao, C., Yang, T.: Fast and accurate graph stream summarization. In: 2019 IEEE 35th International Conference on Data Engineering (ICDE), pp. 1118–1129. IEEE (2019)
7. Groth, P., Moreau, L. (eds.): PROV-Overview. An Overview of the PROV Family of Documents. W3C Working Group Note NOTE-PROV-overview-20130430, World Wide Web Consortium, April 2013. http://www.w3.org/TR/2013/NOTE-prov-overview-20130430/
8. Han, X., Pasquier, T., Ranjan, T., Goldstein, M., Seltzer, M.: Frappuccino: fault-detection through runtime analysis of provenance. In: 9th USENIX Workshop on Hot Topics in Cloud Computing (HotCloud 2017) (2017)
9. Johnson, A.E., et al.: Mimic-iii, a freely accessible critical care database. Sci. Data **3**, 160035 (2016)
10. Ma, X., Fox, P., Tilmes, C., Jacobs, K., Waple, A.: Capturing provenance of global change information. Nat. Clim. Chang. **4**, 409–413 (2014). https://doi.org/10.1038/nclimate2141
11. Mariconti, E., Onwuzurike, L., Andriotis, P., Cristofaro, E.D., Ross, G.J., Stringhini, G.: Mamadroid: detecting android malware by building Markov chains of behavioral models. CoRR abs/1612.04433 (2016). http://arxiv.org/abs/1612.04433
12. Moreau, L.: The foundations for provenance on the web. Found. Trends Web Sci. **2**(2–3), 99–241 (2010). https://doi.org/10.1561/1800000010
13. Moreau, L.: Aggregation by provenance types: a technique for summarising provenance graphs. In: Graphs as Models 2015 (An ETAPS 2015 Workshop), pp. 129–144. Electronic Proceedings in Theoretical Computer Science, London, UK, April 2015. https://doi.org/10.4204/EPTCS.181.9
14. Ramchurn, S., Huynh, T.D., Venanzi, M., Shi, B.: Collabmap: crowdsourcing maps for emergency planning. In: Proceedings of the 3rd Annual ACM Web Science Conference, WebSci 2013, pp. 326–335 (2013). https://doi.org/10.1145/2464464.2464508
15. Ramchurn, S.D., et al.: A disaster response system based on human-agent collectives. J. Artif. Intell. Res. **57**, 661–708 (2016)
16. Shervashidze, N., Schweitzer, P., Leeuwen, E.J.V., Mehlhorn, K., Borgwardt, K.M.: Weisfeiler-Lehman graph kernels. J. Mach. Learn. Re. **12**(Sep), 2539–2561 (2011)
17. Song, C., Ge, T.: Labeled graph sketches. In: 2018 IEEE 34th International Conference on Data Engineering (ICDE), pp. 1312–1315. IEEE (2018)

18. Vijayakumar, N.N., Plale, B.: Towards low overhead provenance tracking in near real-time stream filtering. In: Moreau, L., Foster, I. (eds.) IPAW 2006. LNCS, vol. 4145, pp. 46–54. Springer, Heidelberg (2006). https://doi.org/10.1007/11890850_6
19. Vries, G.K.D.: A fast approximation of the Weisfeiler-Lehman graph kernel for RDF data. In: Blockeel, H., Kersting, K., Nijssen, S., Železný, F. (eds.) ECML PKDD 2013. LNCS (LNAI), vol. 8188, pp. 606–621. Springer, Heidelberg (2013). https://doi.org/10.1007/978-3-642-40988-2_39
20. Yao, Y., Holder, L.: Scalable SVM-based classification in dynamic graphs. In: 2014 IEEE International Conference on Data Mining, pp. 650–659, December 2014. https://doi.org/10.1109/ICDM.2014.69

Reliability and Trustworthiness

Non-repudiable Provenance for Clinical Decision Support Systems

Elliot Fairweather[1], Rudolf Wittner[2,3]([✉]), Martin Chapman[1], Petr Holub[2,3], and Vasa Curcin[1]

[1] Department of Population Health Sciences, King's College London, London, UK
elliot.fariweather@kcl.ac.uk
[2] BBMRI-ERIC, Graz, Austria
rudolf.wittner@bbmri-eric.eu
[3] Institute of Computer Science and Faculty of Informatics, Masaryk University, Brno, Czech Republic

Abstract. Provenance templates are now a recognised methodology for the construction of data provenance records. Each template defines the provenance of a domain-specific action in abstract form, which may then be instantiated as required by a single call to the provenance template service. As data reliability and trustworthiness becomes a critical issue in an increasing number of domains, there is a corresponding need to ensure that the provenance of that data is non-repudiable. In this paper we contribute two new, complementary modules to our template model and implementation to produce non-repudiable data provenance. The first, a module that traces the operation of the provenance template service itself, and records a provenance trace of the construction of an object-level document, at the level of individual service calls. The second, a non-repudiation module that generates evidence for the data recorded about each call, annotates the service trace accordingly, and submits a representation of that evidence to a provider-agnostic notary service. We evaluate the applicability of our approach in the context of a clinical decision support system. We first define a policy to ensure the non-repudiation of evidence with respect to a security threat analysis in order to demonstrate the suitability of our solution. We then select three use cases from within a particular system, CONSULT, with contrasting data provenance recording requirements and analyse the subsequent performance of our prototype implementation against three different notary providers.

Keywords: Data provenance · Non-repudiation · Health informatics · Decision support systems

This work has been supported by European Union's Horizon 2020 research and innovation programme under grant agreement No 654248, project CORBEL, and under grant agreement No 824087, project EOSC-Life.

B. Glavic et al. (Eds.): IPAW 2020/IPAW 2021, LNCS 12839, pp. 165–182, 2021.
https://doi.org/10.1007/978-3-030-80960-7_10

1   Introduction

The *provenance* of a data resource describes the entities, activities and agents that have influenced it over time [21]. *Provenance templates* are a methodology for the construction of data provenance records. A template is an abstract provenance document which may be later instantiated, as many times as required, usually in the context of a larger document, to produce a concrete provenance document [5]. Each template is designed to represent a discrete, domain-specific action which can be recorded as a single call to a provenance template service [6]. Provenance tools are now being used widely in scientific domains, where *trust* in the provenance records constructed is essential [19]. A lack of transparency, which implies a lack of trust, is considered one of the main reasons for the poor uptake of clinical decision support systems (DSS) [22]. In response to this issue, there has been a recent movement towards *secure* provenance, for example [16].

One key security objective is *non-repudiation*, which is defined as *preventing the denial of previous commitments or actions* [17]. In this paper, we focus specifically on non-repudiation of origin – preventing an author from falsely denying the act of creating content or sending a message – referred to simply as non-repudiation in the remainder of the text.

Whilst the correctness of the operations commonly used to achieve non-repudiation at the cryptographic level can be formally proven, at the practical level, the broader context needs to be taken into account, such as international regulations related to digital signatures and communications, or current threats relevant to specific systems, which evolve over time. For example, applying a digital signature to a message, which is a common way to ensure its authenticity, means only that a cryptographic operation was performed by a piece of hardware or software on behalf of a person. In a real-world scenario, we might then presume that person is the real author of a message, because we have assumed that the corresponding private key is known only to them. However, this might not hold true; there is always a chance that confidentiality of a private key can be violated (for example, by malware) and there is no guaranteed mechanism to prevent such an event.

To address this challenge, we first perform a threat analysis for the non-repudiation of recommendations made by a DSS, and define a non-repudiation policy which can be later used during an adjudication process. We then use this policy to guide the design of a provenance-based model for the representation of the evidence required for non-repudiation, and implement this as an optional feature within our provenance template service. We then evaluate our solution using three different evidence storage solutions that satisfy our policy requirements, in the context of a DSS, CONSULT.

2   Related Work

Authenticity, commonly defined as corroboration of a claimant's identity, has long been considered distinct from non-repudiation [17,23]. The former is considered a simpler security requirement than the latter, which is typically a more complex, protocol-based security service [9] and is also defined as one of nine security principles in [2]. The current ISO standard for non-repudiation [12] explicitly states that *non-repudiation can only be provided within the context of a clearly defined security policy for a particular application and legal environment*. Detailed discussion about why non-repudiation and related evidence management must be designed in advance can be found in the thesis of Roe [25].

To our knowledge, secure provenance and related challenges were discussed for the first time in 2007 [10] and were focused on its integrity, availability and confidentiality. Another paper [3] discussed related challenges in a more detailed way and explained that existing security models do not fit to graph structures, which is the standardized representation of provenance information.

The use of a notary service within a system to ensure the integrity and non-repudiation of biomedical knowledge retrieval requests and responses from a database has already been implemented [14] but differs from our solution by employing a so-called in-line notary. This work does not however include an analysis of possible threats or define tactics for their mitigation, which is crucial in the context of achieving non-repudiation. The authors also mention that to the best of their knowledge there currently exists no other work using blockchain-based technology to manage biomedical evidence integrity and non-repudiation. This is supported by a scoping review [11] which references the former as the only paper within the domain of healthcare or health sciences to address the property of non-repudiation.

Another survey paper [27] describes and compares existing methods to ensure integrity, authenticity, non-repudiation and proof of existence in the long-term. The authors make no distinction between the terms *authenticity* and *non-repudiation*, which would have dramatic consequences in a real-world use case. The same is true for the proposed secure provenance schemes in [1] and [13] that claim that non-repudiation can be ensured by applying digital signatures, but any further discussion about what aspects of non-repudiation are achieved is omitted.

3 A Non-repudiation Policy for Decision Support

A clinical decision support system (DSS) is a software tool that evaluates a set of health data inputs and makes recommendations to support clinical decision making. These recommendations range from treatment suggestions to establishing a diagnosis, and are provided to a patient, among other users. Because the recommendation generation process should be transparent [5], information about that process (*evidence*) is often provided to a patient together with a recommendation, so they can check, for example, whether valid data about their diagnosis and health condition was used (a form of *Explainable AI* (XAI) [18]). In other words, a patient can, either themselves or via an authorised entity, check the provenance of a recommendation generation process, given that the evidence provided describes the creation and evolution of a particular recommendation. Evidence is particularly useful if harm is caused to a patient as the result of a particular recommendation, perhaps due to an error in the DSS's implementation or design, when it may, for example, be required in a legal context. In order for evidence to be used in this way, it must be *irrefutable* at the practical level, meaning that it is sufficiently convincing; it is clear that it really came from the system and it was not later changed by anyone to subvert the adjudication process.

We refer to these concerns as *threats*, and identify them within a DSS by examining the following general requirements for irrefutable evidence [17]:

1. The authenticity and integrity of the provided evidence need to be established, such that the alleged author of the evidence cannot later deny that authenticity.
2. Responsibilities and rules related to evidence generation, storage and verification must be defined in order to enable all participating parties to behave responsibly, in accordance with these rules. Violating these rules can lead to decreased trust in the system.
3. Authenticity and integrity verification information must be available during a pre-defined period of time, according to a time period for which non-repudiation should be achieved (achieving non-repudiation for an unlimited period, if feasible, is likely to be expensive). The evidence verifier must be able to verify the evidence.
4. If a dispute related to the origin of evidence occurs, trusted timestamps are required to reconstruct past events.

When applying these requirements to a DSS we observe, for example, that a DSS is generally motivated to maintain evidence in order to demonstrate that the decision generation process is compliant with standards and clinical practice. On the other hand, if harm were to be caused to a patient, a DSS creator or owner then has a motive to falsify, modify or destroy generated incriminating evidence – such as timestamps, in order to discredit the reconstruction of past events – to protect themselves, particularly if a corresponding authority, responsible for maintaining said standards and practice, is involved. There are also external entities with a motive to disrupt evidence, such as insurance companies, who may wish to avoid making a payment to an injured patient or a DSS provider.

To address these threats, we define a non-repudiation *policy*, given as a set of mandatory requirements for the evidence generation process, in order to ensure that the evidence produced by a DSS both engenders trust, and can also be later used by a patient during an adjudication process in case of a future dispute. These requirements are presented along with brief rationale:

1. A DSS is the only party able to generate valid evidence, thus all of evidence needs to be digitally signed. *Authenticity and integrity of the evidence is achieved by this rule.*
2. Cryptographic operations performed by the DSS are realised using a special piece of hardware, which provides additional protection against private key disclosure. *The reason for applying this rule is that protection of the key needs to be established.*

3. Despite additional protection of private keys, there is always a chance that the confidentiality of a particular private key is compromised. *For that reason, a private key owner should define a certain amount of time to report a confidentiality violation of the private key used for creating digital signatures (this time period is called the clearance period [17]). If the clearance period expires, all digital signatures created before are considered valid. Since this is a processional part of the non-repudiation and it is not important from architecture point of view, we will not address it in our solution.*

4. A timestamp describing the token generation must be generated by a trusted third party. *Integrity and authenticity of the timestamp need to be ensured. Due to the importance of the timestamp, we propose this measure in order to build additional trust in reconstructed events, especially if a signing key had been revoked or expired before a dispute arose.*

5. Because a DSS could have a motive to disrupt or destroy existing evidence, it cannot be the only party responsible for storing and maintaining it.

6. The evidence used should be held in storage that is able to prevent the modification of stored content. *The reason for applying this rule is to raise the level of trust concerning evidence integrity.*

7. All information needed for integrity and authenticity of the evidence verification should be sealed as part of the evidence. *This rule is intended to simplify additional evidence management.*

8. After a decision is made and particular provenance is generated, the patient can verify its meaningfulness, authenticity and integrity, and can store it for prospective future claims. *The assumption here is that the non-repudiation of the provenance is in the best interest of the patient, since their health condition is affected by particular decision. This reflects a current movement in healthcare whereby patients are custodians of their own data [8] and reduces trust assumptions about a third party, which would otherwise have to verify it instead of the patient.*

9. The generated evidence must contain an identifier for the particular patient. *By applying this rule, the patient may be certain that a generated decision and its evidence was not intended for a different person.*

10. The evidence generated during a decision generation contains additional information about time when the request from user and when other inputs for the decision generation were obtained.

This policy is used in the following sections to define a secure process for evidence generation, storage and verification within a DSS. In the following section, we show how some of these requirements can be addressed as a provenance-based model.

4   A Provenance-Based Model for Non-repudiable Evidence

The granularity of the provenance template methodology fits the design of an architecture for non-repudiable evidence perfectly. The fact that each template represent a single, yet complete, domain-specific action within the client system allows evidence to be generated and presented at a meaningful, yet manageable scale. However the direct use of provenance data generated from templates as evidence is insufficient, because it provides no information regarding its use within the construction of the parent document. Thus in order to achieve non-repudiation within a client domain, we have first added the facility to record a provenance trace of the workflow of the provenance template service itself; we call this data *meta-provenance.*

The meta-provenance trace generated for a document constitutes a wholly reproducible record of the construction of that document and is described in detail in Subsect. 4.1. This data, later appended with records of the non-repudiable evidence generated at each point in the workflow as formalised in Subsect. 4.2, also allows us to present clients with a comprehensive survey of provenance actions carried out on their behalf and to later validate their authenticity.

4.1   Templates for Meta-provenance

Each call to the provenance template service, besides some necessary administrative functionality, represents an action to be executed in the life-cycle of a provenance document under construction. We begin, therefore, by recalling the typical workflow for the construction of a document using the service in Fig. 1.

1. *newTemplate* (one or more times) to upload templates to the server
2. (a) *newDocument* (once) to begin a new document
   (b) *addNamespace* (zero or more times) to add a namespace to the document
   (c) *registerTemplate* (one or more times) to associate a template with the document
   (d) *generate* (one or more times) to use a substitution to instantiate a template, and merge it into the document
   (e)   i. *generateInitialise* (once) to use a subsitution to instantiate a template with zones as a fragment
      ii. *generateZone* (zero or more times) to use a substiution to instantiate a subsequent iteration of a zone within the fragment
     iii. *generateFinalise* (once) to check and merge the fragment into the document

Fig. 1. How to construct a document using the provenance template service

We now describe how to formalise instances of this workflow and other important meta-data relating to the operation of the service, by recording provenance traces of the execution of the actions contributing to the life-cycle of a document. Recording the life-cycle of documents not only produces valuable meta-data regarding the construction of a document, but is a necessary prerequisite to enabling the non-repudiation and later verification of the data generated.

These traces are recorded in meta-level *history* documents, one for each standard or *object-level* document under construction. History documents are valid provenance documents created and maintained by the new meta-provenance module, and stored within the server providing the service. Following the creation of new object-level document by the document management module, the meta-provenance module will create a new history document. Each service call has a corresponding provenance template defined within the meta-provenance module. When the web service receives a request, following a successful execution of the request at the object-level by the document management module, the request data is sent to the meta-provenance module, which builds a substitution for the respective template. This is then instantiated within the corresponding separate history document. The templates for the *newDocument* and *addNamespace* service calls are shown by way of example in Fig. 2.

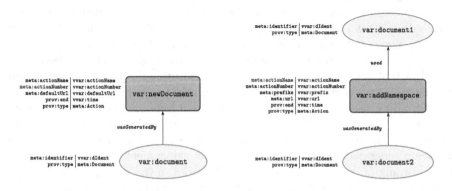

Fig. 2. newDocument (*left*) and addNamespace (*right*) templates

The meta-provenance templates use annotations in the `meta` namespace. The object document being tracked is represented as an entity of type `meta:Document` and each action executed upon that document as an activity of `meta:Action` type. Each action is annotated with its name (`meta:actionName`) and given a numeric value (`meta:actionNumber`), corresponding to its order in the trace. The time that the execution of the action was completed is also recorded as the end time of the activity.[1] Templates are recorded as entities of type `meta:Template` and fragments as entities of `meta:Fragment`. Object documents, templates and fragments are all annotated with the `meta:identifier` attribute which contains their unique document identifier within the server.

---

[1] The provenance template model adds three special attributes (`start, end, time`) to the `prov` namespace in order to allow the start and end times of activities, and the times of influences to be instantiated as template value variables. These attributes are translated in the document model into the respective PROV timings. This is necessary because the PROV data model only allows these timings to be of type `xsd:dateTime` and so cannot be replaced by a variable name directly.

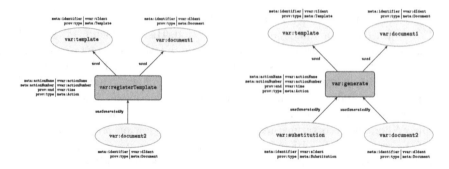

Fig. 3. registerTemplate (*left*) and generate (*right*) templates

Substitutions given as input to generation actions, that is, *generate*, (see Fig. 3) *generateInit*, or *generateZone* are now also persisted as meta-level provenance documents called *substitution* documents. A history document together with its associated substitution documents together form the complete, reproducible meta-procenance record of the construction of an object document. The translation of standard substitutions into substitution documents is carried out by the meta-provenance module again by use of templates, given in Fig. 4. A substitution is created using the *newSubstitution* template, and then each binding added using *addBinding*. These operations instantiations are executed in-memory by the server, and the final document is persisted by the server, under a system-generated identifier. The substitutions documents thus created during the recording of generation actions are referenced in the meta-provenance templates as entities of type `meta:Substitution` and again, being valid documents, annotated by their identifier. The fine granularity of these operations anticipates future improvements to the provenance template service, whereby substitutions may be submitted to the service over time down to the level of a single variable binding.

Any remaining data provided as part of an action, document, is stored as annotations upon the action activity, given in the `meta` namespace. The `meta:defaultUrl` attribute in the *newDocument* template shown in Fig. 2 is one such example.

A meta-provenance record is sufficient to reconstruct an object-level provenance document in its entirety. In order to reproduce the construction of a particular document, its history document is first exported, and the chain of recorded actions then replicated with reference to the necessary substitution documents. This facility allows object documents to be recorded by the server at the meta-level alone, to be expanded at a later date. After the fact document reconstruction from meta-provenance offers the possibility of reducing storage requirements for object documents. Partial reconstruction of documents between specific time points would also reduce the computational requirements for the analysis of object documents.

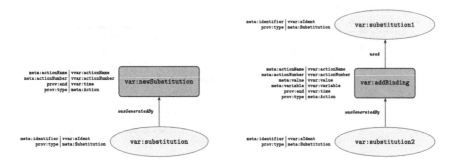

Fig. 4. newSubstitution (*left*) and addBinding (*right*) templates

4.2   A Template for Non-repudiable Evidence

An important requirement of our solution is the capture of the evidence required to achieve the non-repudiation of the provenance data being recorded. The meta-provenance data recorded by each template instantiation within a history document as described in Subsect. 4.1 forms the core of this evidence. However, extra data concerning the security and cryptographic operations later carried out upon each addition to the meta-provenance record must also be stored in order for the evidence to provide a guarantee of non-repudiation. We record this extra data using the template shown in Fig. 5.

The `var:action` activity represents the document management action described in Sect. 4.1 and is instantiated with the same identifier as used for the instantiation of the activity element of the meta-provenance template corresponding to that action. It thus serves as the graft point in the history document between the meta-provenance data recorded about the action and its evidentiary form and required security attributes, as given by the evidence template. The `var:serviceCall` entity represents the service call that requested the document management action, and holds information about the client application and user that made the request. The `var:tokenHeader` entity represents the meta-data required for achieving non-repudiation of the service call and the consequent management action. The token header contains a trusted timestamp, which is generated by a trusted timestamping authority. The header is identified by a unique system-generated identifier. The `var:tokenContent` entity holds a representation of the associated management action, corresponding to the provenance data generated by the meta-provenance module. The `var:signature` entity represents the digital signature of the required evidence, generated by the `var:signToken` activity. The certificate needed to verify the signature is given as the value of `meta:certificate`.

5   A Non-repudiation Architecture for Decision Support

The goal of the proposed solution is to provide a patient with irrefutable evidence that a recommendation made by the DSS and the provenance data recording

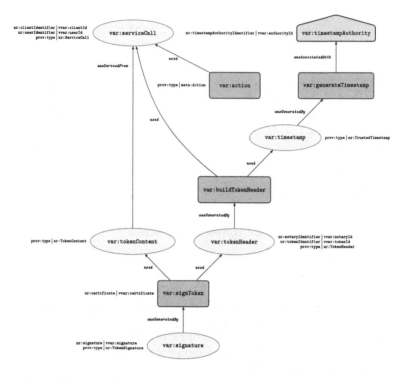

Fig. 5. Template for capturing evidence required for non-repudiation

the generation of that recommendation originated from the DSS. There are four actors present in our solution:

1. *A patient* using the DSS during their treatment process and acting on diagnostic recommendations generated by the system.
2. *A decision support system* consisting of client and server applications, and an instance of the provenance template service, provided by and referred to below as the *provenance server*. A patient will use the client application to request recommendations from the server-side, which in turn may request one or more provenance template actions to be carried out by the provenance server, for which it will generate non-repudiable evidence that is later returned to the patient together with the recommendation.
3. *A trusted timestamping authority service* which provides signed timestamps. These timestamps are included within the required evidence generated to confirm its existence from a specific instant in time.
4. *A trusted notary service* which stores the required evidence. If a dispute about the origin of the provenance data later arises, the notary may be queried to either support or contradict a particular claim.

In the remainder of this section we describe how we use the provenance evidence model given in Sect. 4 to design an extended DSS architecture that meets the policy requirements outlined in Sect. 3 and thus ensures non-repudiation of the recommendation-making process.

5.1 Non-repudiable Evidence Generation and Recording Process

The proposed architecture is illustrated in Fig. 6. The process begins with a request from a DSS client to the DSS service (1) that initiates the generation of a recommendation by the system (2). The recommendation-making process will then in turn request one or more provenance actions to be performed by the provenance server (3). The provenance server first executes the requested action upon the object-level document as usual (4). In the standard architecture this is the point at which the DSS would simply return the recommendation to the user. In the extended architecture however it then records the action as part of the meta-provenance record for the document (5.1) as described in Subsect. 4.1.

The provenance server then constructs a non-repudiation token (5.3.1). The token is made up of two parts, the *token header* and the *token payload*. The header contains a system-generated identifier for the token, an identifier for the patient who made the request, an identifier for the DSS service, a *signed timestamp* requested by the server from a trusted timestamping authority (5.2.1), an identifier for that timestamping authority, an identifier for the trusted notary that the evidence is to be later sent to for storage, and the digital certificates required to verify all signatures within the token. The payload consists of data representing the meta-provenance recorded for a provenance action within the recommendation generation process. In the case of a *registerTemplate* action, this data includes a hash of a normalised and ordered representation of the template used. Similarly, in the case of generation actions, the data includes a hash of an ordered representation of the substitution data used. The token contains all the information required to resolve potential disputes and addresses policy requirements 7, 9 and 10. The use of a trusted timestamping authority addresses policy requirement 4.

The token is then signed using a private key belonging to the server (5.3.2). This addresses policy requirement 1. The signed token is now stored as an instance of the non-repudiable evidence template shown in Fig. 5, within the appropriate meta-provenance record for the requested provenance action (5.4). The signed copy of the token will later be provided to a patient as the irrefutable evidence of the recommendation generation process. Since the provenance data used as evidence contains sensitive information about a patient's health and this information should thus not be provided directly to the notary, we store a signed hash of the signed token only. The server therefore now generates a hash of the signed token (5.5.1) and signs that hash with a second private key (5.5.2). This second signature is important for preventing the generation of false hashes. The signed hash is then sent to the trusted notary (5.6) where it is stored (6).

A copy of the signed token for the provenance action is now returned to the DSS (7). The service then returns the generated recommendation along with all signed tokens created during recommendation process to the client (8). The identifier of each signed token is generated by the DSS and is included in the token header, so that a patient can access the stored signed token from the meta-provenance record whenever they desire. This reflects the current movement in healthcare whereby patients are custodians of their own data [8] and addresses policy requirements 5 and 8.

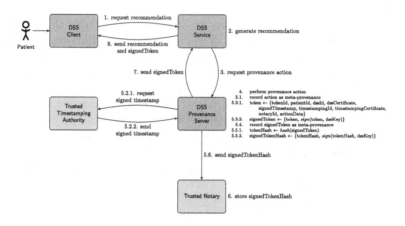

Fig. 6. The non-repudiable DSS recommendation process

5.2 Non-repudiable Evidence Verification Process

Once evidence is presented to a patient, according to our policy, its validity must then be checked. The patient or an authorised agent acting on their behalf, must verify both the integrity and authenticity of the evidence, which consists of the token and its signature. First, they must verify the content of the token. In particular, they need to ensure that the token payload contains the correct information relating to their medical condition, that the timestamps included in the token are valid, and that there is a link in the token payload to their identity; that is, that they are the correct recipient of the evidence. They must then retrieve the token identifier from the token and look up the corresponding record in the trusted notary. They need to check whether the digital signature of the stored hash was created by the DSS, that it is valid, and that the stored hash is the same for the token that was received from the DSS. Checking the validity of the signatures involves not only verifying the correct computation of the signatures, but also checking the revocation and expiration information of the keys, the size of the keys and the algorithms used to make sure that the signatures are secure. If these checks succeed, the patient has complete certainty that the provenance data is authentic and that there is a witness (the notary) confirming that fact. If any inconsistency is detected, or one of the digital signatures is invalid, this fact must be reported to the DSS and the patient must not follow the recommendation provided alongside the evidence.

6   Implementation

We have implemented a prototype version of the non-repudiation architecture described in Sect. 5. This involved the development of two new modules for the provenance server. The first, a meta-provenance module, carries out the construction of meta-provenance records as detailed in Subsect. 4.1. The second, a non-repudiation module, performs the necessary security and cryptographic operations upon each addition to a meta-provenance record, generates the necessary non-repudiable evidence, and appends it to the stored trace. The functionality of both modules is controlled by the web service during the handling of relevant incoming requests to the server. The use of both modules is optional, however, note that whilst meta-provenance may be generated without the addition of non-repudiable evidence, the opposite is not true. Hashing and signing operations are performed using reference implementations of algorithms compliant with the PKCS 11 API standard [7], addressing policy requirement 2. The prototype does not currently make use of a trusted timestamping authority, and instead generates timestamps locally. This will however be implemented in the near future, following the RFC 3161 standard [28]. The overall architecture of the server in the context of this paper is shown in Fig. 7. The remainder of the components are described briefly below.

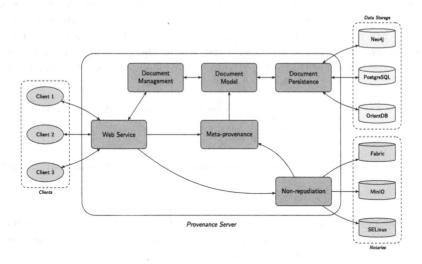

Fig. 7. The architecture of the provenance server

The document model is graph-based and supports both the OPM [20] and PROV [24] provenance specifications. The document persistence module defines an interface for storing documents, and provides a number of backends. The model was designed with graph databases in mind, and our core storage backend is Neo4j (https://neo4j.com), but we also support those that follow the

Tinkerpop (https://tinkerpop.apache.org) standard, and provide a baseline relational implementation. The construction of documents is controlled through the document management module, which is accessed as a web service.

As shown in Fig. 7, our prototype system provides three trusted notary implementations, each of which exhibits the required properties of data immutability and data auditability, and meets policy requirement 6. Our chosen implementations are a distributed ledger, with hashed blocks and a public ledger (*Hyperledger Fabric*, https://www.hyperledger.org/projects/fabric); a single store object service, with single-write functionality and object access (*MinIO*, https://min.io); and a file secured by an append-only access control policy (*SELinux*, http://www.selinuxproject.org). Our notaries are accessed as a web service, providing calls to add, and validate the presence of, data within each notary[2].

7   Evaluation

We hypothesise that each notary implementation is likely to affect the performance of the provenance server differently, depending on the domain within which the server is deployed. Therefore, by providing multiple implementations, our aim is to allow a user to select the notary that works best with the server within a given domain. In order to produce a set of heuristics for notary selection, we now examine the performance of the server when attached to each notary in three use cases with distinct characteristics for the construction of provenance information. These use cases exist within the CONSULT architecture, a DSS designed to support stroke patients in self-managing their treatments [4].

```
a(provenance(source(giveRecommendation), relationship(wasAssociatedWith), target(Patient))) :-
  a(aspt([goal(G), action(A), promotes(A,G)], action(A))), patient(Patient).
a(provenance(source(giveRecommendation), relationship(used), target(S))) :-
  suffers_from(Patient,S).
```

Fig. 8. Sample of rules used to capture provenance data in the recommendation service

At the core of the CONSULT system is an *argumentation*-based recommendation service, which takes facts about a patient and their preferences, and, using a computational form of clinical guidelines, determines a treatment path for them [15]. This first use case is characterised by a high computation time. In this instance, provenance data provides the aforementioned insight into the recommendations provided by this service. To extract this data, we augment the service's rule-base with an additional set of rules, which are satisfied when the system makes particular decisions, and thus output the required provenance data. We structure these rules in the style of [26], and an example is given in Fig. 8.

---

[2] https://github.com/kclhi/nr.

Table 1. Average response time of provenance server (seconds) using different notaries in different CONSULT use cases, and associated (maximum) *p*-values (other notaries; other use cases).

	Recommendation	Sensor	Chatbot
Ledger	7.04 (.05,.05; .05,.05)	6.25 (.05,.05; .05,.05)	3.02 (.05,.05; .05,.05)
Object	0.56 (.05,.05; .6,.4)	0.56 (.05,.05; .6,.6)	0.55 (.05,.05; .4,.6)
File	1.17 (.05,.05; .05,.05)	1.36 (.05,.05; .05,.05)	0.82 (.05,.05; .05,.05)

The facts used by the recommendation service are based upon sensor data (and a patient's EHR), which the CONSULT system gathers from wearable devices. This second use case is characterised by high volumes of data. Here, provenance data is useful for auditing purposes, for example to aggregate sensor data and identify erroneous readings, before subsequently tracking them back to the device from which they originate. To extract this data, we examine the sensor readings that arrives at a central service in the CONSULT system.

To interface with the CONSULT system, users engage with a chatbot. This chatbot is able to provide the patient with healthcare information, which includes the information provided by the recommendation service, although we do not consider this interaction as a part of this third use case. This aspect of the system is characterised by its non-determinism, as we cannot know, prior to the execution of the chatbot, which answers a user will provide. Much like the recommendation service, in this situation provenance data provides insight into the decisions made by the chatbot, and various parts of the CONSULT chatbot logic are augmented to extract this data.

The output from each of these use cases is used as the basis for constructing substitutions for a set of templates designed for the CONSULT DSS. These templates capture the key agents (e.g. a patient), entities (e.g. a sensor reading or a clinical guideline) and activities (e.g. the generation of a recommendation), in the DSS. In the case of the chatbot, each substitution is constructed and submitted incrementally as zones, as the interaction with the chatbot progresses.

7.1 Experiments and Results

We now examine the performance of the provenance server when attached to each notary, within each of these use cases. To do so, we further augment the CONSULT system in order to simulate patients interacting with each use case. The results of these simulations are shown in Table 1, which reflects the average response time, and related statistical tests, of each call to the server from CONSULT, over 1000 simulations ($N = 1000$). Note that these experiments were performed before the completion of the prototype but still offer a relative comparison of performance.

Examining first the performance of different notaries against one another, we note that the introduction of a ledger-based notary results in the most significant overhead in terms of response time, which is to be expected, given that speed is a common criticism of the technology. While this may make a ledger appear to be the least attractive option, it may still be a consideration when deploying the provenance server, as the use of a ledger brings additional benefits, such as decentralisation, which may outweigh the impact of an increased response time. Of the remaining two notaries, the use of single-write object store offers the best performance, over an append-only file, which is interesting given the low-level nature of the latter, and suggests that, when linked to our server, a notary technology optimised for the storage of client data is more efficient.

In terms of the performance of the same notary across different deployment domains, we note that, in addition to offering the best performance, the use of a single-write object store also guarantees consistent performance when operating in domains with differing provenance data collection properties. This may make the object store an attractive option in domains with uncertain properties. In contrast, while responding broadly consistently to the high throughput of data found in the sensor use case, and when working with the complexity of the rule-based recommendation service, both the ledger and file offer improved performance in the chatbot use case. While, in general, this is to be expected, given that a number of smaller submissions are made to the server during the incremental construction of resources, rather than a single larger submission, it is interesting to note that this style of resource construction has the most significant impact on the performance of these two notaries.

8   Conclusions and Future Work

We have identified the importance of the role of provenance data within a DSS, as evidence designed to be used in the resolution of potential disputes about the actions of the system. We have shown that a DSS – the evidence generator – has a motive to disrupt this evidence in order to protect its interests, and thus the authenticity and integrity of the evidence must be established. That is, provenance data used as evidence must exhibit non-repudiation of origin. In order to achieve this goal, we have defined a security policy for non-repudiable evidence in the context of a DSS, developed a fully general provenance-based model to represent such evidence, and then proposed an extended DSS architecture that meets the requirements of our policy.

Our solution allows us to present to the user a comprehensive survey of all provenance actions taken by the system on their behalf and to retrieve and validate the authenticity of that data at any point thereafter.

We have developed a prototype implementation of our architecture, by extending our provenance template service with the functionality described in our evidence model, and creating a web service interface for trusted notary applications. We evaluated the performance of the prototype using three contrasting provenance generation use cases arising within the CONSULT DSS.

Following further improvements to our prototype, we now intend to investigate how our model may be extended to work within a distributed environment, in which provenance data is being generated by multiple systems working in multiple domains.

References

1. Ahmed, I., Khan, A., Khan, M.S., Ahmed, M.: Aggregated signatures for chaining: a secure provenance scheme. In: 2016 IEEE Trustcom/BigDataSE/ISPA, pp. 2012–2017, August 2016
2. Anderson, R.J.: Liability and computer security: nine principles. In: Gollmann, D. (ed.) ESORICS 1994. LNCS, vol. 875, pp. 231–245. Springer, Heidelberg (1994). https://doi.org/10.1007/3-540-58618-0_67
3. Braun, U., Shinnar, A., Seltzer, M.: Securing provenance. In: Proceedings of the 3rd Conference on Hot Topics in Security, HOTSEC 2008, Berkeley, CA, USA, pp. 4:1–4:5. USENIX Association (2008)
4. Chapman, M., et al.: Computational Argumentation-based Clinical Decision Support. In: Proceedings of the 18th International Conference on Autonomous Agents and MultiAgent Systems, AAMAS 2019, pp. 2345–2347, Richland, SC. International Foundation for Autonomous Agents and Multiagent Systems (2019)
5. Curcin, V., Fairweather, E., Danger, R., Corrigan, D.: Templates as a method for implementing data provenance in decision support systems. J. Biomed. Inf. **65**, 1–21 (2017)
6. Fairweather, E., Alper, P., Porat, T., Curcin, V.: Architecture for template-driven provenance recording. In: Belhajjame, K., Gehani, A., Alper, P. (eds.) IPAW 2018. LNCS, vol. 11017, pp. 217–221. Springer, Cham (2018). https://doi.org/10.1007/978-3-319-98379-0_23
7. Gleeson, S., Zimman, C.: PKCS #11 cryptographic token interface base specification. Technical report, OASIS (2015)
8. Gordon, W.J., Catalini, C.: Blockchain technology for healthcare: facilitating the transition to patient-driven interoperability. Comput. Struct. Biotechnol. J. **16**, 224–230 (2018)
9. Hafner, M., Memon, M., Breu, R.: Seaas - a reference architecture for security services in SOA. J. Univ. Comput. Sci. **15**(15), 2916–2936 (2009)
10. Hasan, R., Sion, R., Winslett, M.: Introducing secure provenance: Problems and challenges. In: Proceedings of the 2007 ACM Workshop on Storage Security and Survivability, StorageSS 2007, New York, NY, USA, pp. 13–18. ACM (2007)
11. Hasselgren, A., Kralevska, K., Gligoroski, D., Pedersen, S.A., Faxvaag, A.: Blockchain in healthcare and health sciences - a scoping review. Int. J. Med. Inf. **134**, 104040 (2020)
12. ISO/TC JTC1, SC 27: ISO 13888–1:2009 Information technology - Security techniques - Non-repudiation Part 1 - General. Technical report, International Organisation for Standardization (2009)
13. Jamil, F., Khan, A., Anjum, A., Ahmed, M., Jabeen, F., Javaid, N.: Secure provenance using an authenticated data structure approach. Comput. Secur. **73**, 34–56 (2018)
14. Kleinaki, A.S., Mytis-Gkometh, P., Drosatos, G., Efraimidis, P.S., Kaldoudi, E.: A blockchain-based notarization service for biomedical knowledge retrieval. Comput. Struct. Biotechnol. J. **16**, 288–297 (2018)
15. Kokciyan, N., et al.: Towards an argumentation system for supporting patients in self-managing their chronic conditions. In: Joint Workshop on Health Intelligence (W3PHIAI) (2018)
16. Massi, M., Miladi, A., Margheri, A., Sassone, V., Rosenzweig, J.: Using PROV and Blockchain to Achieve Health Data Provenance. University of Southampton, Technical report (2018)

17. Menezes, A.J., Vanstone, S.A., Oorschot, P.C.V.: Handbook of Applied Cryptography, 1st edn. CRC Press Inc., Boca Raton (1996)
18. Miller, T.: Explanation in artificial intelligence: Insights from the social sciences (2019)
19. Moreau, L.: A canonical form for PROV documents and its application to equality, signature, and validation. ACM Trans. Internet Technol. **17**(4), 1–21 (2017)
20. Moreau, L., et al.: The open provenance model core specification (v1.1). Future Gener. Comput. Syst. **27**(6), 743–756 (2011)
21. Moreau, L., et al.: Prov-DM: The PROV data model. W3C (2013)
22. Moxey, A., Robertson, J., Newby, D., Hains, I., Williamson, M., Pearson, S.A.: Computerized clinical decision support for prescribing: provision does not guarantee uptake. J. Am. Med. Inf. Assoc. **17**(1), 25–33 (2010)
23. Pinto, F.: Digital time-stamping to support non repudiation in electronic communications. Proceedings of SECURICOM 1996-14th Worldwide Congress on Computer and Communications Security and Protection, pp. 397–406 (1990)
24. Provenance Working Group W3C: W3C-PROV (2011)
25. Roe, M.: Cryptography and evidence. Technical report UCAM-CL-TR-780, University of Cambridge, Computer Laboratory (2010)
26. Toniolo, A., Cerutti, F., Oren, N., Norman, T., Sycara, K.: Making Informed Decisions with Provenance and Argumentation Schemes. In: 11th International Workshop on Argumentation in Multi-Agent Systems, pp. 1–20 (2014)
27. Vigil, M., Buchmann, J., Cabarcas, D., Weinert, C., Wiesmaier, A.: Integrity, authenticity, non-repudiation, and proof of existence for long-term archiving: A survey. Comput. Secur. **50**, 16–32 (2015)
28. Zuccherato, R., Cain, P., Adams, D.C., Pinkas, D.: Internet X.509 Public Key Infrastructure Time-Stamp Protocol (TSP). Technical report, Internet Engineering Task Force (Aug 2001)

A Model and System for Querying Provenance from Data Cleaning Workflows

Nikolaus Nova Parulian$^{(\boxtimes)}$, Timothy M. McPhillips, and Bertram Ludäscher

School of Information Sciences, University of Illinois at Urbana-Champaign,
Champaign, USA
{nnp2,tmcphill,ludaesch}@illinois.edu

Abstract. Data cleaning is an essential component of data preparation in machine learning and other data science workflows, and is widely recognized as the most time-consuming and error-prone part when working with real-world data. How data was prepared and cleaned has a significant impact on the reliability and trustworthiness of results of any subsequent analysis. *Transparent data cleaning* not only requires that provenance (i.e., operation history and value changes) be captured, but also that those changes are easy to explore and evaluate: The data scientists who prepare the data, as well as others who want to reuse the cleaned data for their studies, need to be able to easily explore and query its data cleaning history. We have developed a domain-specific provenance model for data cleaning that supports the kind of provenance questions that data scientists need to answer when inspecting and debugging data preparation histories. The design of the model was driven by the need (i) to answer relevant, user-oriented provenance questions, and (ii) to do so in an effective and efficient manner. The model is a refinement of an earlier provenance model and has been implemented as a companion tool to OpenRefine, a popular, open source tool for data cleaning.

Keywords: Domain-specific provenance models · Data cleaning · Workflows · Provenance queries

1 Introduction

Data cleaning and data preparation are critically important, labor-intensive, and error-prone stages in data science pipelines and machine learning workflows. Far from being an incidental detail, how data was prepared and cleaned can make all the difference between analysis results and predictive models that are reliable, trustworthy, and explainable on one side, or unreliable, erroneous, and incomprehensible on the other.[1] The way data is treated during preparation often significantly affects subsequent machine learning steps and analysis results.

---

[1] The old adage of *"garbage in, garbage out"* comes to mind.

© Springer Nature Switzerland AG 2021
B. Glavic et al. (Eds.): IPAW 2020/IPAW 2021, LNCS 12839, pp. 183–197, 2021.
https://doi.org/10.1007/978-3-030-80960-7_11

For example, consider an employee table with null values in some of the address fields. Suppose we want to use address information to find correlations between residence areas of employees and their punctuality. During data preparation, many different actions can be taken when encountering incomplete data: e.g., one could *remove* rows with missing values; *leave* any null values as they are; *replace* them with a default value; or *infer* suitable values, just to name a few options. Clearly, one size doesn't fit all. Instead, the assumptions and analysis goals should inform which route to take to obtain a dataset of adequate quality.[2] In machine learning, making any data cleaning performed on training and input datasets completely *transparent* is critical to ensuring that the algorithm and predictions have the expected dependencies on the intended signals in the data.

Transparent data cleaning entails both: that all potentially relevant data changes are captured and that those changes are easy to evaluate and assess by those who are tasked with *inspecting* the curated dataset, or with *auditing* and *validating* the data cleaning process itself. Transparency has been achieved when a set of key questions about data preparation and cleaning can be answered practically and robustly. To this end, fine-grained provenance information has to be captured during data cleaning *and* made available in a form that allows users to formulate and execute the desired questions as custom provenance queries.

The main contributions of this paper are as follows: We have developed DCM (**D**ata **C**leaning **M**odel), a domain-specific provenance model for describing the history of data cleaning workflows in a way that is conducive to user-driven, goal-oriented queries. Conventional history models view the evolution of a dataset as a sequence of snapshots $D_0 \rightsquigarrow D_1 \rightsquigarrow \cdots \rightsquigarrow D_n$, transforming an initial, "dirty" dataset D_0 via a series of steps $S_1, \ldots, S_n$ into a "clean" version D_n. Our model can answer targeted user-queries about the processing history (*which operations were executed and on what data*), and about the value history (*what values were changed and how*), and do so at *multiple levels* of granularity (e.g., column-level, row-level, and cell-level), all while avoiding to materialize the intermediate snapshots affected. As a result, goal-oriented provenance queries are executed much more efficiently. Queries can be *high-level* (referring to workflow operations) and *fine-grained* (to inspect individual value changes). DCM can thus be seen as a hybrid provenance model, and like other such models it combines *prospective* elements (at the workflow level) with *retrospective* provenance. However, in contrast to existing models (e.g., see [3,10,13]), DCM also includes *domain-specific* elements for data cleaning. Generic, domain-independent provenance relations, such as those from W3C PROV [1], can then simply be obtained as views.

DCM has been prototypically implemented in an open-source tool ORPE (**OpenRefine P**rovenance **E**xplorer [17]), as a companion tool to OpenRefine [15]: Users of OpenRefine perform their interactive data cleaning workflows exactly as before. The *provenance harvester* of ORPE then extracts latent provenance information from internal OpenRefine *project files*, transforms it, and loads it into a relational database implementing DCM. Ad-hoc user queries and customizable, predefined provenance reports can be specified in the form of SQLite queries

---

[2] Roughly speaking, data is of good quality if it is *fit for purpose* [19].

and/or as Datalog queries. A set of system demonstrations that illustrate the use of ORPE is under development and scheduled for release in the near future.

2 Modeling Interactive Data Cleaning Workflows

Consider a researcher or data curator who is using a tool such as OpenRefine for interactive, exploratory data cleaning. The *history* H at any point in the data cleaning process can be described using a sequence of *steps* (or data cleaning *operations*) $S_1, \ldots, S_n$ executed thus far, and the resulting sequence of dataset snapshots D_i obtained that way, starting from the original state D_0, and ending in the current database state D_n:

$$D_0 \overset{S_1}{\rightsquigarrow} D_1 \overset{S_2}{\rightsquigarrow} D_2 \overset{S_3}{\rightsquigarrow} \ldots \overset{S_n}{\rightsquigarrow} D_n \ . \tag{1}$$

This view of the data cleaning history highlights both the snapshots D_i and the (intensional) operations S_i that led to them. A complementary view is to describe the database evolution using a sequence of *deltas* Δ_i that capture the (extensional) data differences between snapshots:

$$D_0 \overset{\Delta_1}{\rightsquigarrow} D_1 \overset{\Delta_2}{\rightsquigarrow} D_2 \overset{\Delta_3}{\rightsquigarrow} \ldots \overset{\Delta_n}{\rightsquigarrow} D_n. \tag{2}$$

During an interactive, exploratory data cleaning session it is not uncommon that a user pauses and considers *backtracking* to an earlier state, i.e., when a sequence of recent operations turns out to be ineffective. To this end, OpenRefine implements an *undo/redo* stack: The user can jump back and forth between different states D_i to consider the effect of the workflow up to any step S_i. This way of inspecting the data cleaning history is analogous to the classic Video Cassette Recorder (VCR)[3] model with functions for *rewind/review* (◄◄) and *fast-forward/cue* (►►). OpenRefine maintains *symmetric* deltas, i.e., which can be used both as forward and reverse deltas. In this way, rewinding the history (*undo*) from D_n to D_i, and further to D_j, can be achieved in reverse delta mode, and the same deltas can be used in forward mode (*redo*) as well to return to the current state D_n:

$$D_n \overset{\Delta_n}{\rightsquigarrow} D_{n-1} \overset{\Delta_{n-1}}{\rightsquigarrow} \ldots \overset{\Delta_{i+1}}{\rightsquigarrow} D_i \overset{\Delta_i}{\rightsquigarrow} \ldots \overset{\Delta_{j+1}}{\rightsquigarrow} D_j \tag{3}$$

While this VCR rewind model is clearly useful during interactive, exploratory data cleaning, it is not a practical model for inspecting, auditing, or validating workflow histories to ensure transparency (this shouldn't come as a surprise as OpenRefine was not specifically designed for such uses). For example, if a user wants to know which steps have affected a given column[4], or what values a given cell has assumed over time and what steps have caused which changes, a model that requires the user to "eyeball" these changes across a number of snapshots is not feasible. Using our data cleaning model DCM, however, such user-driven and goal-oriented queries can be easily specified and efficiently executed.

---

[3] en.wikipedia.org/wiki/Videocassette_recorder.

[4] In ML and statistics, columns and rows often represent *features* (or *variables*) and *observations*, respectively.

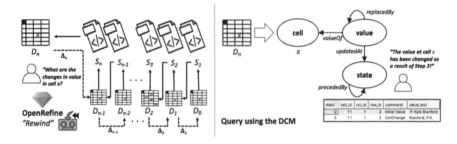

Fig. 1. OpenRefine "State Rewind" vs. Goal-Oriented Provenance Queries: OpenRefine's internal history model supports an undo/redo stack allowing the user to backtrack from the current state D_n to any earlier snapshot D_i (*left*). OpenRefine then recreates all intermediate states $D_{n-1}, D_{n-2}, \ldots, D_i$ through reverse deltas. If a user is looking for a particular change of cell x, she has to "eyeball" all of the intermediate states in the UI. In contrast, using our provenance model for data cleaning (*right*), the user asks a specific question about cell x and the system retrieves only the relevant part of the history, *without* recreating the intermediate states.

Figure 1 depicts an example where the user wants to understand how the value of cell "x" has changed during a data cleaning project. In the VCR rewind model, the user needs to focus on the row of interest, and within that row on a particular cell (corresponding to an attribute/column) of interest to find which operations and steps have affected the cell. To complicate matters further, a user must take into account any schema changes, e.g., addition, removal, or renaming of columns caused by schema-changing operations. In the worst-case scenario, our user has to go back all the way from the current step S_n to the initial step step S_1 to understand the complete history of a cell.

To address this problem, we have developed DCM, a domain-specific provenance model for data cleaning that keeps track of changes at all levels, i.e., at the workflow (operation) level, and at all data levels (snapshots, columns, rows, and cells). As can be seen from the illustration in Fig. 1, our model enables the user to answer provenance questions using direct, goal-oriented queries that employ the relevant entities from the model. Rather than "single-stepping" through the history as in the VCR model, in our DCM model a user is given "random" access by addressing operations, rows, columns, and cells of interest *directly*, without going first through intermediate snapshots.

2.1 DCM: A Data Cleaning Model for OpenRefine Provenance

Starting from an earlier data cleaning model proposed by McPhillips et al. [9], we customize and extend this model for use with OpenRefine [15]. One such extension, e.g., is the addition of *column dependencies* to capture provenance at the workflow level, i.e., which columns were input and output of a step S_i. Figure 2 depicts DCM as a conceptual model. An Array is (a part of) a dataset. Array can also be useful to capture multiple representations of tables on a single dataset. Array in this model is a way to capture multiple representations of tables

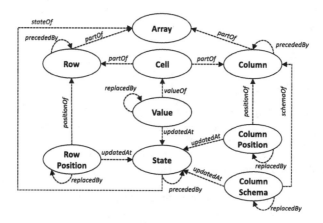

Fig. 2. Core conceptual model of DCM (**Data Cleaning Model**): It contains key entities (Row, Column, Cell, State, ...) and the necessary relations between them (*replacedBy*, *precededBy*, *updatedAt*, ...) to support user-driven, goal-oriented provenance queries. Generic provenance (e.g., W3C PROV relations) can be obtained through multiple *views* at different levels of granularity and abstraction (*workflow*, *table*, *column*, ...).

on a single dataset. For example, a transformation function that can change the table schema such as in **group by** operation. This operation aggregates the preceding input table and constructs a table with a new schema. Thus need to be recorded as a new Array in the DCM. A Cell is part of a Row and of a Column, which in turn are part of an Array. To keep track of changes, all values, cells, rows, and columns have unique identifiers. A Value can be updated at a State, and each State (with the exception of the initial state) is *precededBy* another State. Other elements of the model capture changes in Row Position, Column Position, and in Column Schema. Keeping track of the order of rows and columns is important, as user interactions may depend on what the UI shows to the user at any given moment during data cleaning.

The Row Position and Column Position record the logical order of rows and columns, respectively at a given state, and correspond to the "XY-coordinates" of rows, columns, and cells in the UI. The separation of Value, Column Schema, and Row Position allow us to keep track of them independently, and data transformations that affect the schema (rearranging columns, renaming columns) or the row order, will not affect the capability of querying value provenance. As can be seen from the relations in Fig. 2, several entities (State, Column, Value, etc.) have dependencies on themselves, which provides an efficient mechanism to represent reverse deltas of these entities at a given state. This representation resembles a linked list that links prior data whenever new data is introduced. As a result, in our model, instead of storing full data in the table, we only store the changes of the entities affected by the data transformation. Listing 1 depicts further details of DCM using a Datalog-like syntax.

By design, DCM supports multiple views for generating provenance and there is no single, fixed mapping to W3C PROV [1] (or, as an example for a hybrid

```
% An Array (i.e., a part of a dataset) has an ID:
Array(array_ID).
% A Row is partOf an Array:
Row(row_ID,array_id).
% A Column is partOf an Array:
Column(col_ID,array_id).
% A Cell is partOf a Row and partOf a Column:
Cell(cell_ID, row_id, col_id).
% A State (transition) is associated with an Array and a predecessor:
State(state_ID,array_id,prv_state_id).
% In a State (transition) there are input-output column dependencies:
In_Out_Columns(state_id,input_col_id,output_col_id).
% A Cell Value has content and a previous Value:
Value(value_ID,cell_id,state_id,content,prv_value_id).
% Row Positions can change:
Row_Pos(row_pos_ID,row_id,state_id,prv_row_id,prv_row_pos_id).
% Column Positions and Schema can change:
Col_Pos_Sch(sch_ID,col_id,state_id,col_type,col_name,prv_col_id,prv_sch_id).
```

Listing 1: Logical schema of the data cleaning provenance model DCM (cf. Fig. 2): The suffix "_ID" ("_id") indicates a *primary* (*foreign*) key, respectively. The prefix "prv" denotes a link to a previous entity of the same type (e.g., state).

provenance model: ProvONE [3]). Instead, different views give rise to different mappings into the target provenance model. For example, in the *workflow view* (1), a data cleaning process is seen as a sequence of steps $S_1, \ldots, S_n$ that induce a sequence of database snapshots $D_0, \ldots, D_n$. In the complementary *delta views* (2) and (3), the same data cleaning process is described via deltas, i.e., where each extensional change Δ_i describes the updates between states as a result of applying the (intensional) operation S_i. Many other views can be derived from our model, e.g., *column views* describe the change history from the perspective of one or more *columns* (which in turn can involve *operations* at the workflow level or *deltas* at the value level). A *cell view*, on the other hand, allows a user to inspect "the life of a cell", e.g., in terms of value changes, position changes, or operations that have affected the cell values.

2.2 The **ORPE** Provenance Harvester for OpenRefine

OpenRefine captures multiple operations from the UI and records the changes of values in internal log files in order to implement the undo/redo features. Different UI operations may have their own data structure to implement the necessary (symmetric) deltas. Figure 4 depicts the many-to-one mapping from UI operations to internal log entries, and to concepts currently implemented in our DCM model. For example, a MassCellChange entry is created for different UI operations such as *clustering, to-uppercase, to-lowercase, to-number*, etc. Since this information is only partially preserved as a JSON-formatted text recipe

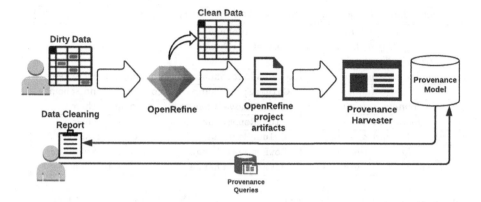

Fig. 3. ORPE Provenance Harvester: A user cleans a dataset using OpenRefine as usual. The harvester then automatically extracts, transforms, and loads internal provenance data ("buried" in internal project files) into our domain-specific data cleaning provenance model (DCM). Using our system the user can then automatically generate data cleaning reports for auditing purposes, and she can inspect or debug details of data cleaning operations, cell changes, etc. by performing ad-hoc queries.

in the log files, we record additional recipe information, including execution timestamps, as a JSON blob in a state_detail table.

The current provenance harvester does not extract information about some of OpenRefine's more specialized interactive features, e.g., *row flagging* (RowFlag-Change), *row starring* (RowStarChange), *transpose* (MassRowColumnChange), *reconciliation* (ReconChange, MassReconChange), etc.

Another limitation is due to OpenRefine not capturing certain provenance information in its project files. Among the potentially useful elements currently missing are various *parameters* of operations. For clustering operations, e.g., OpenRefine does not capture clustering parameters such as *cluster type* or *number of neighbors* (for k-nearest neighbors clustering). OpenRefine also does not record the user-IDs of individuals who have worked on a project, and so we assume that a single user has performed all data transformations in our prototype. Last not least, there is currently no mechanism for a user to adorn a workflow with user-annotations, e.g., to describe the intent or goal of a workflow step. Figure 3 depicts the use of the ORPE provenance harvester as a companion tool to OpenRefine: The harvester is used to extract, transform, and load information from internal project files into a database that implements DCM. The user can then run powerful ad-hoc queries or predefined (and customizable) provenance reports for any previously executed data cleaning workflow.

2.3   The ORPE Provenance Querying and Reporting Module

After the OpenRefine provenance harvester has loaded the data into the DCM schema, the user can ask meaningful, targeted queries about a data cleaning

OpenRefine UI Operation	Internal Log-File Entry	Provenance Model (DCM)
Single cell edit	`CellChange`	value
Clustering, Upper/Lower case Change datatype, ...	`MassCellChange`	value
Add new column	`ColumnAdditionChange`	column, column_schema
Split column	`ColumnSplitChange`	column, column_schema
Remove column	`ColumnRemovalChange`	column_schema
Rename column	`ColumnRenameChange`	column_schema
Move column operation	`ColumnMoveChange`	column_position
Remove row	`RowRemovalChange`	row, row_position
Permanent row ordering	`RowReorderChange`	row_position

Fig. 4. Mapping between OpenRefine operations in the UI, corresponding identifiers in internal logs (**changes** file), and elements of DCM: the subset of operations in the **changes** file that can be mapped to the respective provenance entities on our proposed provenance model. This mapping can also help a user to scope and filter related entities for answering the provenance of a particular transformation from the UI.

workflow history, e.g., *how many values have changed for each data transformation*; *which columns have been renamed*; *which rows have been removed*, etc.

The ORPE prototype supports queries expressed in Datalog (implemented via an answer set reasoner [2,5]) and in SQL (implemented using SQLite [6,20]). The structure of the underlying DCM schema is conducive to expressing very powerful and complex provenance queries natively, i.e., using only pure Datalog (or basic SQL), without resorting to "detours" through a programming language or by applying external methods through Embedded SQL.

In addition to the native query module, we have also developed a library that integrates SQLite queries with the Python APIs for a user who wants to query the DCM programmatically. Using the library in an interactive Jupyter notebook environment yields a user-friendly, interactive Provenance Explorer tool. The library also includes a feature that can reconstruct dataset snapshots as pandas data frames [16], and that can be used to implement a snapshot "time machine", or to produce custom data cleaning provenance reports. We are making the data, tools, rules, queries, and scripts developed for this research available in a Github repository [17], in order to make our methods and research transparent and more easily accessible and reproducible for the provenance research community.

3   Example Provenance Queries

We have prepared two OpenRefine datasets to illustrate a number of basic data cleaning provenance queries. Additional queries for provenance analysis are being added over time. The first dataset is a small, controlled sample proposed by McPhillips et al. [9]. The dataset uses the columns Book Title, Date, and Author. We have applied a few basic data cleaning transformation scenarios for this demo-dataset as shown in Fig. 5.

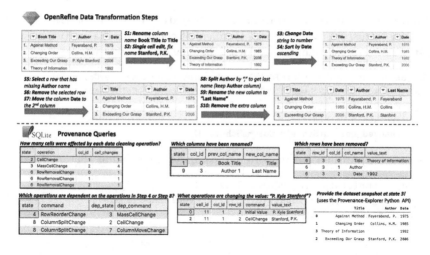

Fig. 5. Data cleaning steps and related query results over DCM: A sequence of data transformations and associated snapshots for a small example are shown (*top*). Below, the results of SQLite queries against the DCM instance are shown, illustrating that questions about cells, columns, rows, etc. can be answered easily and efficiently.

In the following we list and elaborate on a number of queries for the example workflow depicted in Fig. 5. Additional SQL query outputs are available in the appendix. We have also applied our tool to a real-world dataset ("*What's on the menu?*" [12]) with 17,000 rows and 20 columns, obtained from the New York Public Library. This dataset was also subjected to a more complex data cleaning workflow and we have made the results available in an online repository [17].

The following queries are (predominantly) expressed in Datalog, but the repository also includes the SQL versions.

Across all operations, how many cells were affected in each column?
We start with a simple SQL query that joins key relations from DCM and applies an aggregation to count the number of cell changes per state and column:

```
select StateId,ColumnId, count(1) as Cell_count
from States natural join Value natural join Cell
group by StateId,ColumnId order by StateId desc;
```

At the heart of this query (i.e., if we ignore the aggregation) is a simple conjunctive query, whose query pattern is nicely exhibited when we use the logic-based Datalog syntax:

```
changed_values(StateId,ColumnId,ValueId):-
    state(StateId,_,_),
    value(ValueId,CellId,StateId,_,_),
    cell(CellId,_,_ColumnId).
```

What are the names of columns in each state? We can reconstruct column names for each state by excluding identifiers of column_schema entities from the latest state to the state of interest with the prev_column_schema_id:

```
column_at_state(StateId,ColumnId,ColumnSchemaId,ColumnName,PrevColumnId) :-
    col_pos_sch(ColumnSchemaId,ColumnId,AssignStateId,_,ColumnName,
        PrevColumnId,_).
    AssignStateId =< StateId,
    not changed_column(StateId,ColumnSchemaId).
```

This query requires an auxiliary rule to compute the columns that changed:

```
changed_column(StateId,PrevColumnSchemaId):-
    col_pos_sch(_,_,NextStateId,_,_,_,PrevColumnSchemaId),
    NextStateId =< StateId.
```

Which rows have been removed in which state? We encode a newly created row using a previous row position of "−1" (i.e., a special null value). The initial row is flagged with state_id. When combined we can identify deleted rows:

```
value_removed(StateIdRowRemoved,StateId,CellId,ValueId,Value):-
    cell(CellId,RowId,_),
    value(ValueId,CellId,StateId,Value,_),
    row_removed(StateIdRowRemoved,RowId).
```

We use an auxiliary rule to compute the IDs of rows that have been removed:

```
row_removed(StateId,RowId):-
    % newly defined row
    row_pos(_,RowId,StateId,_,-1),
    % which is not the row in the latest state
    not row_pos(_,RowId,-1,_,_).
```

What is the history of a cell? This query reconstructs cell values at each state using a "frame rule" that propagates values if they have *not* changed.[5]

```
 value_at_state(StateId,ValueId,CellId,Value):-
    value(ValueId,CellId,AssignStateId,Value,_).
    AssignStateId =< StateId,
    not changed_value(StateId,ValueId).
```

We use an auxiliary rule to identify values that *have* changed:

```
changed_value(StateId,PrevValueId):-
    value(_,_,NextStateId,_,PrevValueId),
    NextStateId =< StateId.
```

---

[5] This query can also be reused to reconstruct dataset snapshots if needed.

Show the names of columns and their order for each state: In addition to supporting queries at the cell/value level, our model can also provide information about the history of the schema: To provide a column's current position name, we can reuse the column_at_state rule. However, because we store the data using a graph-based model in which order is not explicitly defined, we use the directed edges between PrevColumnId and ColumnId to infer the order. Thus, additional rules are needed to chain previous columns to the current column. The following Datalog rule constructs the column order at a state represented by the Level attribute in the column_order rule:

```
column_order(StateId,ColumnId,ColumnName,0,-1):-
    column_at_state(StateId,ColumnId,_,ColumnName,-1).
column_order(StateId,ColumnId,ColumnName,Level+1,PrevColumnId):-
    column_order(StateId,PrevColumnId,_,Level,_),
    column_at_state(StateId,ColumnId,_,ColumnName,PrevColumnId).
```

Which operations are dependent (or independent) on what operations? This is a key workflow-level provenance question that allows users to understand how *operations* depend on each other across states. Since OpenRefine operations primarily function at the column level, the dependency of a state in our model is determined by the *input* columns used, and the *output* columns produced by an operation. If an operation requires input from a column that a prior another operation has modified, then the two operations are dependent. A recursive query computes the desired lineage information:

```
state_lineage(StateId,AncestorStateId) :-
    state_parent(StateId,AncestorStateId).
state_lineage(StateId,CommonAncestor) :-
    state_parent(StateId,AncestorStateId),
    state_lineage(AncestorStateId,CommonAncestor).
```

The base case uses the in_out_columns signature of operations:

```
state_parent(StateId,ParentStateId):-
    in_out_columns(StateId,ChildColumn,CurrentColumn),
    in_out_columns(ParentStateId,CurrentColumn,ParentColumn).
```

4   Relation to Other Provenance Models and Prior Work

DCM is a domain-specific provenance model for describing histories of data cleaning workflows. As a custom provenance model it contains different levels of abstraction: workflow-level information corresponds to *prospective* provenance, while individual cell changes can be understood as *retrospective* provenance. Even more importantly, changes happen simultaneously at different levels of granularity, ranging from the most fine-grained level of value changes of individual *cells*, via changes at the *row*- and *column*-level, all the way to transaction-level changes of dataset *snapshots*. At the core of the W3C PROV model [1] are the provenance relations *wasDerivedFrom*, *used*, and *wasGeneratedBy*. Using this standard vocabulary, we can describe a state transition $D \xrightarrow{S} D'$ at the snapshot level in the obvious way, e.g., $D \xleftarrow{wdf} D'$, where *wdf* stands for *wasDerivedFrom*. Similar PROV statements can be made for *used* and *wasGeneratedBy* relations to describe the input and output dependencies of a step S relative to D and D', respectively. It should be clear, however, that there is no obvious single mapping from DCM to PROV: depending on the user-perspective and level of abstraction desired to describe the changes in a data cleaning workflow, several mappings are possible, corresponding to the different "accounts" of the processing history, according to the preferred perspectives and levels of granularity. One attempt to combine these different perspectives would be to specialize the W3C PROV vocabulary and introduce different "flavors" of dependency relations and different subclasses of entities in the PROV model to create a rich, multi-perspective extension of PROV.

It is well-known that the practical expressive power of a generic, domain-independent provenance model such as W3C PROV can be significantly increased by extending it with domain-specific concepts. For example by adding prospective provenance that describes workflow-level information, the resulting hybrid provenance models support queries that could not be answered using retrospective provenance alone [3,4,18]. As shown in this paper, DCM extends hybrid provenance models further by adding other domain-specific elements necessary to describe data cleaning workflows, e.g., row-, column-, and cell-changes.

Other Data Cleaning Provenance Models

In prior work, McPhillips et al. [9] proposed a data cleaning model for OpenRefine histories by representing columns, rows, cells, and values for each transformation step using logic facts. This model allows users to ask meaningful retrospective provenance questions about the data and schema changes of a data cleaning workflow, or to reproduce the data snapshots associated with each transformation step. Another prior work [8] shows how retrospective provenance can be reconstructed via prospective provenance, combined with the harvesting of existing information. This approach is somewhat similar to how we harvest available OpenRefine information from internal project files. The present work extends the earlier approaches by adding prospective provenance information from the OpenRefine operation history, including the column and data dependencies at each state to represent the overall data transformation workflow. This additional information can be used to exhibit parallel workflow structures and to explain the history of a cell by providing detailed accounts of cell value changes. Another benefit of our current approach is that it has been implemented as a companion tool to OpenRefine which can automatically extract, transform and load OpenRefine project artifacts into the DCM. Although we use OpenRefine as our main example, our model can also be applied, *mutatis mutandis*, to other data cleaning tools.

The work by Gibbins et al. [14] captures provenance from the OpenRefine UI and uses this information to populate an OPM model [11]. This early work has shown that dataset states and activities performed in OpenRefine can be queried once they are represented in an OPM schema. In contrast to their work, we have focused on automatically harvesting the information-rich existing OpenRefine project files and load them into our custom provenance model DCM. Our tool is an independent companion tool to OpenRefine and, unlike [14] does not depend on, or interact with, the OpenRefine UI.

In [7] Lan et al. proposed a tool that can visualize OpenRefine operation histories as workflows that show snapshot-level dependencies. Their work focuses on workflow-level, prospective provenance, while we focus on multi-level retrospective provenance, enriched with workflow-level information to obtain a complete data cleaning history, suitable for detailed provenance analysis.

5   Conclusions and Future Work

We have developed DCM, a data cleaning model for describing the processing history and changes occurring in data cleaning workflows at multiple levels of detail and abstraction. DCM has been implemented as part of the ORPE toolkit and includes (1) a provenance harvester that can automatically extract, transform, and load information from internal OpenRefine project files, and (2) a provenance query module for specifying powerful ad-hoc queries (in Datalog or SQL) and customizable provenance reports. The schema of DCM makes it easy for users to express complex, hybrid provenance queries suitable for inspecting, auditing, and validating histories from data cleaning workflows.

There are several improvements that we plan to consider in future work. For example, we would like to leverage our data cleaning model for other data cleaning tools, e.g., specialized data preparation and cleaning workflows implemented in (subsets of) Python and R. We are also considering to develop an API with a graphical user interface that allows users to debug their data cleaning workflows interactively. Finally, the rich structure of DCM seems to allow many, yet unexplored provenance queries and even more sophisticated provenance analytics. For example, a system may recommend data cleaning steps based on a repository of data cleaning workflows, or could highlight ineffective operations from the current provenance data.

Appendix A   Sample Provenance Query Output

The following is a log of outputs for a set of SQLite demo-queries:

```
What is the name of the archive dataset ?
   source_url = ipaw_2021_demo.tar.gz
source_format = OpenRefine Project File


How many data transformation steps are there in the dataset?
source_url = ipaw_2021_demo.tar.gz
 num_steps = 10


How many cells affected for each transformation step with detail recipe for each operation?
state      operation   col_id     cell_changes  detail
---------- ----------  ---------- ------------  -------------------------------------
2          CellChange  1          1             {"id": 1616260511775, "description": "Edit s..."
3          MassCellCh  2          4             {"id": 1616260337198, "description": "Text t..."
6          RowRemoval  0          1             {"id": 1616261155430, "description": "Remove..."
6          RowRemoval  1          1             {"id": 1616261155430, "description": "Remove..."
6          RowRemoval  2          1             {"id": 1616261155430, "description": "Remove..."


Show the column schema changes from the step 7 to the step 8 (split column)!
state      col_name
---------- ----------
7          Title
7          Date
7          Author
8          Title
8          Date
8          Author
8          Author 1
8          Author 2


Which columns are being renamed?
        state = 1
       col_id = 0
prev_col_name = Book Title
 new_col_name = Title

        state = 9
       col_id = 3
prev_col_name = Author 1
 new_col_name = Last Name


Which rows are being removed?
state      row_id     col_id     col_name    value_text
---------- ---------- ---------- ----------  ----------------------
6          3          0          Title       Theory of Information
6          3          1          Author
6          3          2          Date        1992


Show dependency of step 4 or step 8!
state      command            dep_state   dep_command
---------- ----------------   ----------  ----------------
4          RowReorderChange   3           MassCellChange
8          ColumnSplitChang   2           CellChange
8          ColumnSplitChang   7           ColumnMoveChan
```

References

1. Belhajjame, K., et al.: PROV-DM: the PROV data model. www.w3.org/TR/prov-dm (2012)
2. Clingo: A grounder and solver for logic programs. https://github.com/potassco/clingo
3. Cuevas-Vicenttín, V., et al.: ProvONE: a PROV extension data model for scientific workflow provenance (2016). http://jenkins-1.dataone.org/jenkins/view/DocumentationProjects/job/ProvONE-Documentation-trunk/ws/provenance/ProvONE/v1/provone.html
4. Dey, S.C., Köhler, S., Bowers, S., Ludäscher, B.: Datalog as a Lingua Franca for Provenance Querying and Reasoning. In: Workshop on Theory and Practice of Provenance (TaPP) (2012)
5. Gebser, M., Kaminski, R., Kaufmann, B., Schaub, T.: Multi-shot ASP solving with clingo. CoRR arXiv:1705.09811 (2017)
6. Hipp, R.: SQLite (2021). www.sqlite.org
7. Li, L., Parulian, N., Ludäscher, B.: or2yw: generating YesWorkflow models from OpenRefine histories (2021). https://github.com/idaks/OR2YWTool
8. McPhillips, T., Bowers, S., Belhajjame, K., Ludäscher, B.: Retrospective provenance without a runtime provenance recorder. In: Theory and Practice of Provenance (TaPP) (2015). https://doi.org/10.5555/2814579.2814580
9. McPhillips, T., Li, L., Parulian, N., Ludäscher, B.: Modeling provenance and understanding reproducibility for OpenRefine data cleaning workflows. In: Workshop on Theory and Practice of Provenance (TaPP) (2019)
10. Missier, P., Dey, S., Belhajjame, K., Cuevas-Vicenttín, V., Ludäscher, B.: D-PROV: extending the PROV provenance model with workflow structure. In: Workshop on the Theory and Practice of Provenance (TaPP) (2013)
11. Moreau, L., et al.: The open provenance model core specification. Future Gener. Comput. Syst. **27**(6), 743–756 (2011)
12. New York Public Library: What's on the menu? (2020). http://menus.nypl.org
13. Olveira, W., Missier, P., de Olveira, D., Braganholo, V.: Comparing provenance data models for scientific workflows: an analysis of PROV-Wf and ProvONE. In: Anais do Brazilian e-Science Workshop (BreSci), pp. 9–16, January 2020
14. Omitola, T., Freitas, A., Curry, E., O'Riain, S., Gibbins, N., Shadbolt, N.: Capturing interactive data transformation operations using provenance workflows. In: Simperl, E., et al. (eds.) ESWC 2012. LNCS, vol. 7540, pp. 29–42. Springer, Heidelberg (2015). https://doi.org/10.1007/978-3-662-46641-4_3
15. OpenRefine: A free, open source, power tool for working with messy data (2021). https://github.com/OpenRefine
16. Pandas: powerful Python data analysis toolkit (2019). https://github.com/pandas-dev/pandas
17. Parulian, N.: OpenRefine Provenance Explorer (ORPE) Data Cleaning Model (DCM) (2021). https://github.com/idaks/IPAW2021-ORPE
18. Pimentel, J.F., et al.: Yin & Yang: demonstrating complementary provenance from noWorkflow & YesWorkflow. In: IPAW. LNCS, vol. 9672. Springer, Cham (2016). https://doi.org/10.1007/978-3-319-40593-3_13
19. Sadiq, S.: Handbook of Data Quality. Springer, Heidelberg (2013). https://doi.org/10.1007/978-3-642-36257-6
20. Winslett, M., Braganholo, V.: Richard Hipp speaks out on SQLite. ACM SIGMOD Record **48**(2), 39–46 (2019)

Joint IPAW/TaPP Poster and Demonstration Session

ReproduceMeGit: A Visualization Tool for Analyzing Reproducibility of Jupyter Notebooks

Sheeba Samuel[1,2(✉)] and Birgitta König-Ries[1,2]

[1] Heinz-Nixdorf Chair for Distributed Information Systems,
Friedrich Schiller University Jena, Jena, Germany
[2] Michael Stifel Center, Jena, Germany
{sheeba.samuel,birgitta.koenig-ries}@uni-jena.de

Abstract. Computational notebooks have gained widespread adoption among researchers from academia and industry as they support reproducible science. These notebooks allow users to combine code, text, and visualizations for easy sharing of experiments and results. They are widely shared in GitHub, which currently has more than 100 million repositories, making it the world's largest host of source code. Recent reproducibility studies have indicated that there exist good and bad practices in writing these notebooks, which can affect their overall reproducibility. We present *ReproduceMeGit*, a visualization tool for analyzing the reproducibility of Jupyter Notebooks. This will help repository users and owners to reproduce and directly analyze and assess the reproducibility of any GitHub repository containing Jupyter Notebooks. The tool provides information on the number of notebooks that were successfully reproducible, those that resulted in exceptions, those with different results from the original notebooks, etc. Each notebook in the repository, along with the provenance information of its execution, can also be exported in RDF with the integration of the ProvBook tool.

Keywords: Jupyter notebooks · Reproducibility · GitHub · Visualization · Provenance · RDF

1 Introduction

Several large studies have emerged to analyze different aspects of Jupyter Notebooks, particularly from GitHub [1–3]. Rule et al. [1] analyzed over 1 million publicly available notebooks from GitHub. The focus of their study was on the exploration of the usage and structure of Jupyter notebooks, especially analyzing the use of code, text, and comments inside the notebooks. Another recent study by Pimental et al. [2] analyzed 1.4 million Jupyter notebooks from the GitHub repositories created between January 1st, 2013 and April 16th, 2018. They presented a detailed analysis of the quality and reproducibility of these

© Springer Nature Switzerland AG 2021
B. Glavic et al. (Eds.): IPAW 2020/IPAW 2021, LNCS 12839, pp. 201–206, 2021.
https://doi.org/10.1007/978-3-030-80960-7_12

notebooks. Their focus was not only on the structure of notebooks but also on their execution and replication. Inspired by these works, we present ReproduceMeGit. With this online tool, users can examine any GitHub repository and obtain an extensive analysis of different aspects of notebooks, including their structure and reproducibility features. This tool provides a dashboard that shows the statistics of the notebooks in a selected repository. It will execute the notebooks and provide provenance information from the run, including modules used and errors that occur during runs. This tool also provides direct access to Binder [4] and ProvBook [5]. Binder is an open-source web service provided by Project Jupyter to create shareable reproducible environments for Jupyter Notebooks in the cloud. It captures the code repository with its technical environment by creating containers and generates user sessions to run the notebooks in those containers. ProvBook, an extension of Jupyter Notebooks, captures and visualizes the provenance of the execution of the notebooks. By using ProvBook in ReproduceMeGit, users can download the notebooks' execution provenance information in RDF.

2   ReproduceMeGit: An Overview

We present ReproduceMeGit, a visualization tool for analyzing different aspects of Jupyter Notebooks, including their structure and reproducibility. The goal of this tool is to provide an overview of the reproducibility of notebooks in a selected repository by providing information on the number of notebooks that were successfully reproducible, errors that occurred during runs, the difference in the results from the original notebooks, provenance history of runs, etc. This would help repository users and owners to better understand the different aspects that impact the reproducibility of Jupyter Notebooks. With the help of metrics and the provenance information collected from ReproduceMeGit, users would be able to adopt good practices in writing Jupyter notebooks in the context of reproducibility [6].

ReproduceMeGit is built on top of the work from [2]. ReproduceMeGit provides a user interface where users can provide a repository URL and reproduce Jupyter Notebooks using a *Reproduce* button. The tool fetches the repository's content using the GitHub API, processes the repository, and scans it for Jupyter Notebooks. It then loads the notebooks and extracts information on their structure, cells, modules, etc. In the next step, to execute these notebooks, the requirements for the environment setup are collected. The dependencies for the execution of these notebooks are commonly defined in the repositories using files like *requirements.txt*, *setup.py* or *pipfile*. All the dependencies are installed using the setup environment files collected from the repository. Conda, an open-source package manager, and environment management system environment, is used to install and manage the dependencies of Python packages. If the repository does not provide any setup information, the tool installs all Anaconda[1] dependencies. Anaconda comes with more than 250 packages automatically installed, and

---

[1] https://www.anaconda.com.

additional open-source packages can be installed from PyPI, Conda package, or virtual environment manager. After setting up the environment, the notebooks are executed using the Python version of the original notebook. Supported by ProvBook, ReproduceMeGit stores the provenance information of the execution. This information includes the start and end time of the cell execution, total execution time, and the source and result of each cell execution. The provenance difference module in ProvBook helps users to compare their previous results with the current ones. In [2], direct string matching is used to calculate the difference between the execution of the original notebook from the repository and their execution. In contrast, we use the nbdime [7] tool provided by Project Jupyter to calculate the difference between the two executions. This is because nbdime provides diffing of notebooks based on the content, especially for image-diffs.

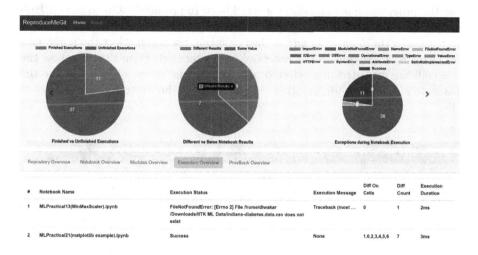

Fig. 1. Visualizations of the analysis of reproducibility of Jupyter notebooks in ReproduceMeGit

Figure 1 depicts the GUI of the ReproduceMeGit tool. The tool shows the highlights of the reproducibility study in the top panel and the respective detailed analysis in the bottom panel. It displays the respective count of notebooks (un-)successfully finishing the executions. Out of the successfully executed notebooks, it provides information on the number of notebooks that had the same or different results compared to the original. For notebooks that failed to execute, the tool shows the exceptions that occurred in their executions. These exceptions include *ImportError, ModuleNotFoundError, FileNotFoundError, IOError, SyntaxError,* etc. It also displays the information of the notebooks, which provide output and execution count in their code cells. The execution count is the cell identifier that denotes the count of the execution of the cell [8]. It also provides more analysis on the structure of the notebooks. It shows the number of valid notebooks based on their nbformat, kernel specification, and language version. The distribution of the most common programming languages and their version used in these notebooks are also shown in the tool.

The second panel provides detailed information on the repository, notebooks, cells, modules, and executions. It displays the list of Python modules used in each notebook to help users see which modules are commonly used in a repository. In the *Execution Overview* tab, it provides information on which cell in the notebook resulted in the difference in outputs. In case of failure in the execution of a notebook, it shows the detailed message on the reason for the occurring exception. ReproduceMeGit provides an export feature supported by ProvBook to capture the prospective and retrospective provenance in RDF described by the REPRODUCE-ME ontology [9]. The notebook data in RDF can be used in combination with the experiments that used them and help to get a track of the complete path of the scientific experiments. In our future work, we plan to post the provenance information collected from ReproduceMeGit to the GitHub repository to allow users to compare provenance between the original run and later runs. In the *User Interaction Overview* tab, users can select the notebooks and check how the cells in the notebooks are executed. Figure 2 shows how the code cells are executed in a selected notebook in the repository. Users have the option to select the code or other cells and check the execution order of code cells.

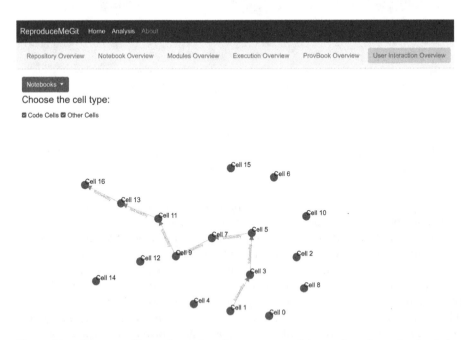

Fig. 2. Visualization of how the code cells are executed in a selected notebook of the repository

3 Demonstration

In our demonstration, users will be able to provide the URL of any GitHub repository containing Jupyter Notebooks and reproduce them. They will be able to explore the results of ReproduceMeGit, including the overview of

- the GitHub repository and the Jupyter Notebooks available in it
- the reproducibility study
- the notebooks which had the same or different results
- the provenance of the execution of each notebook
- the modules used by each notebook
- the feature to export each notebook along with its provenance in RDF
- the provenance history and provenance difference using ProvBook
- the execution order of cells in each notebook in a repository

The source code and a demo video [10] of ReproduceMeGit with an example are available online[2].

Acknowledgments. The authors thank the Carl Zeiss Foundation for the financial support of the project "A Virtual Werkstatt for Digitization in the Sciences (K3)" within the scope of the program-line "Breakthroughs: Exploring Intelligent Systems" for "Digitization – explore the basics, use applications".

References

1. Rule, A., et al.: Exploration and explanation in computational notebooks. In: Proceedings of the 2018 CHI, pp. 32:1–32:12. ACM (2018)
2. Pimentel, J.F., et al.: A large-scale study about quality and reproducibility of Jupyter notebooks. In: Proceedings of the 16th International Conference on MSR, pp. 507–517 (2019)
3. Rehman, M.S.: Towards understanding data analysis workflows using a large notebook corpus. In: Proceedings of the 2019 International Conference on Management of Data, SIGMOD 2019, pp. 1841–1843. Association for Computing Machinery, New York (2019)
4. Jupyter, P., Bussonnier, M., et al.: Binder 2.0 - reproducible, interactive, sharable environments for science at scale. In: Proceedings of the 17th Python in Science Conference, pp. 113–120 (2018)
5. Samuel, S., König-Ries, B.: ProvBook: provenance-based semantic enrichment of interactive notebooks for reproducibility. In: Proceedings of the ISWC 2018 Posters & Demonstrations, Industry and Blue Sky Ideas Tracks (2018)
6. Sandve, G.K., Nekrutenko, A., Taylor, J., Hovig, E.: Ten simple rules for reproducible computational research. PLOS Comput. Biol. **9**(10), 1–4 (2013)
7. Project Jupyter: nbdime: Jupyter notebook diff and merge tools (2021). https://github.com/jupyter/nbdime. Accessed 18 May 2021
8. Samuel, S.: A provenance-based semantic approach to support understandability, reproducibility, and reuse of scientific experiments. Ph.D. thesis, Friedrich-Schiller-Universität Jena (2019)

---

[2] https://github.com/fusion-jena/ReproduceMeGit.

9. Samuel, S., König-Ries, B.: Combining P-plan and the REPRODUCE-ME ontology to achieve semantic enrichment of scientific experiments using interactive notebooks. In: Gangemi, A., et al. (eds.) ESWC 2018. LNCS, vol. 11155, pp. 126–130. Springer, Cham (2018). https://doi.org/10.1007/978-3-319-98192-5_24

10. Samuel, S., König-Ries, B.: ReproduceMeGit: a visualization tool for analyzing reproducibility of jupyter notebooks (2020). https://doi.org/10.6084/m9.figshare.12084393.v1,

Mapping Trusted Paths to VGI

Bernard Roper[1]([✉]), Adriane Chapman[1], David Martin[1], and Stefano Cavazzi[2]

[1] Southampton University, University Road, Southampton SO17 1BJ, UK
b.a.roper@soton.ac.uk

[2] The Ordnance Survey, Explorer House, Adanac Drive, Nursling, Southampton SO16 0AS, UK

Abstract. We propose a novel method of assessing OpenStreetMap data using the concept of Data Maturity. Based on research into data quality and trust in user generated content, this is a set of measurements that can be derived from provenance data extracted from OpenStreetMap edit history.

Keywords: VGI · OpenStreetMap · Wikipedia

1 Introduction

The production of geographic data has traditionally been the purview of government regulated institutions such as the Ordnance Survey and the US Geological Survey. The World Wide Web has since given rise to Volunteered Geographic Information and now the world's most extensive geographic dataset is OpenStreetMap, also part of the user generated content (UGC) phenomenon.

Geographic data has traditionally been used in science and academia, but the free and open nature of OpenStreetMap has generated novel and often mission-critical use cases among people with little understanding of or interest in ISO data standards. This shift away from authoritative data sources and traditional paradigms of quality assurance raises problems for geospatial data consumers who must make informed trust judgements in an ever-wider range of use cases. The move away from institutional accreditation demands new forms of quality labelling to facilitate these decisions.

2 Maturity

Maturity is a stable stage in the lifecycle of some data when it no longer requires editing except to reflect real world change. It has been studied in both Wikipedia [1–7] and OpenStreetMap [8–15], and we draw on this research to propose provenance-based metrics which are indicators of maturity.

2.1 Linus's Law Maturity

A measure of how many people have "seen" a feature. It is characterised by the open source maxim, "many eyes make bugs shallow" [16].

© Springer Nature Switzerland AG 2021
B. Glavic et al. (Eds.): IPAW 2020/IPAW 2021, LNCS 12839, pp. 207–210, 2021.
https://doi.org/10.1007/978-3-030-80960-7_13

- Edit Count: Number of versions of an OSM data primitive within a grid cell normalised by the number of primitives.
- Editor Count: The number of editors who influenced data within the cell.
- Average editors per feature: the number of agents who have edited any version of the feature or any child features of that feature divided by the number of features in the cell.
- Average edits per feature: the number of feature versions divided by the number of features.

2.2 Currency

A measure of how recently editing activity has taken place, and how "up to date" data is.

- Days since last update: The difference between the timestamp of the most recent version of a data primitive within the cell, and now.
- Average days since Last Update: The average difference between the timestamp of the most recent version of all primitives within the cell.
- New Edits: The number of edit versions within a cell with timestamps within one months of the download date High values indicate high maturity.

2.3 Life-Cycle Maturity

Changes in edit frequency over the lifecycle of data have been studied in Wikipedia and OSM, where the most mature data has a stable phase after a period of more intense activity.

- Life-Cycle Edits: The number of edits that occurred in the last 20% of an artefact's lifetime divided by the total edits.

2.4 Volatility

A measure of the rate at which edits are retained. It is calculated by counting the number of tags which are changed and then reverted to their previous state. A tag revert is defined as a tag (a feature attribute) is edited and then returned to its previous state in a subsequent edit.

- Tag Revert Count: The number of tag reverts in a cell.
- Revert Rate: The average number of tag reverts per feature.
- Transient Edit ratio derived from the number of edits to tags reverted to their previous state within one month.

2.5 Maintenance Edit Ratio

A maintenance edit is defined as any edit to data that occurs after its creation, i.e. resulting in a version number greater than 1.

- Maintenance ratio: the number of Maintenance Edits in a cell divided by the number of Creation Edits in that cell.

3 Conclusions and Future Work

Using provenance data, we provide different measurements for each of these maturity metrics to provide useful automated quality labelling of OpenStreetMap data. We have developed a data analysis pipeline which discovers provenance graphs from OpenStreetMap XML history data, using the PROV-DM, and stores this data as RDF triples. Using research into user generated content. We have derived measurements of our maturity metrics from this provenance data. In our preliminary work, we have extracted OpenStreetMap provenance data using a hexagonal polygon grid and noted interesting spatial clusters.

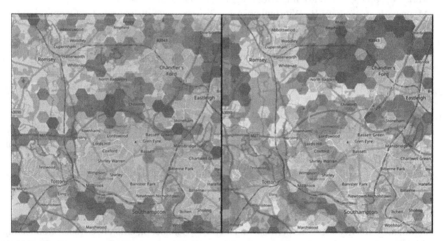

Fig. 1. Maps of the study area using hexagonal grid cells, showing the distribution of maintenance ratio (left), and currency as days since last update (right)

We intend to build on this work using UK 2011 census output area polygons to extract the data, which will enable investigation of potential geodemographic drivers for the variations in our measurements.

References

1. Anderka, M., Stein, B., Lipka, N.: Predicting quality flaws in user-generated content: the case of Wikipedia. In: Proceedings of the 35th International ACM SIGIR Conference on Research and Development in Information Retrieval, New York, NY, pp. 981–990 (2012). https://doi.org/10.1145/2348283.2348413

2. Lih, A.: Wikipedia as participatory journalism: reliable sources? Metrics for evaluating collaborative media as a news resource. In: Proceedings of the 5th International Symposium on Online Journalism, pp. 16–17 (2004)
3. Stvilia, B., Twidale, M.B., Smith, L.C., Gasser, L.: Assessing information quality of a community-based Encyclopedia (2005). http://www.scopus.com/inward/record.url?scp=848 71554587&partnerID=8YFLogxK
4. Wilkinson, D.M., Huberman, B.A.: Cooperation and quality in Wikipedia. In Proceedings of the 2007 International Symposium on Wikis, New York, NY, pp. 157–164 (2007). https://doi.org/10.1145/1296951.1296968
5. Dalip, D.H., Gonçalves, M.A., Cristo, M., Calado, P.: Automatic quality assessment of content created collaboratively by web communities: a case study of Wikipedia. In: Proceedings of the 9th ACM/IEEE-CS Joint Conference on Digital Libraries, New York, NY, pp. 295–304 (2009). https://doi.org/10.1145/1555400.1555449
6. Li, X., Luo, Z., Pang, K., Wang, T.: A lifecycle analysis of the revision behavior of featured articles on Wikipedia. In: 2013 International Conference on Information Science and Cloud Computing Companion, pp. 846–851, December 2013. https://doi.org/10.1109/ISCC-C.201 3.16
7. Wöhner, T., Peters, R.: Assessing the quality of Wikipedia articles with lifecycle based metrics. In: Proceedings of the 5th International Symposium on Wikis and Open Collaboration, New York, NY, pp. 1–10 (2009). https://doi.org/10.1145/1641309.1641333
8. Mooney, P., Corcoran, P., Winstanley, A.C.: Towards quality metrics for OpenStreetMap, p. 514 (2010). https://doi.org/10.1145/1869790.1869875
9. Mooney, P., Corcoran, P.: Characteristics of heavily edited objects in OpenStreetMap. Future Internet 4(1), 285–305 (2012). https://doi.org/10.3390/fi4010285
10. Haklay, M.M., Basiouka, S., Antoniou, V., Ather, A.: How many volunteers does it take to map an area well? The validity of Linus law to volunteered geographic information. Cartographic J. 47(4), 315-322 (2010). https://doi.org/10.1179/000870410X12911304958827
11. Rehrl, K., Gröechenig, S., Hochmair, H., Leitinger, S., Steinmann, R., Wagner, A.: A conceptual model for analyzing contribution patterns in the context of VGI. In: Krisp, J.M. (ed.) Progress in Location-Based Services, pp. 373–388. Springer , Heidelberg (2013). https://doi.org/10.1007/978-3-642-34203-5_21
12. Arsanjani, J.J., Mooney, P., Helbich, M., Zipf, A.: An exploration of future patterns of the contributions to OpenStreetMap and development of a contribution index. Trans. GIS 19(6), 896–914 (2015). https://doi.org/10.1111/tgis.12139
13. Gröchenig, S., Brunauer, R., Rehrl, K.: Estimating completeness of VGI datasets by analyzing community activity over time periods. In: Huerta, J., Schade, S., Granell, C. (eds.) Connecting a Digital Europe Through Location and Place. LNGC, pp. 3–18. Springer, Cham (2014). https://doi.org/10.1007/978-3-319-03611-3_1
14. Keßler, C., de Groot, R.T.A.: Trust as a proxy measure for the quality of volunteered geographic information in the case of OpenStreetMap. In: Vandenbroucke, D., Bucher, B., Crompvoets, J. (eds) Geographic Information Science at the Heart of Europe, pp. 21–37. Springer International Publishing, Cham (2013). https://doi.org/10.1007/978-3-319-006 15-4_2
15. Quattrone, G., Dittus, M., Capra, L.: Work always in progress: analysing maintenance practices in spatial crowd-sourced datasets. In Proceedings of the 2017 ACM Conference on Computer Supported Cooperative Work and Social Computing, New York, NY, pp. 1876–1889 (2017). https://doi.org/10.1145/2998181.2998267
16. Raymond, E.S.: The Cathedral and the Bazaar : Musings on Linux and Open Source by an Accidental Revolutionary. Sebastopol, UNITED STATES: O'Reilly Media, Incorporated (2001). http://ebookcentral.proquest.com/lib/soton-ebooks/detail.action?docID=443450

Querying Data Preparation Modules Using Data Examples

Khalid Belhajjame[1]([✉]) and Mahmoud Barhamgi[2]

[1] PSL, Université Paris-Dauphine, LAMSADE, Paris, France
khalid.belhajjame@dauphine.fr
[2] Claude Bernard Lyon 1 University, Villeurbanne, France
mahmoud.barhamgi@liris.cnrs.fr

Abstract. Data preparation modules are ubiquitous and are used to perform, amongst other things, operations such as record retrieval, format transformation, data combination to name a few. To assist scientists in the task of discovering suitable modules, semantic annotations can be leveraged. Experience suggests, however, that while such annotations are useful in describing the inputs and outputs of a module, they fail in crisply describing the functionality performed by the module. To overcome this issue, we outline in this poster paper a solution that utilizes semantic annotations describing the inputs and outputs of modules together with data examples that characterize modules' behavior as ingredients for querying data preparation modules. Data examples are constructed using retrospective provenance of module executions. The discovery strategy that we devised is iterative in that it allows scientists to explore existing modules by providing feedback on data examples.

1 Introduction

Data preparation is a long-standing issue that has been the focus of considerable body of work in industry and academia, and has gained recently momentum with the rise of data-driven analyses and experiments in the Big Data era. It is estimated that in average 80% of the tasks that compose a data-driven analysis are dedicated to data preparation

Despite the impressive body of work in data management on data preparation tasks, it is recognized that there is not a single generic one-shop-stop solution that can be utilized by the scientists to prepare their data prior their analysis. Instead, data preparation tasks are numerous, can be difficult to generalize (e.g., data cleansing, data integration), and tends to vary depending on the processing tasks at hand, but also on the semantic domains and the format of the data subject to processing. As a result, scientists tend to develop their own program/script using their favorite language, e.g., Python, R or Perl, to prepare their data. This operation is time-consuming and recurrent since sometimes the scientist has to redevelop data preparation scripts that s/he has previously performed on the same or similar data.

© Springer Nature Switzerland AG 2021
B. Glavic et al. (Eds.): IPAW 2020/IPAW 2021, LNCS 12839, pp. 211–217, 2021.
https://doi.org/10.1007/978-3-030-80960-7_14

To overcome the above problem, a number of researchers have been calling for the creation of repositories dedicated to data preparation modules with the view to save the time scientists spend on data preparation to allow them to focus their effort on the analysis tasks. Examples of such repositories are BigGorilla[1], an open-source ecosystem for data preparation and integration, Bio.Tools[2], a catalogue which provides access to, amongst other things, services for the preparation of bioinformatics data, and Galaxy tools[3].

In this poster, we set out to examine the problem of querying data preparation modules. Specifically, the objective is to locate a module that can be perform a data preparation task at hand, if such a module exists. Semantic annotations can be used to reach this objective [5]. A module is semantically annotated by associating it to concepts from ontologies. Different facets of the module can be described using semantic annotations, e.g., input and output parameters, task and quality of service (QoS). In practice, however, we observe that most of semantic annotations that are available are confined to the description of the domain of input and output parameters of modules. Annotations specifying the behavior of the module, as to the task it performs, are rarely specified. Indeed, the number of modules that are semantically described with concepts that describe the behavior of the module lags well behind the number of modules that are semantically annotated in terms of the domains of the input and output parameters, e.g., in BioTools. Even when they are available, annotations that describe the behavior of the module tend to give a general idea of the task that the module implements, and fall short in describing the specifics of its behavior. For example, the modules in BioTools, which is a registry that provides information about data preparation modules, are described using terms such as *merging* and *retrieving*. While such terms provide a *rough* idea of what a module does, they do not provide the user with sufficient information to determine if a it is suitable for the data preparation at hand. The failure in crisply describing the behavior of scientific modules should not be attributed to the designers of task ontologies. Indeed, designing an ontology that captures precisely the behavior of modules, without increasing the difficulty that the human annotators who use such ontologies may face thereby compromising the usability of the ontology, is challenging.

To overcome this issue, we outline in this poster a solution that utilizes semantic annotations describing the inputs and outputs of modules together with data examples that characterize modules' behavior as ingredients for the discovery of data preparation modules. Given a module m, a data example provides concrete values of inputs that are consumed by m as well as the corresponding output values that are delivered as a result. Data examples are constructed by harvesting the retrospective provenance of modules' executions. They provide an intuitive means for users to understand the module behavior: the user does not need to examine the source code of the module, which is often not available, or

---

[1] https://www.biggorilla.org.

[2] https://bio.tools.

[3] https://galaxyproject.org/tools.

Fig. 1. Data example.

the semantic annotations, which require the user to be familiar with the domain ontology used for annotation. Moreover, they are amenable to describing the behavior of a module in a precise, yet concise, manner. It has been shown in [2] that data examples are an effective means for characterizing and understanding the behavior of modules. We explore in this poster that data examples can also be used to effectively and efficiently discover modules that are able to perform a data preparation task of interest.

2   Data Model

A data-prepration module can be defined by the pair: $m = \langle id, name \rangle$, where id is the module identifier and name its name. A module m is associated with two ordered sets inputs(m) and outputs(m), representing its input and output parameters, respectively. A parameter p of a module m is characterized by a structural type, $str(i)$, and a semantic type, $sem(i)$. The former specifies the structural data type of the parameter, e.g., String or Integer, whereas the latter specifies the semantic domain of the parameter using a concept, e.g., Protein, that belongs to a domain ontology [3].

A data example δ that is used to describe the behavior a module m can be defined by a pair: $\delta = \langle I, O \rangle$, where: $I = \{\langle i, ins_i \rangle\}$ and $O = \{\langle o, ins_o \rangle\}$. i (resp. o) is an input (resp. output) parameter of m, and ins_i and ins_o are parameter values. δ specifies that the invocation of the module m using the instances in I to feed its input parameters, produces the output values in O. We use in what follows $\Delta(m)$ to denote the set of data examples that are used to describe the behavior of a module m.

Example 1. *To illustrate how data examples can be used to understand a module behavior, consider the module* GetRecord, *which has one input and one output. Figure 1 illustrates an input instance that is consumed by* GetRecord *and the corresponding value obtained as a result of the module invocation. By examining such a data example, a domain expert will be able to understand that the* GetRecord *module retrieves the protein record that corresponds to the accession number given as input.*

3   Generation of Data Examples

Enumerating all possible data examples that can be used to describe a given module may be expensive or impossible since the domains of input and output parameters can be large or infinite. A solution that can be used is to create data examples that cover the classes of behavior of the module in question, and then construct data examples that cover the classes identified. When the modules are white boxes, then their specification can be utilized to specify the classes of behavior and generate the data examples that cover each class (see e.g., [1]). If, on the other hand, the modules are black boxes and their specification is not accessible, then a heuristic such as the one described in [2] can be utilized.

Using the solution proposed in [2], to construct data examples that characterize the behavior of a module m, the domain of its input i is divided into partitions, $p_1, p_2, \ldots, p_n$. The partitioning is performed in a way to cover all classes of behavior of m. For each partition p_i, a data example δ is constructed such that the value of the input parameter in δ belongs to the partition p_i. A source of information that is used for partitioning is the semantic annotations used to describe module parameters. Indeed, the input and output parameters of many scientific modules are annotated using concepts from domain ontologies [4] (Fig. 2).

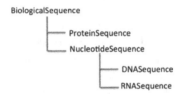

Fig. 2. Fragment of the myGrid ontology.

To generate data examples that characterize the behavior of a module m, m is probed using input instances from a pool, the instances of which cover the concepts of the ontology used for annotations. The retrospective provenance obtained as a result of the module' executions are then used to construct data examples. In doing so, only module executions that terminates without issues (that is without raising any exception) are utilized to construct data examples for m. For more details on this operation, the reader is referred to [2].

It is worth stressing that while the domain ontologies used for describing module behavior provides terms that vaguely describe the data transformation carried out by the module, the domain ontologies used for describing module parameters are much more elaborated. They often provide terms that capture the domain of legal values of a module parameter in a precise manner. Examples of such ontologies are the Gene Ontology[4], the Microarray Gene Expression Data Ontology[5] and the Open Biomedical Ontologies[6].

---

[4] http://www.geneontology.org/.

[5] http://mged.sourceforge.net/ontologies/MGEDontology.php.

[6] http://obo.sourceforge.net/.

4   Querying Modules

To discover a module, a user can provide data examples that characterize the module s/he had in mind. However, specifying data examples that characterize the desired module can be time-consuming, since the user needs to construct the data examples by hand. We present in this section a method that allows users to discover modules by simply providing feedback on a list of data examples they are presented with.

4.1   Feedback-Based Discovery of Scientific Modules

To identify the modules that meet his/her needs, the user starts by specifying the semantic domains and the structural types of the inputs and outputs of the modules s/he wishes to locate. The modules with inputs and outputs that are compatible with the specified semantic domains and structural types are then located. Consider, for example, that the user is interested in locating a module that consumes input values that belong to the semantic domain c_i and structural type t_i, and produces output values that belong to the semantic domain c_o and structural type t_o. A module m meets such a query if it has an input (resp. output) with a semantic domain and structural type that are equivalent to or subsumed by c_i and t_i (resp. c_o and t_o). Specifically, the set of modules that meet those criteria can be specified by the following set comprehension (Fig. 3):

	Data examples		User feedback	
	protein name	**accession**	**expected**	**unexpected**
δ_1	Chorion protein S36	CH36_CERCA	X	
δ_2	Zinc metalloproteinase	VMDM_VIRST		X

Fig. 3. Data examples and user feedback.

$$\{\text{m s.t. } (\exists \, i \in \text{inputs}(m), (\text{sem}(i) \sqsubseteq c_i) \wedge (\text{str}(i) \sqsubseteq t_i))$$
$$\wedge (\exists \, o \in \text{outputs}(m), (\text{sem}(o) \sqsubseteq c_o) \wedge (\text{str}(o) \sqsubseteq t_o))\}$$

It is likely that not all the modules retrieved based on the semantic domain of input and output parameters perform the task that is expected by the user. Because of this, we refer to such modules using the term *candidate modules*.

To identify the candidate module(s) that perform the task expected by the user, the data examples characterizing candidate modules are displayed to the user. The user then examines the data examples and specifies the ones that meet the expectations, and the ones that do not. To do so, the user provides feedback instances. A feedback instance uf is used to annotate a data example, and can be defined by the following pair $\text{uf} = \langle \delta, \text{expected} \rangle$, where δ denotes the data example annotated by the feedback instance uf, and expected is a boolean that is true if δ is expected, i.e., compatible with the requirements of the user who supplied uf, and false, if it is unexpected.

4.2   Incremental Ranking of Candidate Modules

The discovery strategy we have just described can be effective when the number of candidate modules and the number of data examples characterizing each candidate are small. If the number of candidate modules to be annotated and/or the number of data examples used for their characterization are large, then the user may need to provide a large amount of feedback before locating the desired module among the candidates. Moreover, there is no guarantee that the set of candidates is complete in the sense that it contains a module that implements the behavior that meets user requirements. Therefore, the user may have to annotate a (possibly) large number of data examples only to find out that none of the candidates meet the requirements. Because of the above limitations, we set out to develop a second discovery strategy with the following properties:

1. **Ranking candidate modules**: Instead of simply labeling candidate modules as suitable or not to user requirements, they are ranked based on metrics that are estimated given the feedback supplied by the user, to measure their fitness to requirements. In the absence of candidates that meet the exact requirements of users, ranking allows the user to identify the modules that best meet the requirements among the candidate modules.
2. **Incrementality**: The user does not have to provide feedback annotating every data example characterizing the candidate modules before being presented with the modules that best meet the requirements. Instead, given feedback supplied by the user to annotate a subset of the data examples, the candidate modules are ranked and the obtained list of candidates is shown to the user. The list of candidates is incrementally revisited as more feedback instances are supplied by the user.
3. **Learning feedback**: To reduce the cost in terms of the amount of feedback that the user needs to provide to locate suitable modules, new feedback instances annotating data examples that the user did not examine are inferred based on existing feedback that the user supplied to annotate other data examples.

5   Conclusions

We have outlined, in this poster paper, a solution for discovering data preparation modules. This is to our knowledge one of the few attempts in the state of the art that investigates the use of data examples that have been harvested from retrospective provenance of modules' execution for improving module discovery. We have shown how feedback provided by the user can be utilized to efficiently navigate the space of candidate modules.

References

1. Alexe, B., ten Cate, B., Kolaitis, P.G., Chiew Tan, W.: Characterizing schema mappings via data examples. ACM Trans. Database Syst. **36**(4), 23:1–23:48 (2011)
2. Belhajjame, K.: Annotating the behavior of scientific modules using data examples: a practical approach. In: EDBT, pp. 726–737. OpenProceedings.org (2014)
3. Gruber, T.: Ontology. In: Encyclopedia of Database Systems (2009)
4. Kuropka, D., Tröger, P., Staab, S., Weske, M. (eds.) Semantic Service Provisioning. Springer, Heidelberg (2008). https://doi.org/10.1007/978-3-540-78617-7
5. Studer, R., Grimm, S., Abecker, A. (eds.): Semantic Web Services, Concepts, Technologies, and Applications. Springer, Heidelberg (2007). https://doi.org/10.1007/3-540-70894-4

Privacy Aspects of Provenance Queries

Tanja Auge$^{(\boxtimes)}$, Nic Scharlau, and Andreas Heuer

University of Rostock, 18051 Rostock, Germany
{tanja.auge,nic.scharlau,andreas.heuer}@uni-rostock.de

Abstract. Given a query result of a big database, **why**-provenance can be used to calculate the necessary part of this database, consisting of so-called witnesses. If this database consists of personal data, privacy protection has to prevent the publication of these witnesses. This implies a natural conflict of interest between publishing original data (*provenance*) and protecting these data (*privacy*).

In this paper, privacy goes beyond the concept of personal data protection. The paper gives an extended definition of privacy as intellectual property protection. If the provenance information is not sufficient to reconstruct a query result, additional data such as witnesses or provenance polynomials have to be published to guarantee traceability. Nevertheless, publishing this provenance information might be a problem if (significantly) more tuples than necessary can be derived from the original database. At this point, it is already possible to violate privacy policies, provided that quasi identifiers are included in this provenance information. With this poster, we point out fundamental problems and discuss first proposals for solutions.

Keywords: Provenance · Privacy

1 Privacy vs. Provenance

For us, the term privacy goes beyond the concept of (mostly personal) data protection. Rather, we mean the protection of data in general. Reasons for the protection of data can be economic ones (intellectual properties), since generating such data is often very time-consuming and expensive. The identification of personal or internal company information should also be strictly prevented.

Since queries that occur in the context of projects can become arbitrarily complex – simple selections and projections, even joins and aggregations – the inversion of these queries is often not 100% possible or necessary. However, using provenance enables us to perform this inversion as accurately as possible [1]. This implies a natural conflict of interest between publishing original data (*provenance*) and protecting these data (*privacy*), and it may be possible to reconstruct parts of the source instance that contradict the privacy concepts (see Fig. 1).

© Springer Nature Switzerland AG 2021
B. Glavic et al. (Eds.): IPAW 2020/IPAW 2021, LNCS 12839, pp. 218–221, 2021.
https://doi.org/10.1007/978-3-030-80960-7_15

Fig. 1. Motivation

Privacy refers to the protection of (personal) data against unauthorized collection, storage, and publication. This becomes difficult if even the combination of apparently harmless attributes (*quasi-identifiers*) can lead to a clear identification.

Data Provenance is concerned with the origin of a data analysis. This analysis may be a database query using aggregation or selection. We distinguish three provenance-questions answered by using the names of the source relations (*where*), witness bases (*why*, [2]), or provenance polynomials (*how*, [5]), as well as additional information which are sometimes necessary for reconstructing concrete lost attribute values.

Privacy and Provenance conflicts have already been discussed in various papers. For example, a formalization of security properties such as disclosure and obfuscation is shown in [3]. Besides Data Provenance, there also exist other types of provenance we need to face. At the workflow level, privacy and provenance have already been investigated by [4].

2   Problems Using *where*, *why* and *how*

Data provenance can have different characteristics, generating different provenance information and therefore different privacy problems.

Let us imagine a data set with personal data such as a university database. It contains data about its students and staff, equipment and buildings, and much more. A sensitive attribute w.r.t. privacy aspects is the `Grade` attribute in the `Grades` relation storing the results of the exams. Instead of extracting the exact grade for every exam, a query calculating the average grade per student should be allowed to be performed by the university administration. Different sub-databases can now be calculated depending on the choice of stored provenance. Figure 2 shows the result tables extended to the original schema using *where*-provenance (left), the extension to the exact number of tuples when using *why*-provenance (center), or the representation of all individual grades per student in the case of *how*-provenance (right). In all situations the `Module` attribute can not be reconstructed. Hence, modules are reconstructed introducing null values (highlighted in gray).

These data can be reconstructed by *where*-, *why*- and *how*-provenance with the techniques described in [1]. We will now consider the privacy aspects of these results of the provenance queries: (1) Using *where*, there is generally not enough data worth protecting and reproducibility of the data is not guaranteed. Data protection aspects are therefore negligible. If we interpret **where** as tuple names and we save not only the scheme but the tuple itself, this can lead to major privacy problems. However, this second **where** approach is subject of our current work. (2) In the case of **why**-provenance, we may encounter privacy problems, if the variance of the distribution of attribute values is equal to zero. However, this only applies for special cases not known to the user interpreting the results of the provenance queries. (3) **How** often calculates too much recoverable information, so that privacy aspects are likely to be a major problem with this technology.

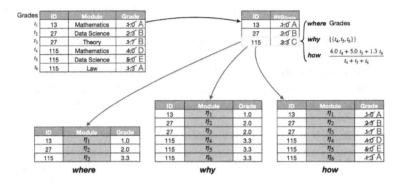

Fig. 2. Possible provenance-based database reconstructions (red) including generalization (blue) as solution approach (Color figure online)

3   Possible Solutions to the Privacy Problem

For solving the problems generated by the different provenance queries, we examined different approaches such as generalization and suppression, differential privacy, permutation of attribute values, and intensional (instead of extensional) answers to provenance queries [6].

Intensional provenance answers represent one solution approach to combine data provenance and privacy. It can be realized, e.g., by the generalization of attribute values. The idea of generalization is shown in Fig. 2 by generalizing the grade from a concrete number like 1.0 or 1.3 to a grade area of A (highlighted in blue). This results in a (hopefully acceptable) loss of information, while approaching a solution to the privacy problem of protecting sensitive attribute values.

Acknowledgments. We thank Goetz Graefe and Tom Ettrich for their support and comments during the development of this work.

References

1. Auge, T., Heuer, A.: ProSA: using the CHASE for provenance management. In: Welzer, T., Eder, J., Podgorelec, V., Kamišalić Latifić, A. (eds.) ADBIS 2019. LNCS, vol. 11695, pp. 357–372. Springer, Cham (2019). https://doi.org/10.1007/978-3-030-28730-6_22
2. Buneman, P., Khanna, S., Wang-Chiew, T.: Why and where: a characterization of data provenance. In: Van den Bussche, J., Vianu, V. (eds.) ICDT 2001. LNCS, vol. 1973, pp. 316–330. Springer, Heidelberg (2001). https://doi.org/10.1007/3-540-44503-X_20
3. Cheney, J.: A formal framework for provenance security. In: CSF, pp. 281–293. IEEE Computer Society (2011)
4. Davidson, S.B., Khanna, S., Roy, S., Stoyanovich, J., Tannen, V., Chen, Y.: On provenance and privacy. In: ICDT, pp. 3–10. ACM (2011)
5. Green, T.J., Tannen, V.: The semiring framework for database provenance. In: PODS, pp. 93–99. ACM (2017)
6. Scharlau, N.: Privacy und Provenance in ProSA. Bachelor Thesis, University of Rostock, DBIS (2020)

ISO 23494: Biotechnology – Provenance Information Model for Biological Specimen And Data

Rudolf Wittner[1,2](✉), Petr Holub[1,2], Heimo Müller[3], Joerg Geiger[4], Carole Goble[5], Stian Soiland-Reyes[5,11], Luca Pireddu[6], Francesca Frexia[6], Cecilia Mascia[6], Elliot Fairweather[7], Jason R. Swedlow[8], Josh Moore[8], Caterina Strambio[9], David Grunwald[9], and Hiroki Nakae[10]

[1] BBMRI-ERIC, Graz, Austria
rudolf.wittner@bbmri-eric.eu
[2] Institute of Computer Science and Faculty of Informatics, Masaryk University, Brno, Czech Republic
[3] Medical University Graz, Graz, Austria
[4] Interdisciplinary Bank of Biomaterials and Data Würzburg (ibdw), Würzburg, Germany
[5] Department of Computer Science, The University of Manchester, Manchester, UK
[6] CRS4 – Center for Advanced Studies, Research and Development in Sardinia, Pula, Italy
[7] King's College London, London, UK
[8] School of Life Sciences, University of Dundee, Dundee, UK
[9] University of Massachusetts, Amherst, USA
[10] Japan bio- Measurement and Analysis Consortium, Tokyo, Japan
[11] Informatics Institute, University of Amsterdam, Amsterdam, Netherlands

Abstract. Exchange of research data and samples in biomedical research has become a common phenomenon, demanding for their effective quality assessment. At the same time, several reports address reproducibility of research, where history of biological samples (acquisition, processing, transportation, storage, and retrieval) and data history (data generation and processing) define their fitness for purpose, and hence their quality. This project aims to develop a comprehensive W3C PROV based provenance information standard intended for the biomedical research domain. The standard is being developed by the working group 5 ("data processing and integration") of the ISO (International Standardisation Organisation) technical committee 276 "biotechnology". The outcome of the project will be published in parts as international standards or technical specifications. The poster informs about the goals of

Supported by European Union's Horizon 2020 research and innovation programme under grant agreement No. 654248, project CORBEL; grant agreement No. 824087, project EOSC-Life; and grant agreement No. 823830, project BioExcel-2.

The original version of this chapter was revised: The DOI "10.5281/zenodo.4705074" has been added in Reference 7 "Wittner, R., et al.: EOSC-life common provenance model. EOSC-Life deliverable D6.2 (2021)". The correction to this chapter is available at https://doi.org/10.1007/978-3-030-80960-7_24

the standardisation activity, presents the proposed structure of the standards, briefly describes its current state and outlines its future development and open issues.

Keywords: Provenance · Biotechnology · Standardization

1   Introduction

Research in life sciences has undergone significant changes during recent years, evolving away from individual projects confined to small research groups to transnational consortia covering a wide range of techniques and expertise. At the same time, several reports addressing the quality of research papers in life sciences have uncovered an alarming number of ill-founded claims. The reasons for the deficiencies are diverse, with insufficient quality and documentation of the biological material used being the major issue [1–3]. Hence there is urgent need for standardized and comprehensive documentation of the whole workflow from the collection, generation, processing and analysis of the biological material to data analysis and integration.

The PROV[4] family of documents serves as a current standard for provenance information used to describe the history of an object. On the other hand, as discussed in the results from EHR4CR and TRANSFoRm projects [5,6], its implementation for the biotechnology domain and the field of biomedical research in particular is still a pending issue. To address this, the International Standardisation Organisation (ISO) initiated the development of a *Provenance Information Model for Biological Specimen and Data* standard defining the requirements for interoperable, machine-actionable documentation intended to describe the complete process chain from the source of biological material through its processing, analysis, and all steps of data generation and data processing to final data analysis.

The standard is intended for implementers and suppliers of HW/SW tools used in biomedical research (e.g. lab automation devices or analytical devices used for research purposes) and also for organisations adopting generated provenance (e.g. to require or use standardised tools).

2   Goals of the Standard and Its Structure

The main goals of the standard are to (a) enable effective assessment of quality and fitness for purpose of the objects provided, such as biological material and data; (b) support reproducible research by exacting the capture of all relevant information; (c) track error propagation within scientific results; (d) track the source of biological material in order to prevent fabrication of data and enabling notification of subjects in case of relevant incidental findings; (e) propagate withdrawal of or changes to an informed consent along the process chain.

The proposed structure of the standard reflects the intention to interconnect and integrate distributed provenance information furnished by all kinds of organisations involved in biotechnology research. Examples of such organisations are hospitals, biobanks, research centers, universities, data centers or pharmaceutical companies, where each of them is participating in research, thus generating provenance information describing particular activities or contributions.

In its current the standard is composed of the following 6 parts:

- **Part 1** stipulates common requirements for provenance information management in biotechnology to effectuate compatibility of provenance management at all stages of research and defines the design concept of this standard;
- **Part 2** defines a common provenance model which will serve as an overarching principle interconnecting provenance parts generated by all kinds of contributing organisations and enable access to provenance information in a distributed environment;
- **Parts 3, 4 and 5** are meant to complement the *horizontal* standards (1) and (2) as *vertical* standards defining domain specific provenance models describing diverse stages or areas of research in biotechnology (e.g. sample acquisition and handling, analytical techniques, data management, cleansing and processing; database validation);
- **Part 6** will contain optional data security extensions especially to address non-repudiation of provenance.

The proposed structure is also depicted in Fig. 1. Parts indicated by red boxes are considered as *horizontal* standards, i.e. providing a common basis for provenance information at all stages of research. The blue boxes indicate domain specific *vertical* standards build on top of the *horizontal* standards.

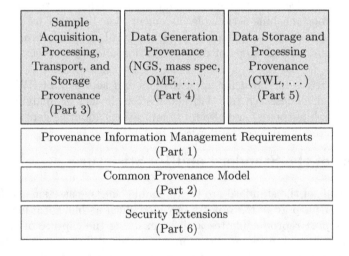

Fig. 1. Overall structure of the standard (Color figure online)

3   Current Status and Future Development

The standard is currently at an early stage of development. The PROV model has been already used to define new types of provenance structures, called *con-*

nectors, that are used to interconnect provenance generated by different organizations. The concept of the connectors and a common mechanism for bundles versioning has been published as an EOSC-Life project provenance deliverable [7]. A publication describing use of the connectors at a specific use case is under development at the moment and its pre-print will be published in summer 2021. Continuously, the model will be enriched by new types of structures (e.g. relations, entities, etc.) to capture common objects. These structures will be subsequently used to design provenance templates[1] to define a common representation of usual scenarios in life sciences. Further aspects will be also targeted. The major focus areas are: opaque provenance components; privacy preservation and non-repudiation of provenance information; full syntactic and semantic interoperability of provenance information captured; rigorous formal verification process of provenance instance validity (provable compliance with the proposed model).

Another publication describing the standardization process in a more detailed way is under development. The publication will contain more detailed explanation of our motivation and the standardization activity itself, more detailed description of the standard structure, and finally, an important discussion on openness of the standard and related issues.

References

1. Freedman, L.P., Cockburn, I.M., Simcoe, T.S.: The economics of reproducibility in preclinical research. PLoS Biol. **13**(6), e1002165 (2015). https://doi.org/10.1371/journal.pbio.1002165
2. Begley, G.C., Ioannidis, J.P.A.: Reproducibility in science. Circ. Res. **116**(1), 116–126 (2015). https://doi.org/10.1161/CIRCRESAHA.114.303819
3. Freedman, L.P., Inglese, J.: The increasing urgency for standards in basic biologic research. Cancer Res. **74**(15), 4024–4029 (2014). https://doi.org/10.1158/0008-5472.CAN-14-0925. ISSN 0008-5472
4. Groth, P., Moreau, L.: Prov-overview. An overview of the prov family of documents. W3C Working Group Note 30 April 2013 (2013). https://www.w3.org/TR/2013/NOTE-prov-overview-20130430/
5. Curcin, V., Miles, S., Danger, R., Chen, Y., Bache, R., Taweel, A.: Implementing interoperable provenance in biomedical research. Future Gener. Comput. Syst. **34**, 1–16 (2014). https://doi.org/10.1016/j.future.2013.12.001
6. Cuccuru, G., et al.: An automated infrastructure to support high-throughput bioinformatics. In: 2014 International Conference on High Performance Computing & Simulation (HPCS), pp. 600–607. IEEE (2014). https://doi.org/10.1109/HPCSim.2014.6903742
7. Wittner, R., et al.: EOSC-life common provenance model. EOSC-Life deliverable D6.2 (2021). https://doi.org/10.5281/zenodo.4705074

---

[1] The templates can be considered as synonyms for named graphs or graph patterns. These concepts are used to abstract from actual instances of provenance and to describe repeating occurrences of components of provenance.

Machine Learning Pipelines: Provenance, Reproducibility and FAIR Data Principles

Sheeba Samuel[1,2](✉) [iD], Frank Löffler[1,2] [iD], and Birgitta König-Ries[1,2] [iD]

[1] Heinz-Nixdorf Chair for Distributed Information Systems,
Friedrich Schiller University Jena, Jena, Germany
[2] Michael Stifel Center Jena, Friedrich Schiller University Jena, Jena, Germany
{sheeba.samuel,frank.loeffler,birgitta.koenig-ries}@uni-jena.de

Abstract. Machine learning (ML) is an increasingly important scientific tool supporting decision making and knowledge generation in numerous fields. With this, it also becomes more and more important that the results of ML experiments are reproducible. Unfortunately, that often is not the case. Rather, ML, similar to many other disciplines, faces a reproducibility crisis. In this paper, we describe our goals and initial steps in supporting the end-to-end reproducibility of ML pipelines. We investigate which factors beyond the availability of source code and datasets influence reproducibility of ML experiments. We propose ways to apply FAIR data practices to ML workflows. We present our preliminary results on the role of our tool, ProvBook, in capturing and comparing provenance of ML experiments and their reproducibility using Jupyter Notebooks. We also present the ReproduceMeGit tool to analyze the reproducibility of ML pipelines described in Jupyter Notebooks.

Keywords: Machine Learning · Reproducibility · Provenance · FAIR · ReproduceMe-ML

1 Introduction

Over the last few years, advances in artificial intelligence and machine learning (ML) have led to their use in numerous applications. With more and more decision making and knowledge generation being based on ML, it becomes increasingly important, that ML experiments are reproducible. Only reproducible results are trustworthy and a suitable basis for future work. Unfortunately, similar to other disciplines, ML faces a "reproducibility crisis" [1–3]. In this paper, we investigate which factors contribute to this crisis and propose first solutions to address some of them. We have conducted an initial study among domain experts for a better understanding of the requirements for reproducibility of ML experiments. Based on the results from the study and the current scenario in the field of ML, we propose the application of FAIR data practices [4] in end-to-end ML pipelines. We use the ontologies to achieve interoperability of scientific

B. Glavic et al. (Eds.): IPAW 2020/IPAW 2021, LNCS 12839, pp. 226–230, 2021.
https://doi.org/10.1007/978-3-030-80960-7_17

experiments. We demonstrate the use of ProvBook to capture and compare the provenance of executions of ML pipelines through Jupyter Notebooks. Tracking the provenance of the ML workflow is needed for other scientists to understand how the results are derived. Along with the provenance, the version for each provenance item needs to be maintained for the end-to-end reproducibility of an ML pipeline. We also demonstrate the use of ReproduceMeGit to analyse the factors that impact reproducibility of ML pipelines.

2   The Situation: Characteristics of Machine Learning Experiments and Their Reproducibility

An ML pipeline consists of a series of ordered steps used to automate the ML workflow. Even though the general workflow is the same for most ML experiments, there are many activities, tweaks, and parameters that are involved which require proper documentation. Pineau et al. [5] present Machine Learning Reproducibility checklist as part of improving reproducibility in ML research. We conducted an internal study among 15 domain experts to understand what is needed to achieve reproducibility of ML experiments. We asked questions regarding the reproducibility of results, the challenges in reproducing published results and the factors required for describing experiments for reproducibility in the field of ML. We present here some relevant challenges and problems faced by scientists in reproducing published results of others: (1) Unavailability, incomplete, outdated or missing parts of source code (2) Unavailability of datasets used for training and evaluation (3) Unavailability of a reference implementation (4) Missing or insufficient description of hyperparameters that need to be set or tuned to obtain the exact results (5) Missing information on the selection of the training, test and evaluation data (6) Missing information of the required packages and their version (7) Tweaks performed in the code not mentioned in the paper (8) Missing information in methods and the techniques used, e.g., batch norm or regularization techniques (9) Lack of documentation of preprocessing steps including data preparation and cleaning (10) Difficulty in reproducing training of large neural networks due to hardware requirements. All the participants mentioned that if ML experiments are properly described with all the entities of the experiments and their relationships between each other, it will benefit them not only in the reproducibility of results but also for comparison to other competing methods (baseline). The results of this survey are available online[1].

3   Towards a Solution: Applying FAIR Data Principles to ML

The FAIR data principles not only apply to research data but also to the tools, algorithms, and workflows that lead to the results. This aids to enhance transparency, reproducibility, and reuse of the research pipeline. In the context of the

---

[1] https://github.com/Sheeba-Samuel/MLSurvey.

current reproducibility crisis in ML, there is a definite need to explore how the FAIR data principles and practices can be applied in this field. In this paper, we focus on two of the four principles, namely Interoperability and Reusability which we equate with reproducibility. To implement FAIR principles regarding interoperability, it is important that there is a common terminology to describe, find and share the research process and datasets. Describing ML workflows using ontologies could, therefore, help to query and answer competency questions like: (1) Which hyperparameters were used in one particular run of the model? (2) Which libraries and their versions are used in validating the model? (3) What is the execution environment of the ML pipeline? (4) How many training runs were performed in the ML pipeline? (5) What is the allocation of samples for training, testing and validating the model? (6) What are the defined error bars? (7) Which are the measures used for evaluating the model? (8) Which are the predictions made by the model?

In previous work, we have developed the REPRODUCE-ME ontology which is extended from PROV-O and P-Plan [6]. REPRODUCE-ME introduces the notions of Data, Agent, Activity, Plan, Step, Setting, Instrument, and Materials, and thus models the general elements of scientific experiments required for their reproducibility. We extend this ontology to develop ReproduceMe-ML to include ML concepts which scientists consider important according to our survey. We also aim to be compliant with existing ontologies like ML-Schema [7] and MEX vocabulary [8]. With ReproduceMe-ML ontology, the ML pipeline developed through Jupyter Notebooks can be described in an interoperable manner.

4   Achieving Reproducibility Using ProvBook

Building an ML pipeline requires constant tweaks in the algorithms and models and parameter tuning. Training of the ML model is conducted through trial and error. The role of randomness in ML experiments is big and its use is common in steps like data collection, algorithm, sampling, etc. Several runs of the model with the same data can generate different results. Thus, repeating and reproducing results and reusing pipelines is difficult.

The use of Jupyter Notebooks is rapidly increasing as they allow scientists to perform many computational activities including statistical modeling, machine learning, etc. They support computational reproducibility by allowing users to share code along with documentation and results. However, the surveys [9] on Jupyter Notebooks point out the need of provenance information of the execution of these notebooks. To overcome this problem, we developed ProvBook [10]. With ProvBook, users can capture, store, describe and compare the provenance of different executions of Jupyter notebooks. This allows users to compare the results from the original author with their own results from different executions. ProvBook provides the difference in the result of the ML pipeline from the original author of the Jupyter notebook in GitHub with the result from our execution using ProvBook. Even though the code and data remain the same in both the executions, there is a subtle difference in the result. In ML experiments, users need to figure out the reason behind different results due to modification in data or models or because of a random sample. Therefore, it is important to describe the data being used, the code and parameters of the model, the execution environment to know how the results have been derived. ProvBook helps in achieving this reproducibility level by providing the provenance of each run of the model along with the execution environment.

5 Analysing Reproducibility Using ReproduceMeGit

Jupyter Notebooks play an important role in data science and machine learning research with the development and wide adoption of libraries like Scikit-Learn, Pandas, Tensorflow, and PyTorch in recent years. They provide an ideal environment for exploratory data analysis and ML Engineering. These notebooks which are used as tutorials or for sharing results to the scientific community are widely saved in repositories like GitHub[2], Zenodo[3], etc. Recent studies have pointed out the good and bad practices in writing Jupyter Notebooks that can impact reproducibility [9]. To help users analyze the reproducibility of ML pipelines shared using Jupyter Notebooks in GitHub, we present ReproduceMeGit [11]. It is a visual analytic tool for analyzing the reproducibility of Jupyter Notebooks. With this tool, we aim to help repository users and owners to reproduce and directly analyze and assess the reproducibility of any GitHub repository containing Jupyter Notebooks. It provide provenance information on different aspects that impact reproducibility. This information includes the number of notebooks that were successfully reproducible, those that resulted in exceptions, those with different results from the original notebooks, the different libraries and modules used in the ML pipeline, etc. With this tool, the users can see which errors are caused, for example, *ImportError, ModuleNotFoundError, FileNotFoundError, IOError, SyntaxError*, etc., and which cell caused the difference from the original result. Each notebook in the repository along with the provenance information of its execution can also be exported in RDF described using the REPRODUCE-ME ontology with the integration of ProvBook.

Acknowledgments. The authors thank the Carl Zeiss Foundation for the financial support of the project "A Virtual Werkstatt for Digitization in the Sciences (K3)" within the scope of the program-line "Breakthroughs: Exploring Intelligent Systems" for "Digitization – explore the basics, use applications".

References

1. Hutson, M.: Artificial intelligence faces reproducibility crisis. Science **359**(6377), 725–726 (2018)

---

[2] https://github.com.
[3] https://zenodo.org/.

2. Raff, E.: A step toward quantifying independently reproducible machine learning research. In: Advances in Neural Information Processing Systems 32: Annual Conference on Neural Information Processing Systems 2019, NeurIPS 2019, Vancouver, BC, Canada, 8–14 December 2019, pp. 5486–5496 (2019)
3. Samuel, S., König-Ries, B.: Understanding experiments and research practices for reproducibility: an exploratory study. PeerJ **9**, e11140 (2021)
4. Wilkinson, M.D., et al.: The FAIR Guiding Principles for scientific data management and stewardship. Sci. Data **3**, 1–9 (2016)
5. Pineau, J., et al.: Improving reproducibility in machine learning research (a report from the NeurIPS 2019 reproducibility program). arXiv preprint arXiv:2003.12206 (2020)
6. Samuel, S.: A provenance-based semantic approach to support understandability, reproducibility, and reuse of scientific experiments. PhD thesis, Friedrich-Schiller-Universität Jena (2019)
7. Publio, G.C., et al.: ML-schema: exposing the semantics of machine learning with schemas and ontologies. CoRR arXiv:1807.05351 (2018)
8. Esteves, D., et al.: MEX vocabulary: a lightweight interchange format for machine learning experiments. In: Proceedings of the 11th International Conference on Semantic Systems, SEMANTICS 2015, Vienna, Austria, 15–17 September 2015, pp. 169–176 (2015)
9. Pimentel, J.F., et al.: A large-scale study about quality and reproducibility of Jupyter notebooks. In: Proceedings of the 16th International Conference on Mining Software Repositories, USA, pp. 507–517 (2019)
10. Samuel, S., König-Ries, B.: ProvBook: provenance-based semantic enrichment of interactive notebooks for reproducibility. In: Proceedings of the ISWC: Posters & Demonstrations, Industry and Blue Sky Ideas Tracks Co-located with 17th International Semantic Web Conference (ISWC 2018), Monterey, USA, p. 2018 (2018)
11. Samuel, S., König-Ries, B.: ReproduceMeGit: a visualization tool for analyzing reproducibility of Jupyter notebooks. CoRR arXiv:2006.12110 (2020)

ProvViz: An Intuitive Prov Editor and Visualiser

Ben Werner$^{(\boxtimes)}$ ⓘ and Luc Moreau$^{(\boxtimes)}$ ⓘ

King's College London, London, UK
`luc.moreau@kcl.ac.uk`

Abstract. This proposed demonstration introduces *ProvViz* [9], an intuitive in-browser PROV editor and visualiser that targets both users familiar and unfamiliar with the syntax of PROV documents. The layout of the editor is composed of a text-editor and an interactive visualiser which is also released as a standalone UI component on the Node Package Manager (NPM) registry (https://npmjs.org/provviz).

Keywords: Provenance · Editor · Visualisation

1 Introduction

PROV [7] was standardised in 2013 and since then can demonstrate some high-profile and impactful deployments, as discussed in [4]. However, adoption still requires significant effort, in terms of creating provenance, storing provenance or analysing provenance. Thus, any tool that lowers the adoption threshold is welcomed. Our focus in this demonstration is on an editing and visualization tool, *ProvViz*, which does not require any software to be pre-installed by the user, and allows PROV documents to be constructed and explored in any of the serializations it supports.

This document outlines the related work and proposed demonstration, and concludes by discussing the significance and applications of the *ProvViz* system. A thorough report of the *ProvViz* design and implementation can be found in [9].

2 Background and Related Work

A variety of related work exists which aims to visualise data provenance.

Provenance Explorer [1] is a standalone Java-based desktop application that visualises RDF provenance data, with an emphasis on security features that produce a variety of views based on a user's access privileges. It focuses exclusively on provenance events associated with laboratories or manufacturing.

Supported by the Department of Informatics at King's College London. Luc Moreau was partially supported by the UK Engineering and Physical Sciences Research Council (EPRSC Grant EP/S027238/1) and the US Department of Navy award (N62909-18-1-2079) issued by the Office of Naval Research Global.

B. Glavic et al. (Eds.): IPAW 2020/IPAW 2021, LNCS 12839, pp. 231–236, 2021.
https://doi.org/10.1007/978-3-030-80960-7_18

Prov Viewer [3] is also a standalone Java-based desktop application, with the aim of enabling visual exploration of PROV documents. The application facilitates filtering nodes and edges, zooming and panning to navigate the graph, basic visualisation editing functionality, and merging multiple provenance graphs into a single visualisation. The GUI of the application presumes prior knowledge of the PROV ontology, and no modification functionality is implemented.

AVOCADO [8] is another visualisation tool which generates provenance visualisations based on data flows with the goal of assisting the reproducibility of bioinformatic workflows by allowing the user to introspect the provenance visually. It supports very large provenance graphs through clustering methods.

More general-purpose tools such as the *ProvToolBox* Java library [5] and the *prov* Python library [2] also implement provenance visualisation generation functionality, producing an SVG image for a corresponding PROV document.

In general, existing provenance visualisation tools focus on scientists as their target users because of the important role provenance plays in the scientific discovery process as a means of reproducing and peer-reviewing experimental procedures. None of the applications are directed towards beginners who may simply want to interact with existing PROV documents to learn more about the standard and how it can be used. Some of the applications are targeted towards specific domains (*Provenance Explorer* and *AVOCADO*), and most require downloading and installing software packages on a desktop computer before they can be used. The applications that support the PROV data model focus on provenance visualisation, and do not facilitate intuitive editing functionality relying on the user to manually modify the underlying PROV document if they wish to do so, hence requiring familiarity with PROV document syntax.

Table 1. Comparison between *ProvViz* and existing provenance visualisation systems

System	Requires Software Installation	Domain-Free	Intuitive Editing Functionality
Provenance Explorer [1]	Yes	No	No
Prov Viewer [3]	Yes	Yes	No
AVOCADO [8]	No	No	No
ProvViz	No	Yes	Yes

As illustrated by Table 1, what sets the *ProvViz* application apart from the related work is its aim to be an introductory tool for the PROV data model, providing an easy-to-use user interface that enables intuitive PROV editing and visualisation functionality without requiring the user to modify the PROV document directly. In addition usage of the *ProvViz* application does not require downloading or installing any software, and can be used for free at https://provviz.com.

3   Demonstration

The proposed demonstration serves as a walk-through of the primary functionality provided by the *Prov Viz* application. The following sections outline the
topics covered by the demonstration in order.

3.1   Loading a PROV Document

First the primary methods of loading a PROV document into the editor will be
demonstrated. This includes loading a previous or example document, uploading
a document, or creating a new empty document. Supported PROV document
formats include *PROV-N, PROV-JSON, TriG, PROV-XML* and *Turtle*. When
a PROV document is loaded, it is displayed in the *Prov Viz* editor view, which
is pictured in Fig. 1.

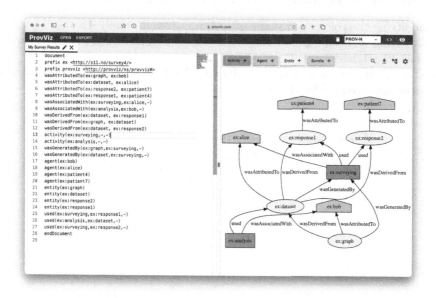

Fig. 1. *Prov Viz* editor view of an example PROV document

3.2   Modifying a PROV Document

The majority of the demonstration will consist of demonstrating the PROV editing functionality made available in the editor view of the *Prov Viz* application
(Fig. 1). The layout of the editor view is comprised of a text-editor and a visualiser component. The PROV document can be modified directly by interacting
with the text-editor. The visualiser component can be used to interact with the
visualisation (by panning, zooming, or selecting visualisation items), and make
PROV document modifications intuitively. Supported intuitive PROV editing
functionality includes:

- creating or removing *Entities*, *Activities*, *Agents*, *Bundles* and relationships,
- editing the global and *Bundle* specific namespace declarations,
- editing the identifier of an *Entity*, *Activity*, *Agent* or *Bundle*,
- editing the PROV attributes of an *Entity*, *Activity*, *Agent* or *Bundle*,
- moving *Entities*, *Activities* and *Agents* from one *Bundle* to another, and more.

The majority of editing functionality can be accessed by selecting an *Entity*, *Activity*, *Agent*, *Bundle* or relationship, which opens a tabbed inspector component that provides information and editing functionality related to the selected item. Figure 2 illustrates an example inspector tab of a selected *Entity*, where its identifier, attributes and outgoing relationships can be intuitively modified.

3.3 Visualising a PROV Document

Next the visualisation editing functionality will be demonstrated, which includes:

- modifying the colour and shape of *Entities*, *Activities* and *Agents*,
- displaying a specific provenance view (*Responsibility*, *Data Flow* or *Process Flow View*), and
- filtering the *Entities*, *Activities*, *Agents*, *Bundles*, relationships and namespaces displayed in the visualisation.

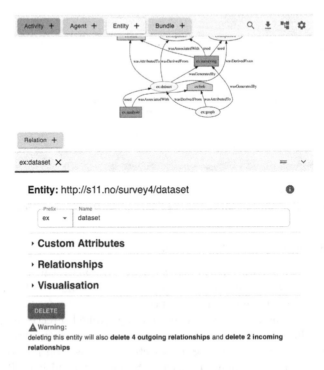

Fig. 2. *ProvViz* visualiser inspector tab for an *Entity*

3.4   Exporting the PROV Document and Visualisation

Finally, the functionality available for exporting the modified PROV document and visualisation will be demonstrated.

4   Discussion

The *ProvViz* application has the potential to fulfil a significant role in the PROV tooling ecosystem. It provides intuitive PROV editing and visualisation functionality well-suited for those already familiar with the PROV ontology as well as beginners, in a free-to-use browser-based application. Making PROV models more accessible in this way would not only promote the PROV data modelling standard, but data provenance as a whole.

The source code for the *ProvViz* web application is available in the GitHub repository https://github.com/benwerner01/provviz-web and is deployed as a live service at https://provviz.com. The source code for the visualiser UI component is available at https://github.com/benwerner01/provviz, where its latest release is published as an NPM package at https://npmjs.com/package/provviz. We welcome forks and contributions to this project.

There are opportunities to expand the functionality of *ProvViz* as follows. Edits of the layout could be allowed and saved as part of PROV documents, themselves. *ProvViz* could be extended to support the editing of provenance templates [6], with dedicated functionality related to templates, such as template variables and template control parameters. Cloud storage providers could be integrated into *ProvViz* as a further method of uploading and saving PROV documents.

References

1. Cheung, K., Hunter, J.: Provenance explorer – customized provenance views using semantic inferencing. In: Cruz, I., et al. (eds.) ISWC 2006. LNCS, vol. 4273, pp. 215–227. Springer, Heidelberg (2006). https://doi.org/10.1007/11926078_16
2. Huynh, D.: Prov Python Library. https://github.com/trungdong/prov
3. Kohwalter, T., Oliveira, T., Freire, J., Clua, E., Murta, L.: Prov viewer: a graph-based visualization tool for interactive exploration of provenance data. In: Mattoso, M., Glavic, B. (eds.) IPAW 2016. LNCS, vol. 9672, pp. 71–82. Springer, Cham (2016). https://doi.org/10.1007/978-3-319-40593-3_6
4. McAteer, L.: Impact evaluation of prov. a provenance standard published by the world wide web consortium. Technical report, Impact Science (2020). https://www.impact.science/wp-content/uploads/2020/08/Evaluation-of-Impact-of-PROV.pdf
5. Moreau, L.: ProvToolbox. http://lucmoreau.github.io/ProvToolbox/
6. Moreau, L., Batlajery, B.V., Huynh, T.D., Michaelides, D., Packer, H.: A templating system to generate provenance. IEEE Trans. Softw. Eng. (2017). https://doi.org/10.1109/TSE.2017.2659745
7. Moreau, L., et al. (eds.): PROV-DM: The PROV Data Model. W3C Recommendation REC-prov-dm-20130430, World Wide Web Consortium, April 2013. http://www.w3.org/TR/2013/REC-prov-dm-20130430/

8. Stitz, H., Luger, S., Streit, M., Gehlenborg, N.: AVOCADO: visualization of workflow-derived data provenance for reproducible biomedical research. Comput. Graph. Forum **35**, 481–490 (2016). https://doi.org/10.1111/cgf.12924
9. Werner, B., Moreau, L.: ProvViz: an intuitive PROV editor and visualiser. Technical report, April 2021. https://ben-werner.com/papers/provviz-an-intuitive-prov-editor-and-visualiser.pdf

Curating Covid-19 Data in Links

Vashti Galpin[1(✉)] and James Cheney[1,2]

[1] University of Edinburgh, Edinburgh, UK
{Vashti.Galpin,James.Cheney}@ed.ac.uk
[2] The Alan Turing Institute, London, UK

Abstract. Curated scientific databases play an important role in the scientific endeavour and support is needed for the significant effort that goes into their creation and maintenance. This demonstration and case study illustrate how curation support has been developed in the Links cross-tier programming language, a functional, strongly typed language with language-integrated query and support for temporal databases. The chosen case study uses weekly released Covid-19 fatality figures from the Scottish government which exhibit updates to previously released data. This data allows the capture and query of update provenance in our prototype. This demonstration will highlight the potential for language-integrated support for curation to simplify and streamline prototyping of web-applications in support of scientific databases.

1 Introduction

Curated scientific databases take significant human effort to develop and then to maintain [2]. These databases are crucial in providing knowledge bases for science to proceed and users of the data need to be able to trust in their contents. One way to support this trust is for users to be able to review provenance information.

We consider update provenance [2] as a specific use case, based on the fact that regularly released datasets can include updates to previously released datasets, and our case study is based on data that has been released weekly by the Scottish government on Covid-19 deaths [8].

We are developing a prototype curation interface using Links[1], a cross-tier programming language with language-integrated query that is being extended with experimental temporal database features [3].

Both the prototype and Links's temporal features are works-in-progress, and as we develop the interface, we are considering the more general issues that would apply to any curated scientific databases where update provenance is to be captured using temporal databases.

2 Links

Links is a cross-tier programming language developed at the University of Edinburgh [3]. It is *cross-tier* in the sense that it allows a developer to write a single

---

[1] https://links-lang.org/.

© Springer Nature Switzerland AG 2021
B. Glavic et al. (Eds.): IPAW 2020/IPAW 2021, LNCS 12839, pp. 237–243, 2021.
https://doi.org/10.1007/978-3-030-80960-7_19

type-checked program which that can then be executed efficiently on multi-tier Web architectures. Typically, a web application consists of three distinct applications coded in different languages: HTML and JavaScript for the browser, a different language for the application logic and SQL for the database queries, leading to complex coordinating issues. Links provides a single language in which to implement these three aspects, thus simplifying the development process. For our curation interface, the built-in translation to JavaScript completely abstracts away the details and there is no JavaScript code in the source Links program.

Furthermore, Links supports *language-integrated query* whereby database queries can be written in Links itself resulting in safe and efficient queries. In particular when writing database-related code, the support provided by type inference for row types in Links makes referring to the fields of interest in a table while abstracting from the others straightforward. This leads to compact and readable programming style. Links requires the types of the database tables to be declared explicitly in the program, which enables checking of language-integrated queries and supports the temporal query transformations. This adds some work at the beginning and if there is schema evolution, work is needed re-synchronize these declarations. Support for schema evolution in Links is a future area of research. Links currently supports PostgreSQL, MySQL 5.x and SQLite 3. Links covers a wide range of SQL but some aspects are ongoing research such as support for set and bag semantics [9].

In terms of use for curated scientific databases, IUPHAR/BPS Guide to PHARMACOLOGY (GtoPdb) [1] has been reimplemented in Links as a case study to demonstrate that Links is suitable for this task both in terms of functional correctness and performance [4]. However, because of its size and complexity, GtoPdb is not a good candidate for exploring the strengths and weaknesses of Links's new temporal support; instead in this demonstration we present the current Covid-19 curation prototype, which is the next step in developing curation functionality for this type of database in Links. We consider both the interface as the end product, and how the development of the interface is supporting by the features of Links.

3   Temporal Databases

Temporal databases provide the ability to record when a row in a table is valid, either with respect to the database itself using a transaction time period, or with respect to the real world using a valid time period [5]. We can use this functionality to track the validity of the data items that are updated. Figure 1 illustrates how an update differs between a standard database on the left, and a temporal database on the right. In the former, the data is replaced and the previous values are lost. However, in the temporal case, additional columns to record the start and end of the time period of validity form part of the key and allow previous values to be recorded. The interpretation of the validity is dependent on the particular application.

Although temporal extensions to SQL have been standardized [6], many current popular relational database implementations have no built-in support for

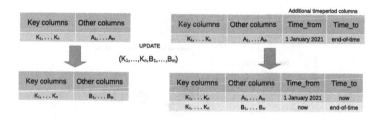

Fig. 1. Standard database update (left) compared with temporal database update (right)

temporality, although it is possible to implement temporal tables by the use of explicit additional fields and complex hand-generated SQL queries [10]. In comparison, Links now provides support for transaction-time tables and valid-time tables, allowing both sequenced (taking time period into account) and non-sequenced queries over these tables. This is achieved by interacting with a standard relational database such as PostgreSQL, using the approach currently provided by Links for generating standard queries and translating temporal queries into standard queries as described above [10], thereby avoided the need for the application developer to generate these complex SQL statements. An example is given in the next section.

4   Curation Functionality

To investigate how to develop curation functionality in Links, we choose a dataset that raised questions of interest around updating of data. To set the context for discussion of the type of queries that can be considered, we first provide more information about the data we used in implementing the prototype.

4.1   The Case Study

We identified data that was released weekly by the Scottish Government through the National Records of Scotland website [8], as suitable and interesting for the prototype exploration. Each week, since early in the pandemic a spreadsheet (as a CSV file and Excel document) has been released (amongst other data) with counts of Covid-19 fatalities for individual weeks and data categories including sex, age, health board, local authority, and location. An example of a data category is "Location of death" and its subcategories are "Care Home", "Home/Non-institution", "Hospital" and "Other institution". Our application supports upload of this CSV data and its transformation into a temporal table as illustrated in Fig. 2.

4.2   Provenance-Based Queries

One of the aims of this research is to identify the queries that are interesting for update provenance. An obvious query is how an individual data item has changed

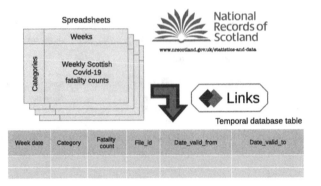

Fig. 2. Uploading new data

over time, but other potential queries include finding out whether one category of data has changed more often than another. Dependency is also relevant: are the changes of a data item associated or correlated with changes in other data.

Examples of queries that the interface can support (or will support in the future):

1. What was the number of female fatalities in the week of 20 April 2020 when that data was first uploaded
2. What is the current number of female fatalities in the week of 20 April 2020?
3. What is the range of female fatalities in the week of 20 April 2020 over all uploads?
4. Which updates to female fatalities were rejected and when?
5. Have there been more updates to female fatalities or male fatalities considering all weeks?
6. Which health board has seen most updates in the first six months of the pandemic?
7. How are updates for the Lothian health board figures correlated with those for the local authority of Edinburgh?

4.3   The Prototype Curation Interface

The interface has been developed using the Bootstrap HTML, CSS and JavaScript library. We present two screenshots illustrating the functionality of the prototype interface in Fig. 3. The left-hand figure shows updates for a specific week that have arisen in a subsequent week. By grouping them together, a user is able to assess the consistency of this update[2]. These updates can be accepted or rejected together, or each can be considered individually in the context of other updates to that data item.

---

[2] The dataset has the feature that it contains counts for categories that subsume other categories. We decided to capture all categories rather than just the minimal ones to support checking for inconsistencies.

Fig. 3. Screenshots: decision making (left) and provenance (right)

The following shows the Links code which updates the main table of fatalities from a table of accepted updates for counts relating to the Lothian health board.

```
for (x <-- AcceptedUpdates)
    [update sequenced (y <-v- CovidDeaths)
     between (valid_from_date,forever())
     where (x.week==y.week && x.category=="Lothian")
     set (count = x.new_value, file_id=x.new_id)]);
```

The double arrows, `<--` and `<-v-`, indicate iteration over the rows of the named tables, with `<-v-` indicated that the table is a temporal table. The keyword **sequenced** indicates that this update should result in the modification of one record and the insertion of a new record as illustrated in Fig. 1. To write this query in SQL for a non-temporal database would be more complex, requiring explicit updates and insertions.

The right-hand screenshot in Fig. 3 shows a provenance query on a single data item. For the updates on this data item, it is possible to see the updates in the context of other updates that occurred in the same week. Other provenance queries can be done on data categories (such as queries 5, 6 and 7 above), and a similar approach can be applied to weeks. The final menu item allows for queries such as query 4.

The prototype has taken around 120 h to develop to date, approximately 1 person month of effort by the first author, who was not previously familiar with Links. It consists of around 1800 lines of Links code, as well as supporting CSS and JavaScript code. Reuse of existing code will make the implementation of additional queries less time-consuming.

5   Conclusion

We have developed a prototype curation interface in Links to demonstrate and investigate curation functionality for a selected dataset with interesting features relating to data update. Links, as a cross-tier programming language, has provided a typed and functional language for implementing all of the appearance of the web interface (using the Bootstrap library), the logic of the interface and querying of the database.

By using Links, we have avoided the need to code temporal features in SQL for databases without temporal features, to transition to a database such as MariaDB [7] which has temporality, or to deal with the integration errors that occur during conventional web development using SQL.

Another option would be to use a temporal middleware/stratum translator that maps temporal SQL queries to plain ones [11]. This requires the same kind of information about the database schema that Links requires, but does not provide the advantages of language integration and type checking that we get from Links.

We have successfully created an interface that supports a number of queries and further work involves determining how to support the generation of a curation interface with an arbitrary database schema where selected tables have temporal features.

Acknowledgements. This work was supported by ERC Consolidator Grant Skye (grant number 682315) and by an ISCF Metrology Fellowship grant provided by the UK government's Department for Business, Energy and Industrial Strategy (BEIS). We thank Simon Fowler for his assistance in using the temporal extensions to Links.

References

1. Armstrong, J., et al.: The IUPHAR/BPS guide to PHARMACOLOGY in 2020: extending immunopharmacology content and introducing the IUPHAR/MMV Guide to MALARIA PHARMACOLOGY. Nucleic Acids Res. **48**, D1006–D1021 (2020)
2. Buneman, P., Cheney, J., Tan, W.-C., Vansummeren, S.: Curated databases. In: Proceedings of the Twenty-Seventh ACM SIGMOD-SIGACT-SIGART Symposium on Principles of Database Systems, PODS 2008, pp. 1–12 (2008)
3. Cooper, E., Lindley, S., Wadler, P., Yallop, J.: Links: web programming without tiers. In: de Boer, F.S., Bonsangue, M.M., Graf, S., de Roever, W.-P. (eds.) FMCO 2006. LNCS, vol. 4709, pp. 266–296. Springer, Heidelberg (2007). https://doi.org/10.1007/978-3-540-74792-5_12
4. Fowler, S., Harding, S., Sharman, J., Cheney, J.: Cross-tier web programming for curated databases: a case study. Int. J. Digital Curation **16** (2020)
5. Jensen, C., Snodgrass, R.: Temporal database. In: Liu, L., Özsu, M.T. (eds.) Encyclopedia of Database Systems. Springer, Boston (2009). https://doi.org/10.1007/978-0-387-39940-9_395
6. Kulkarni, K., Michels, J.: Temporal features in SQL: 2011. SIGMOD Rec. **41**(3), 34–43 (2012)
7. MariaDB: What's new in MariaDB Server 10.3 (2018). https://mariadb.com/resources/blog/whats-new-in-mariadb-server-10-3/. Accessed 23 Apr 2021

8. National Records of Scotland: Deaths involving coronavirus (COVID-19) in Scotland: archive (2021). https://www.nrscotland.gov.uk/statistics-and-data/statistics/statistics-by-theme/vital-events/general-publications/weekly-and-monthly-data-on-births-and-deaths/deaths-involving-coronavirus-covid-19-in-scotland/archive. Accessed 23 Apr 2021

9. Ricciotti, W., Cheney, J.: Query lifting. In: ESOP 2021. LNCS, vol. 12648, pp. 579–606. Springer, Cham (2021). https://doi.org/10.1007/978-3-030-72019-3_21

10. Snodgrass, R.: Developing Time-Oriented Database Applications in SQL. Morgan Kaufmann Publishers Inc., Burlington (1999)

11. Torp, K.: Temporal strata. In: Liu, L., Özsu, M.T. (eds.) Encyclopedia of Database Systems. Springer, Boston (2009). https://doi.org/10.1007/978-0-387-39940-9_409

Towards a Provenance Management System for Astronomical Observatories

Mathieu Servillat[1(✉)], François Bonnarel[2], Catherine Boisson[1],
Mireille Louys[2,3], Jose Enrique Ruiz[4], and Michèle Sanguillon[5]

[1] Laboratoire Univers et Théories, Observatoire de Paris, Université PSL, CNRS,
Université de Paris, 92190 Meudon, France
mathieu.servillat@obspm.fr

[2] Centre de Données astronomiques de Strasbourg, Observatoire Astronomique de
Strasbourg, Université de Strasbourg, CNRS-UMR 7550, Strasbourg, France

[3] ICube Laboratory, Université de Strasbourg, CNRS-UMR 7357, Strasbourg, France

[4] Instituto de Astrofísica de Andalucía, Granada, Spain

[5] Laboratoire Univers et Particules de Montpellier, Université de Montpellier,
CNRS/IN2P3, Montpellier, France

Abstract. We present here a provenance management system adapted
to astronomical projects needs. We collected use cases from various astronomy projects and defined a data model in the ecosystem developed by the
IVOA (International Virtual Observatory Alliance). From those use cases,
we observed that some projects already have data collections generated
and archived, from which the provenance has to be extracted (provenance
"on top"), and some projects are building complex pipelines that automatically capture provenance information during the data processing (capture
"inside"). Different tools and prototypes have been developed and tested
to capture, store, access and visualize the provenance information, which
participate to the shaping of a full provenance management system able
to handle detailed provenance information.

Keywords: Astronomy · Provenance · Virtual observatory

1 Context

Astronomical observatories and data providers are increasingly involved in the
development of Open Science. The process of making data FAIR[1] (Findable,
Accessible, Interoperable and Reusable) often has to be integrated early in the
development of astronomical projects. Since more than 20 years, the IVOA[2]
(International Virtual Observatory Alliance) provides various standards to foster
interoperability and enable the production of FAIR data.

The Reusable principle is more subjective and requires rich metadata to
demonstrate the quality, reliability and trustworthiness of the data. Detailed

---

[1] https://www.go-fair.org/fair-principles.

[2] https://www.ivoa.net.

B. Glavic et al. (Eds.): IPAW 2020/IPAW 2021, LNCS 12839, pp. 244–249, 2021.
https://doi.org/10.1007/978-3-030-80960-7_20

provenance is thus a key information to provide along with the astronomical data. The IVOA validated in April 2020 a Provenance Data Model [9] to structure this information. It is based on the W3C PROV concepts of Entity, Activity and Agent [4] with a dedicated set of classes for activity description (e.g. method, algorithm, software) and activity configuration (e.g. parameters).

2   Requirements and Current Perception of Provenance

Several use cases have been discussed within the IVOA and the European ESCAPE project [8]. Astronomical projects that produce data generally develop structured pipelines, scripts and specific methodologies to prepare data products for the end-user from raw data (acquired from observations or generated by simulation).

Key information on what processes were applied and how they were performed is thus relevant to the end-user and could be captured directly during the process (capture "inside"). For older or other projects, a posteriori metadata extraction from data/metadata/logs (provenance "on top") can also provide similar information, with the risk of missing details and links. We often realize too late that there are missing elements or links in the provenance, this is why the capture of the provenance should be as detailed as possible and as naive as possible (simply record what happens). In any case, the granularity of the provenance has to be adapted from one project to another.

2.1   Basic Handling of Provenance

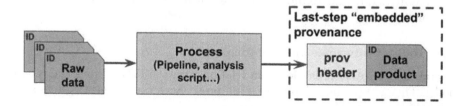

Fig. 1. Basic handling of provenance information.

In general, the perception in the community is that provenance information is easily stored with the data, as a set of keywords recorded in the header of a data product file. This is represented in Fig. 1. This perception is particularly strong in astronomy with the large adoption of the FITS (Flexible Image Transport System) file format [10], that provides a human readable header based on keywords.

2.2 Last-Step Provenance

The complex modeling of provenance information makes it improper to be stored as a flat list of keywords, as provenance is better represented by a graph, based on chains of activities and entities that are used and generated. We thus define the full provenance as this graph, up to the raw data, and the last-step minimum provenance as an embedded list of keywords [8]. The last-step provenance contains information on: the entity itself, one contact agent, the last activity that generated this entity. It also contains identifiers of other used and generated entities. All this information is compatible with the IVOA Provenance data model. Such a last-step provenance can thus be stored in a file header, and should moreover enable the reconstruction of the full provenance through the recursive exploration of used entities.

3 A Provenance Management System

If a basic handling of provenance information may be sufficient for some projects, it is necessary to build a more advanced provenance management system that stores this information separately, as files or in a database. Such a system is composed of the following parts:

1/ **Capture "inside"**: provenance information is recorded during the execution of a pipeline that runs various processing steps, generates intermediate data files...
2/ **Ingestion**: the captured information is transported in a structured format that can be parsed and managed.
3/ **Storage**: the ingested information is then safely stored in a database that preserves its logic.
4/ **Visualization and exploration**: the full provenance can be queried and visualized.

3.1 Tools, Prototypes and Protocols

Several tools have been developed in relation with the IVOA Provenance data model. They are the bricks to build a full provenance management system able to handle detailed provenance information:

– voprov[3]: This Python package extends the W3C PROV compatible prov package to implement the IVOA Provenance data model. It provides a way to create a ProvDocument object and exchange it as an XML, JSON or graphical file.
– logprov[4]: This Python package captures provenance events when running Python functions or methods that are specifically decorated and defined. Those events are recorded through the logging system as structured dictionaries, and can then be transformed using voprov. This package was initially developed with the high level interface of the gammapy package [3].

---

[3] https://github.com/sanguillon/voprov.
[4] https://github.com/mservillat/logprov.

- **ProvSAP**: a Simple Access Protocol that returns a W3C PROV file from a regular GET query on an HTTP endpoint. Arguments can be passed, such as: ID, DEPTH (ALL/1...), DIRECTION (FORWARD/BACKWARD), RESPONSEFORMAT (PROV-SVG/PROV-JSON...), MODEL (IVOA/ W3C), AGENTS (0/1), CONFIGURATION (0/1), DESCRIPTIONS (0/1/2), ATTRIBUTES (0/1). This system if for example implemented in the OPUS job manager[5] [7] and in other tools [5].
- **ProvTAP**: IVOA Table Access Protocol using ADQL for queries and a TAP Schema, itself based on the IVOA Provenance data model [1]. It's a reverse mechanism to locate data through queries on its provenance. Every feature of the model instantiated in the TAP service can then be explored. This approach enables queries to test the data quality, based on the analysis of parameters of some key activities. It is also possible to recompute datasets whose progenitors have been found erroneous.

3.2   Description of the System

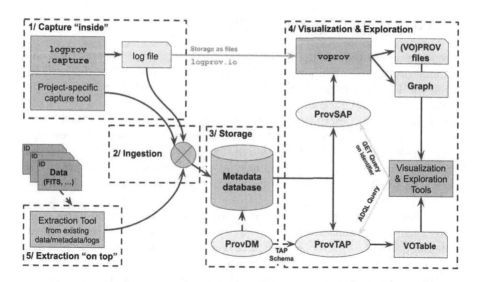

Fig. 2. Provenance management system.

As shown in Fig. 2, the IVOA Provenance Data Model (ProvDM) is implemented as a relational database and connected to an access service based on the IVOA Table Access Protocol (ProvTAP) [1]. A Simple Access Protocol (ProvSAP) is also being specified within the IVOA to provide directly W3C PROV files, using the voprov package.

In the system, provenance information is exchanged via structured logs, W3C PROV files (XML, JSON) or graphs (SVG, PNG). The voprov and logprov

---

[5] https://voparis-uws-test.obspm.fr/provsap?ID=a9b7e2.

packages are being developed to propose a generic solution to the implementation of the system, along with project-specific capture tools (e.g. `ctapipe`[6] or CTADIRAC[7] in the context of the Cherenkov Telescope Array [6]). The Visualization & Exploration subsystem is based on standards to foster interoperability and the reuse of existing tools.

Different implementations based on this schema are possible to adapt the provenance management to the needs and size of the project.

3.3 Extraction "On Top"

A last block in Fig. 2 (labelled 5/) indicates the use case of already existing data from which provenance can be extracted and ingested in the system. In many astronomy projects, some provenance information can be extracted from file headers, or from log files. Such an extraction would be more efficient if embedded provenance information were stored in a standard list of keywords such as the last-step provenance list (see Sect. 2.2).

4 Software and Reproducibility

Depending on the project, the workflow executed to produce science ready data (the final products) can be extracted from the provenance system designed following the IVOA strategy. For each activity execution, the input and output entities and the configuration parameters are recorded, as well as a representation of the ActivityDescription class, where the software name, version, documentation, etc., are traced. To be fully reproducible, we envisage to access such coding blocks through the ActivityDescription class by pointing to a code repository. This can be set up as a dictionary of codes within a specific project, as in the CTA pipeline or other under development projects such as Euclid, LSST, etc.

Software can also be shared within the community and curated in code registries, such as the Software Heritage [2], or the astronomy dedicated software published in ASCL[8] (Astrophysics Source Code Library), or for multi-messenger astronomy, the future ESCAPE OSSR project[9].

Many astronomical projects deal with large amounts of data and require increasing computation power. This has pushed forward the development of science platforms that implement the code-to-the-data strategy. In this new computing and distributing architecture, rich metadata profiles to describe the provenance of datasets and the code applied to process them, is a key for reproducibility and interoperability.

---

[6] https://cta-observatory.github.io/ctapipe.
[7] https://gitlab.cta-observatory.org/cta-computing/dpps/CTADIRAC.
[8] http://ascl.net.
[9] https://wiki.escape2020.de/index.php/WP3_-_OSSR.

Acknowledgements. We acknowledge support from the ESCAPE project funded by the EU Horizon 2020 research and innovation program (Grant Agreement n824064). Additional funding was provided by the INSU (Action Spécifique Observatoire Virtuel, ASOV), the Action Fédératrice CTA at the Observatoire de Paris and the Paris Astronomical Data Centre (PADC).

References

1. Bonnarel, F., Louys, M., Mantelet, G., Nullmeier, M., Servillat, M., Riebe, K., Sanguillon, M.: ProvTAP: a TAP service for providing IVOA provenance metadata. In: Teuben, P.J., Pound, M.W., Thomas, B.A., Warner, E.M. (eds.) ADASS XXVII. ASP Conference Series, vol. 523, p. 313 (2019)
2. Di Cosmo, R., Zacchiroli, S.: Software heritage: why and how to preserve software source code. In: iPRES 2017: 14th International Conference on Digital Preservation. Kyoto, Japan (2017). https://hal.archives-ouvertes.fr/hal-01590958
3. Lefaucheur, J., Deil, C., Donath, A., Jouvin, L., Khélifi, B., King, J.: Gammapy - an Open-source Python Package for γ-Ray Astronomy. In: Ballester, P., Ibsen, J., Solar, M., Shortridge, K. (eds.) ADASS XXVII. ASP Conference Series, vol. 522, p. 525 (2020)
4. Moreau, L., et al.: PROV-DM: The prov data model. W3C Recommendation (2013). http://www.w3.org/TR/prov-dm
5. Sanguillon, M., Bonnarel, F., Louys, M., Nullmeier, M., Riebe, K., Servillat, M.: Provenance tools for astronomy. In: Ballester, P., Ibsen, J., Solar, M., Shortridge, K. (eds.) ADASS XXVII. ASP Conference Series, vol. 522, p. 545 (2020). https://arxiv.org/abs/1812.00878
6. Sanguillon, M., Arrabito, L., Boisson, C., Bregeon, J., Kosack, K., Servillat, M.: Storing Provenance information in a data processing workflow: one CTA use case. In: Ruiz, J.E., Pierfederici, F. (eds.) ADASS XXX. ASP Conference Series, vol. TBD, p. TBD (2021)
7. Servillat, M., Aicardi, S., Cecconi, B., Mancini, M.: OPUS: an interoperable job control system based on VO standards. In: Ruiz, J.E., Pierfederici, F. (eds.) ADASS XXX. ASP Conference Series, vol. TBD, p. TBD (2021). https://arxiv.org/abs/2101.08683
8. Servillat, M., Bonnarel, F., Louys, M., Sanguillon, M.: Practical provenance in astronomy. In: Ruiz, J.E., Pierfederici, F. (eds.) ADASS XXX. ASP Conference Series, vol. TBD, p. TBD (2021). https://arxiv.org/abs/2101.08691
9. Servillat, M., et al.: IVOA Provenance Data Model Version 1.0. IVOA Recommendation, April 2020. https://www.ivoa.net/documents/ProvenanceDM
10. Wells, D.C., Greisen, E.W., Harten, R.H.: FITS - a flexible image transport system. A&AS **44**, 363 (1981)

Towards Provenance Integration for Field Devices in Industrial IoT Systems

Iori Mizutani[1]([⊠])[iD], Jonas Brütsch[2][iD], and Simon Mayer[1][iD]

[1] University of St.Gallen, St.Gallen, Switzerland
{iori.mizutani,simon.mayer}@unisg.ch
[2] ETH Zürich, Zürich, Switzerland
brujonas@ethz.ch
https://interactions.ics.unisg.ch/

Abstract. Industrial Internet of Things (IoT) systems are becoming increasingly complex with interconnected field devices. To cope with the complexity and to facilitate further interoperability between heterogeneous field devices, it is necessary to have a holistic understanding of different types of provenance information about field devices and associated processes. In this paper, we investigate the potential integration of such provenance with the W3C Web of Things and current industrial standards to realize more explainable, efficient, and safer industrial IoT systems.

Keywords: Web of Things · Industrial IoT · OPC UA · Thing description · Semantic web · Provenance

1 Introduction

The Internet of Things (IoT) is a key enabler for the integration of control and automation processes in a wide variety of industrial sectors adding flexibility, robustness, and responsiveness to industrial automation systems [7]. A principle called "separation of concerns" draws the boundary between the information technology (IT) and the operational technology (OT) allowing functional modularity by isolating responsibility. However, with increased connectivity among heterogeneous field devices and software components in complex (industrial) IoT systems, convergence of IT and OT is required to orchestrate the whole automation execution. For instance, to examine to what extent a particular manufacturing process increases the degradation of a field device and its maintenance cost, a factory manager would need the following provenance information: *Where is the yield report for the process located?*; *What control logic was used?*; *Which field devices are involved?*; and *What is the context of these devices, and how do they relate to one another on the shop floor?*. Since these questions stretch across different levels of abstraction and also conflate IT and OT concerns, it is necessary to have a holistic understanding of industrial IoT systems, which, importantly, includes different types of provenance information about field devices and associated processes in the automation system.

© Springer Nature Switzerland AG 2021
B. Glavic et al. (Eds.): IPAW 2020/IPAW 2021, LNCS 12839, pp. 250–255, 2021.
https://doi.org/10.1007/978-3-030-80960-7_21

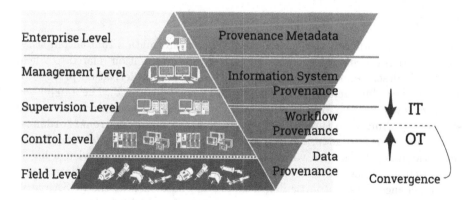

Fig. 1. Relationship between the types of provenance proposed in [3] with the layers of the automation pyramid.

In Fig. 1, we show the well-known ISA-95 automation pyramid [1] for industrial automation systems, where the upper three layers are dominated by IT concerns and the lower two are dominated by OT concerns. We observe that different types of provenance are generated on different layers of the automation pyramid, and propose a mapping of these layers to the provenance types proposed by [3]. Based on this observation, we propose to integrate provenance information across the automation pyramid by linking it to current research and standardization efforts in the Web of Things (WoT) domain. Concretely, we claim that the W3C WoT Architecture [6] is useful to overcome this separation with its platform-neutral environment to integrate cross-vendor and cross-domain IoT applications. In the W3C WoT Architecture, descriptive metadata for IoT devices and services is serialized into machine-understandable Thing Descriptions (TDs) [5] that allow clients to interact with heterogeneous thing-provided services by providing metadata about interactions, including protocol bindings, based on a vocabulary.

2   Provenance and Field Devices

In the following, we address four types of provenance information that are defined in [3] and adapt these for field devices based on the W3C WoT Architecture: (*i.*) provenance metadata (metadata describing an arbitrary derivation process for provenance information), (*ii.*) information system provenance (information pipeline that enables capturing and dissemination of information in the IT layers), (*iii.*) workflow provenance (provenance about the workflow in the OT layers), and (*iv.*) data provenance (provenance information of events to/from field devices).

2.1 Provenance Metadata

Provenance metadata is the most general type of information that encompasses the derivation process for any possible provenance information related to a field device. To describe an arbitrary provenance information derivation process for a field device, *Interaction Affordances* of TD can be utilized. The *Interaction Affordances* suggests a WoT client how it can interact with event, function, and state of the thing with three sub-types: `EventAffordance`, `ActionAffordance`, and `PropertyAffordance`, respectively. The TD context can be extended with semantic annotations with vocabularies defined in industrial knowledge bases, and a rich set of Semantic Web tooling allows to adapt an arbitrary data model for provenance data. In particular, a knowledge base such as the SOSA ontology [4] can be used to align the data provenance from field devices with other ontologies (e.g., W3C PROV-O), and to elicit implicitly hidden domain knowledge on the provenance information derived from field devices, which can then be shared among industrial IoT applications at different layers. Meanwhile, computing such provenance in a real-time context requires a seamless information exchange between field devices and applications.

2.2 Information System Provenance

Information system provenance refers to metadata about information-disseminating processes within an information system, and such provenance usually belongs to the IT layer. As described in Fig. 1, such information-disseminating processes can be observed between different levels in industrial automation systems. For example, a Supervisory Control and Data Acquisition (SCADA) system at the supervision level monitors and aggregates the information collected from the control level underneath. The SCADA system then exchanges the information with a Manufacturing Execution System (MES) at the management level to provision the underlying automation systems and also to coordinate the manufacturing process with the business planning, such as an alignment with the demanded Key Performance Indicator (KPI). To facilitate the information exchange in industrial IoT systems, the Open Platform Communications (OPC) foundation defines the OPC Unified Architecture (OPC UA) specification [8] as a communication framework for automation components.

OPC UA is used for an information system to aggregate complex information as `Objects` in an address space which can be accessed with defined OPC UA Services [9] . The interactions between the OPC UA Services could be exploited for constructing the information system provenance by collecting inputs, outputs, and configurations of the services. However, the OPC UA Service definitions are abstract descriptions and do not represent a specification for implementation. This opaqueness of the OPC UA Services makes it difficult to investigate internal information processing, which may degrade the quality of the information system provenance. In other words, the information system provenance can be observed within the OPC UA silo, but transitive provenance discovery into the OPC UA

Services may be blocked. Consequently, this would decrease the transparency during the information disseminating process capturing.

To improve the transparency, we need to describe and expose the internal logic of the OPC UA Services for external IoT applications, such as a WoT client. Nevertheless, whether or not this can be achieved depends on how the service is actually implemented, i.e., in what programming language, in what framework, and on what platform. Hence, the investigation of the OPC UA Service implementation is required while further specification may be desirable.

2.3 Workflow Provenance

Whereas the information system provenance resides mostly in the IT layers, workflow provenance predominantly involves information in the OT layers. For the development, operation, and maintenance of an automation system, field devices are usually first configured "offline" and the logical configurations will be validated against their physical representative in a real deployment, such as their form factors and (spatial) locations. These properties are individual to each instance of field devices and are essential for the field-level elucidation in tracing the physical source of data, e.g., where and how a device is installed including the physical wiring topology and spatial constraints. Such descriptions are referred to as *offline engineering information*, and they are often represented in various data formats, e.g., Computer-aided Design (CAD) models, electrical and mechanical planning, Programmable Logic Controller (PLC) programming, and models of the human-machine interface. These formats and information models are defined and maintained by a number of vendors and domain standardization groups[1], and the OPC UA Companion Standards extend the OPC UA Device Information Model (DI) [10] for enhanced interoperability among different industrial domains.

Once the offline engineering is completed, field devices establish communications with other automation components in the system. The OPC Field Level Communication (FLC) initiative[2] has been recently established to standardize the semantics and behaviors of field devices and controllers from different manufacturers. The OPC FLC is planning to extend the existing DI model for the management of different types of communication modes (e.g., Client/Server, PubSub) conforming within the required QoS. However, since it is extending the DI model, that information also needs to be accessed through the OPC UA Services. To semantify the field level communications for workflow provenance, the TD can also be extended to the future FLC specification. In the WoT architecture, Protocol Bindings define the mapping between affordance and concrete protocol message. Although, only an HTTP binding is currently standardized [5], further development is expected to support field level industrial protocols such as OPC UA and NETCONF for Time-Sensitive Networking (TSN) [13].

---

[1] https://opcfoundation.org/markets-collaboration/.
[2] https://opcfoundation.org/flc/.

For example, the control logic (e.g., machining of a metal rod by a turning machine) is written as a program inside the PLC, and can be described in Automation Markup Language[3] with the companion specification for the OPC UA object model , and an OPC client application is able to query the control logic as workflow provenance. The engineering of the control logic can also be translated into a formalism (e.g., a UML state machine). This formalism then can be represented by Semantic Web technology, such as Web Ontology Language (OWL), and reasoning on the ontology realizes automated formal verification of the control logic for safety and reliability of the system [12]. In the verification process, the TD for field devices can be treated as an entity in the OWL ontology. Therefore, integration of the OPC DI model and the TD would enhance the interoperability between field level automation components (i.e., field devices) in the OT layers and the industrial IoT applications in the IT layers.

2.4   Data Provenance

In order to complete a specific task, a controller may provide commands and set point information to a field device, which then reports feedback after completion, or even coordinates further activities with other devices. Current industry trends expect more and more field devices to provide a rich set of information, and IT layer applications to extract and derive meaning from the data directly, without needing to go through the controllers.

From the viewpoint of the shop floor, every field device is a functional entity that consumes input data and produces output data. Instances of such data inputs and outputs are handled as events in industrial IoT systems. These events to/from field devices represent specific transient occurrences, such as device configuration changes, operational instructions, or individual sensor readings. They can also be instantiated as `Object` instances in OPC UA with the OPC UA DI model. A separate specification called Historical Data Access provides access to the historical values in `Object` instances, and allows the user to query the data within a specified time range. However, in a practical scenario, it is more convenient to store and access these data in a well-known storage, but this also requires translation of (tabular) data from databases into meaningful object-property forms in OPC UA [2].

To facilitate access to such events to/from field devices for the industrial IoT applications (including those non-compliant with OPC UA), we propose that `EventAffordances` of the W3C WoT TD could be utilized to capture the events in the OPC UA systems, and to allow WoT clients to directly interact with data stores that are external to the OPC UA. The TD would also allow subscription to events and retrieval of data for Web-based IoT applications while maintaining compatibility with the DI model, using a formal mapping between OPC UA and the Semantic Web [11], for example.

---

[3] https://www.automationml.org/.

3   Conclusion and Outlook

Concepts from research on the Web of Things and from current standardization efforts within the W3C Web of Things have the potential to support the integration of provenance information across different layers of industrial IoT systems. Such integration would promote the convergence of IT and OT so that we can create more intelligent industrial IoT applications, which are not restricted by the IT/OT boundary. We believe that an important step is the semantic interoperability for existing technologies and standards in the industrial IoT. With respect to the integration of provenance information, this has the potential to make complex industrial IoT systems more explainable, efficient, and also safer.

References

1. ANSI: ANSI/ISA 95.00.01-2010 (IEC 62264–1 Mod). Standard, ANSI, May 2010
2. El Kaed, C., Ponnouradjane, A.: A model driven approach accelerating ontology-based IoT applications development. In: SEMANTICS Workshops (2017)
3. Herschel, M., Diestelkämper, R., Ben Lahmar, H.: A survey on provenance: what for? what form? what from? VLDB J. **26**(6), 881–906 (2017). https://doi.org/10.1007/s00778-017-0486-1
4. Janowicz, K., Haller, A., Cox, S.J., Le Phuoc, D., Lefrançois, M.: SOSA: a lightweight ontology for sensors, observations, samples, and actuators. J. Web Semant. **56**, 1–10 (2019). https://doi.org/10.1016/j.websem.2018.06.003
5. Kamiya, T., McCool, M., Käbisch, S., Kovatsch, M., Charpenay, V.: Web of Things (WoT) Thing Description. Recommendation, W3C, April 2020. https://www.w3.org/TR/2020/REC-wot-thing-description-20200409/
6. Kovatsch, M., Matsukura, R., Lagally, M., Kawaguchi, T., Toumura, K., Kajimoto, K.: Web of Things (WoT) Architecture. Recommendation, W3C (2020). https://www.w3.org/TR/wot-architecture/
7. Lee, J., Bagheri, B., Kao, H.A.: A cyber-physical systems architecture for industry 4.0-based manufacturing systems. Manufact. Lett. **3**, 18–23 (2015). https://doi.org/10.1016/j.mfglet.2014.12.001
8. OPC Foundation: OPC 10000–1: OPC Unified Architecture - Part 1: Overview and Concepts. Specification, OPC Foundation (2017)
9. OPC Foundation: OPC 10000–4: OPC Unified Architecture - Part 4: Services. Specification, OPC Foundation (2017)
10. OPC Foundation: OPC 10000–100 - Part 100: Device Information Model. Specification, OPC Foundation (2021)
11. Schiekofer, R., Grimm, S., Brandt, M.M., Weyrich, M.: A formal mapping between OPC UA and the semantic web. In: 2019 IEEE 17th International Conference on Industrial Informatics (INDIN), vol. 1, pp. 33–40 (2019). https://doi.org/10.1109/INDIN41052.2019.8972102
12. Schneider, G.F., Wicaksono, H., Ovtcharova, J.: Virtual engineering of cyber-physical automation systems: the case of control logic. Adv. Eng. Inform. **39**, 127–143 (2019). https://doi.org/10.1016/j.aei.2018.11.009
13. Sciullo, L., Bhattacharjee, S., Kovatsch, M.: Bringing deterministic industrial networking to the W3C web of things with TSN and OPC UA. In: Proceedings of the 10th International Conference on the Internet of Things. pp. 1–8 (2020). https://doi.org/10.1145/3410992.3410997

COVID-19 Analytics in Jupyter: Intuitive Provenance Integration Using *ProvIt*

Martin Chapman$^{(\boxtimes)}$, Elliot Fairweather, Asfand Khan, and Vasa Curcin

King's College London, London, UK
`martin.chapman@kcl.ac.uk`

Abstract. Whilst the need to record and understand the evolution of data, together with the processes and users associated with those changes, is now widely appreciated, the uptake of solutions to these issues remains slow. Data provenance techniques have the potential to provide such an understanding, but their use is often considered a specialist activity, requiring detailed knowledge of standards such as W3C PROV. In this work, we introduce *ProvIt*, a suite of tools designed to lower the barriers to entry for the use of provenance technology. We demonstrate the utility of ProvIt by using it to add provenance capabilities to the Jupyter IDE, in order to provide insight into the tools used by a group of researchers analysing a COVID-19 dataset.

Keywords: Software toolkit · COVID-19 · Data analytics

1 Introduction

It is often desirable to record the impact of user interactions on the data in a system for future analysis. However, traditional logging tools, which typically operate at a conceptually low level, are not well suited to capturing this information. Instead, *data provenance*, which is able to capture richer information, must often be looked to. Despite its utility, the use of data provenance is often considered a specialist task, which includes formalising the underlying representation (such as a provenance *template* [1]), extracting relevant provenance information from a system in order to populate these representations, and querying the data collected to understand prior actions.

To make the use of data provenance more intuitive, we introduce *ProvIt*, a set of tools that allow provenance capabilities to be added to an existing software system, without requiring developers to have prior experience of the field. ProvIt consists of the following components: a graphical authoring tool for the visual construction of provenance templates; a set of client libraries to support the extraction and storage of relevant provenance data; and a server-based query template system allowing for questions to be asked of the stored provenance data in an intuitive, high-level way.

© Springer Nature Switzerland AG 2021
B. Glavic et al. (Eds.): IPAW 2020/IPAW 2021, LNCS 12839, pp. 256–262, 2021.
https://doi.org/10.1007/978-3-030-80960-7_22

2   ProvIt

To introduce and demonstrate the utility of ProvIt, in the following sections we detail how it can be used to add provenance capabilities to *Jupyter*. Jupyter is a web-based IDE, where code, and associated plaintext, is organised into individual *notebooks*, and further segmented into a number of different *cells*, each of which can be executed in a REPL-like manner, using one of a number of underlying kernels (e.g. Python)[1]. *JupyterHub* is a version of the IDE with multi-user access. Jupyter(Hub) is often used by groups of researchers to work with data science tools in order to derive results for publication. Therefore, in order for individual research methodologies to be reproducible, the use of these tools must be suitably recorded. As such, Jupyter is a common test bed for different provenance tools (e.g. [5]). Once provenance capabilities are added to Jupyter, we validate ProvIt by showing how it enables the tools used by a set of researchers analysing a COVID-19 patient dataset to be effectively captured.

2.1   Provenance Authoring Webapp

To specify which provenance data is to be captured from within Jupyter, we construct a set of provenance templates using the first component of ProvIt, a graphical provenance authoring webapp (PAW).

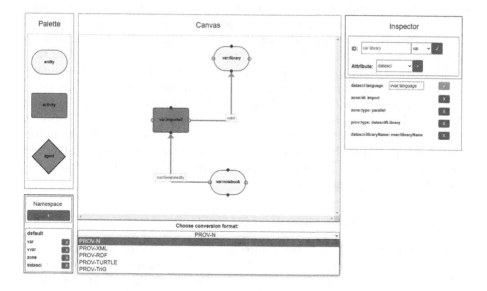

Fig. 1. Import template constructed with PAW

---

[1] https://jupyter.org.

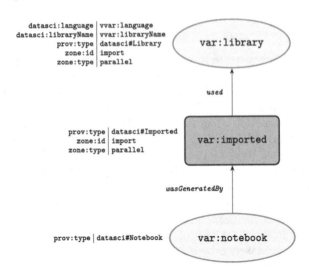

Fig. 2. Completed import template

PAW allows users to draw provenance documents as graphs, by dragging and dropping elements and relations, and then entering annotations. It has a mode that presents the attributes commonly used when defining templates, and supports multiple output formats. The user interface of the webapp is written in JavaScript, using the JointJS framework. The backend is written in Java and uses ProvToolbox to provide format interoperability. PAW does not require knowledge of a particular PROV syntax, and lets users define templates as they would with pen and paper, allowing more complex designs to be expressed more quickly, more easily and with fewer mistakes. The ability to prototype and iteratively develop templates in this fashion is a core feature of ProvIt, as it provides a way for the non-specialist to generate formal descriptions of domain-specific actions of interest to be recorded, and so enhance the usefulness of the provenance trace produced. Figure 1 shows one of our templates under construction that represents a user importing a software library into their notebook. The completed template is shown in Fig. 2.

2.2 Template Service Clients

To extract provenance data from Jupyter, we use the second component of ProvIt, a template service *client*. ProvIt provides clients spanning a number of different languages, and in this instance we select the Python client. The client allows users to associate each variable in a template with one or more regular expressions, each of which is used by the client to derive identifier and data values from system outputs – in this case the content of a Jupyter notebook whenever it is saved or one of its cells is executed. Each expression is associated with an *action* and a *parameter*, which define how the client should derive the required values once the expression is matched. For example, to extract the name of a library imported into a notebook for the import template (`vvar:libraryName`, Fig. 2), we supply the first two expressions shown in Table 1 to process Python and R notebooks, respectively. Each of these expressions is associated with an *extract* action, indicating to the client that once the expression is matched, it should extract the value present in the numbered capture group identified by the stored parameter (3 and 2, respectively) in order to identify the library name. Similarly, to identify the language used by a given notebook for the import template (`vvar:language`, Fig. 2), we supply the second two expressions shown in Table 1. This time, each of these expressions is associated with a *text* action, indicating to the client that once the expression is matched, the library language is the stored parameter itself (*Python* and *R*, respectively).

Table 1. Regular expressions used to determine values for template substitutions

Variable	Expression	Action	Parameter
LibraryName	`(from\s(\S)\s)?import\s([^\s#\\,]+)+`	Extract	3
LibraryName	`library\((’|")?([^\s,’"\)]+)`	Extract	2
Language	`(from\s(\S)\s)?import\s([^\s#\\,]+)+`	Text	Python
Language	`library\((’|")?([^\s,’"\)]+)`	Text	R

Once each variable is associated with a value, the client automatically creates a substitution from these values, by inferring information from the template to which they relate, such as whether an element relates to an *identifier* or a *value* variable, and whether a variable appears within an iterable template *zone*. For each substitution that is constructed, the client creates a git commit in a local repository containing the system output it received (the notebook content). This is then referenced in the substitution, in a fashion akin to [2].

2.3   Query Templates

Once a substitution is constructed, it is forwarded by the client to the template service application (TSA) originally described in [3]. The application stores both provenance templates, and the provenance documents generated from submitted substitutions, in one of several interchangeable persistence backends (e.g. Neo4j[2]). The TSA exposes a message-queueing interface which, using a message broker (RabbitMQ[3]), ensures that the collection of provenance data does not impact the runtime of the target system, in this case Jupyter, even under high request load.

The TSA is presented as a part of ProvIt with the addition of *query template* support, which allows users to express queries using the same syntax as

---

[2] https://neo4j.com.
[3] https://www.rabbitmq.com.

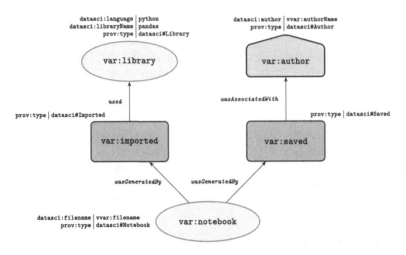

Fig. 3. Example query template

a standard, capture template. Query templates are used to find matching sub-graphs within provenance documents and return the corresponding instantiating substitutions for identifiers and values of interest. Figure 3 shows such a template, which expresses a query that returns the names of users who imported the Python *pandas* library, together with the name of the notebook containing that import. This approach allows users to analyse the captured provenance data without requiring knowledge of the underlying storage backend.

3   COVID-19 Analytics

To confirm that ProvIt enables provenance data to be effectively captured, we used the provenance-enabled Jupyter IDE[4] to capture data relating to the notebooks produced by a team of 10 researchers analysing a COVID-19 dataset between April 2020 and February 2021 at King's College London. The dataset consisted of 1468 patients who tested positive at Guy's and St. Thomas' NHS Foundation Trust (GSTT). In total, 923 substitutions were constructed based on changes in notebook state, with an example capturing library import information shown in Fig. 4.

Figure 4 shows the state of two separate Jupyter notebooks, *InitialExploration* and *DescriptionStatistics*. Each of these notebooks is associated with a *save* activity, connecting the notebook with an author (*Author1* and *Author2*, respectively) and a commit, as well as an *import* activity, which identifies the libraries imported by each notebook within this snapshot. Here, we can see several examples of key (queryable) reproducibility information captured. For example, we can see the software tools imported, who they were imported by

---

[4] https://github.com/kclhi/jupyter.

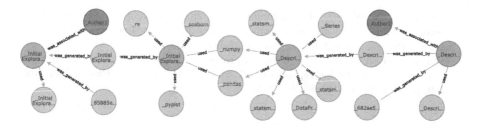

Fig. 4. Tools used by researchers against the COVID dataset

and, when this substitution is combined with others, the order in which they were imported. We can also see common libraries (*numpy* and *pandas*), connecting the actions of different authors.

4 Conclusion

In this work we introduce ProvIt, a set of tools that enable provenance capabilities to be added to a system by non-specialists. To demonstrate ProvIt, we use it to add provenance capabilities to the Jupyter IDE. Using our provenance authoring webapp (PAW), we graphically construct a set of templates that represent data of interest in Jupyter. We then supply a set of regular expressions to our template service client, to enable it to extract values from Jupyter's outputs and construct substitutions for each template. These substitutions are then stored in our template service application (TSA), which facilitates intuitive queries via the use of query templates. To validate the provenance capabilities added to Jupyter by Provit, we use it to capture key reproducibility information relating to the actions of a group of researchers analysing a COVID-19 dataset.

Future work will further validate ProvIt by using it to add provenance capabilities to different systems. In particular, we will focus on those scenarios (such as the use of clinical decision support systems) where *trust* in the provenance trace produced is key, and consider how ProvIt might play a role in establishing this trust. For example, ProvIt might support the creation of non-repudiable evidence stores [4].

References

1. Curcin, V., Fairweather, E., Danger, R., Corrigan, D.: Templates as a method for implementing data provenance in decision support systems. J. Biomed. Inform. **65**, 1–21 (2017)
2. De Nies, T., et al.: Git2PROV: exposing version control system content as W3C PROV. In: CEUR Workshop Proceedings, vol. 1035, pp. 125–128 (2013)
3. Fairweather, E., Alper, P., Porat, T., Curcin, V.: Architecture for template-driven provenance recording. In: Belhajjame, K., Gehani, A., Alper, P. (eds.) IPAW 2018. LNCS, vol. 11017, pp. 217–221. Springer, Cham (2018). https://doi.org/10.1007/978-3-319-98379-0_23

4. Fairweather, E., Wittner, R., Chapman, M., Holub, P., Curcin, V.: Non-repudiable provenance for clinical decision support systems. In: Proceedings of the 8th International Provenance and Annotation Workshop (2020)
5. Samuel, S., König-Ries, B.: ProvBook: provenance-based semantic enrichment of interactive notebooks for reproducibility. In: CEUR Workshop Proceedings, vol. 2180, pp. 231–234 (2018)

CPR-A Comprehensible Provenance Record for Verification Workflows in Whole Tale

Timothy M. McPhillips[1](✉), Thomas Thelen[2], Craig Willis[1], Kacper Kowalik[3], Matthew B. Jones[2], and Bertram Ludäscher[1,3]

[1] School of Information Sciences, University of Illinois at Urbana–Champaign, Illinois, USA
tmcphill@illinois.edu
[2] NCEAS, University of California at Santa Barbara, Santa Barbara, USA
[3] NCSA, University of Illinois at Urbana–Champaign, Illinois , USA

1 Introduction

A growing number of journal publishers verify computational artifacts as part of the peer-review process [9]. Although the problems of defining and achieving computational reproducibility have proved troublesome generally [2], the particular issues publishers aim to detect in this context are well defined. Questions that representative publishers answer via verification workflows include:

- Is the description in the text and supplementary materials sufficient to enable others to repeat the reported computations?
- Does repeating the computations yield the reported results?

Platforms such as Binder [4] and Whole Tale [1] provide environments for assessing reproducibility of computational artifacts by these standards via approaches analogous to *black-box testing* of the reported computational workflow. A *verifier* (i.e. a person carrying out the verification workflow) uses information provided in the paper to (1) set up the required computational environment; (2) stage input data; (3) trigger a sequence of automated computations; and (4) allow these computations to run to completion. The verifier then confirms that the products of the computations match the description in the paper.

Whole Tale further aims to enable verifiers to observe aspects of *how* automated computational workflows produce intermediate and final artifacts. Ultimately this will allow publishers to ask a third general question:

- Is the authors' description of the roles played by various software components consistent with the observed flow of data through those components?

This will provide verifiers with capabilities analogous to *white-box* testing of the computations reported in a paper. Specifically, it will enable a verifier to detect cases where the sequence of computational steps and flow of data between these steps does not conform to the description given in the paper. Here we demonstrate the tools Whole Tale is using or developing for this purpose.

Work supported by NSF Award OAC-1541450.

B. Glavic et al. (Eds.): IPAW 2020/IPAW 2021, LNCS 12839, pp. 263–269, 2021.
https://doi.org/10.1007/978-3-030-80960-7_23

2   The CPR Toolkit

The Comprehensible Provenance Record (CPR) Toolkit is a suite of tools for recording, storing, querying, and visualizing the provenance of artifacts produced by a run of a computational workflow. As the name suggests, a key objective of the toolkit is to make provenance easily comprehensible, not to systems programmers, but to practitioners of a research domain seeking to understand how the computational artifacts associated with a study in that domain were obtained.

While the primary purpose of CPR at present is to automate the monitoring and management of provenance-relevant events and records associated with a Whole Tale *recorded run*, the toolkit can be deployed in any Linux-based computing environment and used to capture, query, and reason about provenance of computational artifacts produced in that environment.

CPR employs ReproZip [7] to observe system calls invoked as part of the recorded run and to record metadata about (1) the operating-system level processes comprising the overall computation; (2) the files accessed by these processes; and (3) the access mode for file accesses, i.e. whether processes opened files for reading, writing, or both. ReproZip captures and records all of this information in a SQLite database with a schema specific to ReproZip.

Once a recorded run is complete, the cpr command-line utility extracts these OS-level records from the ReproZip trace, transforms them into RDF triples, and loads the triples into an RDF dataset in an instance of Blazegraph[1]. The triples are expressed using a vocabulary developed to represent provenance information in the context of Whole Tale recorded runs (Fig. 1).

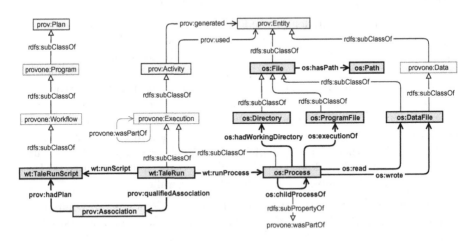

Fig. 1. Relationship of key elements of the CPR vocabulary to classes and properties defined by the PROV and ProvONE vocabularies.

---

[1] https://github.com/blazegraph/database.

The CPR vocabulary extends PROV[2] and ProvONE [3] with subclasses specific to Whole Tale to unambiguously represent run-time provenance records captured from multiple recorded runs and distinct versions of a particular Tale. CPR can represent this vocabulary either as Datalog facts or as RDF triples. Because Blazegraph provides an eager reasoner, all triples implied by the subclass relationships are generated automatically when loading a CPR trace into Blazegraph. Consequently, a CPR trace, asserted using the CPR vocabulary, can be queried in terms of the PROV and ProvONE vocabularies without using a reasoner at query time.

The CPR toolkit and vocabulary recognize the distinct roles played by particular files during a run. A simple YAML file is used to declare a run profile that associates roles with individual files, particular directories, or entire directory trees. Using these declarations while converting a ReproZip trace to the CPR vocabulary, the toolkit is able to distinguish data files of scientific significance from, e.g., shared libraries associated with the operating system or provided by software dependencies, and automatically mask these (often numerous) files in queries and visualizations by default.

Finally, the Geist[3] report-templating tool is used to pose SPARQL queries against the Blazegraph instance, to format the query results as reports, and to create visualizations of query results using Graphviz. Geist queries, reports, and visualizations may be parameterized. In Whole Tale we plan to create a predefined set of reports and visualizations following each recorded run.

3 Demonstration

The CPR demo is provided as a Git repository[4] and associated Docker image that enable the examples to be run on Linux, macOS, and Windows-based systems that have Git, Docker, and GNU Make installed. Each example uses the CPR toolkit to record OS-level provenance information from a run of a different computational workflow, to load a Blazegraph instance with the resulting CPR trace, and to produce a set of reports and visualizations via SPARQL queries.

A Makefile in the top directory of the demo repository provides targets for pulling the Docker image from Dockerhub (`pull-image`), building the Docker image locally (`build-image`), for running the examples (`run-examples`), and for deleting all of the reports, visualizations, and other artifacts generated for each example (`clean-examples`). Because the expected results are included in the repository, successful reproduction of the example products is demonstrated by issuing the commands `make clean-examples` and `make run-examples` and confirming that `git diff` reports no differences.

Query results and visualizations for each example provide answers to standard questions including:

---

[2] https://www.w3.org/TR/prov-dm/.

[3] https://github.com/CIRSS/geist.

[4] https://github.com/CIRSS/cpr-demo-2021.

1. *What programs and script invocations occurred as part of the run?*
2. *What files represent inputs and outputs of the run as a whole?*
3. *What are the input and output data files for each process in the run?*
4. *Which files input to a run are used to produce a particular output file?*
5. *Which run output artifacts are affected by a particular input file?*
6. *What programs contribute to the production of a particular output artifact?*

```
#!/bin/bash
cat inputs/i1.txt inputs/i2.txt > temp/t12.txt
cat inputs/i1.txt inputs/i2.txt inputs/i3.txt > temp/t123.txt
cat inputs/i4.txt > temp/t4.txt
cat temp/t12.txt > outputs/o12.txt
cat temp/t123.txt temp/t4.txt > outputs/o1234.txt
cat temp/t4.txt > outputs/o4.txt
```

Fig. 2. Workflow script.

The example computations range from trivial and domain-independent, to relatively complex and domain-specific. An example of minimal complexity that still demonstrates key capabilities of CPR is illustrated in Figs. 2 and 3. A simple bash script (Fig. 2) invokes the `cat` command six times on different combinations of three input files to produce three intermediate files and three final output files. The run profile (Fig. 3a) allows CPR to identify data files and to ignore system files that are needed to run the script but are otherwise irrelevant to the questions a verifier typically asks. The visualizations satisfying queries 2 and 3 are included for a run of this script (Fig. 3b and Fig. 3c) and depict the answers as dataflow graphs. We expect the visualization answering query 3 to be the main CPR artifact a verifier will use to compare the record of execution with the description of the computation in a paper. Visualizations answering queries 4 and 5 can be considered subgraphs of the visualization for query 3 limited to nodes and edges relevant to a single output or input file.

4   Observations

The computations and queries demonstrated here highlight a key challenge in making provenance useful to domain researchers and verifiers: revealing the small subset of recorded events that are of direct relevance to the scientific purpose of an overall computational workflow. At a low level, execution of even a one-line Python 3 script that prints "Hello World" can involve reading tens of different files from disk in addition to the single-line Python file that the user supplied. CPR minimizes such provenance "noise" using SPARQL queries that select files and processes with particular relationships to other files and processes, optionally informed further by a user-provided run profile that assigns distinct roles to files

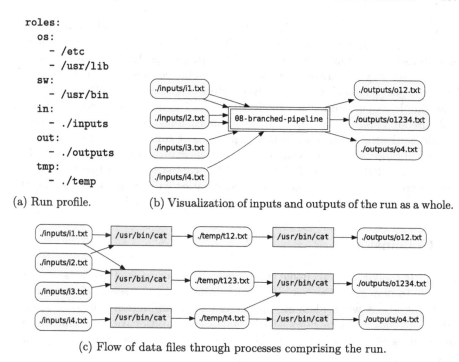

```
roles:
  os:
    - /etc
    - /usr/lib
  sw:
    - /usr/bin
  in:
    - ./inputs
  out:
    - ./outputs
  tmp:
    - ./temp
```

(a) Run profile.

(b) Visualization of inputs and outputs of the run as a whole.

(c) Flow of data files through processes comprising the run.

Fig. 3. The run profile (a) indicates that files in the ./temp directory should be hidden in the "black-box" view (b), but displayed in the "white-box" view (c).

loaded from particular locations on the system. For example, it can be useful to hide processes that do not themselves read or write data files; a bash script that serves only to invoke other programs that do process data files can be masked even in the absence of a profile. The bash script listed in Fig. 2 is not depicted graphically in Fig. 3b and Fig. 3c because these queries filter out processes that do not perform I/O on data files.

A second key challenge to making provenance useful to domain specialists is providing vocabularies that convey the significance of particular processes and data artifacts in domain-specific terms. PROV and ProvONE provide essential abstract base classes from which more meaningful provenance vocabularies can be derived. Domain researchers–and the verifiers of computations reported in their papers–likely will find views of provenance employing such specialized vocabularies the most useful. Nevertheless, the base classes are essential for performing general queries that must succeed on traces captured from any domain, e.g. to answer the question, *What are all the files–data files, scripts, executables, shared libraries, etc.–that must be archived and restored later to repeat the computation?* By describing computations in terms of files used to store data and processes executed on real computers, the CPR vocabulary provides a set of concepts intermediate to the more general ones comprising PROV and ProvONE, and the more specific concepts of domain-specific vocabularies.

Moreover, deriving the CPR vocabulary from existing standard vocabularies provides multiple options when depositing data and its provenance in public repositories such as DataONE. Because Blazegraph eagerly infers triples implied by RDF schema declarations, exporting provenance simply as PROV, or as ProvONE, or as a combination of PROV, ProvONE, and the CPR vocabularies, is as simple as performing a trivial CONSTRUCT query that extracts triples that already exist in the RDF dataset. Finally, much as common base classes in object-oriented programming languages make it convenient to work with collections of objects that are instances of more specialized classes, we expect that access to the PROV, ProvONE, and CPR vocabularies when querying provenance expressed in more specialized vocabularies will in many cases simplify those queries and make them more transparent and reusable.

5   Conclusion

The CPR toolkit aims to make the provenance of computed artifacts comprehensible to domain researchers. By highlighting entities these researchers actually think about when planning and describing computations—data files, programs, executions, data flows—CPR makes computational traces transparent and enables others to judge whether computations were performed appropriately.

CPR complements existing tools for recording provenance at the OS level including ReproZip and SciUnit [8] which employ execution tracing to identify files that must be packaged to make the computation repeatable on a different system; and the CamFlow [5] system which captures whole-system provenance for the purpose of system audit. These tools in turn complement provenance-recording and management tools that target specific programming languages and environments, including noWorkflow [6] (for Python), and the Matlab DataONE Toolbox[5]. By observing computational steps that occur *within* processes, these latter tools provide views of computational provenance that system-level provenance recorders cannot. Making provenance records not just comprehensible but also comprehensive ultimately will require integrating provenance recording tools and vocabularies at multiple levels of abstraction and granularity.

References

1. Brinckman, A., et al.: Computing environments for reproducibility: capturing the "Whole Tale". FGCS **94**, 854–867 (2019)
2. Committee on Reproducibility and Replicability in Science: Reproducibility and Replicability in Science. The National Academies Press (2019)
3. Cuevas-Vicenttín, V., et al.: ProvONE: A PROV Extension Data Model for Scientific Workflow Provenance (2015)

---

[5] https://github.com/DataONEorg/matlab-dataone

4. Jupyter, P.: Binder 2.0 - reproducible, interactive, sharable environments for science at scale. In: Proceedings of 17th Python in Science Conference, vol. 113, p. 120 (2018)
5. Pasquier, T., et al.: Practical whole-system provenance capture. In: Symposium on Cloud Computing (SoCC 2017). ACM (2017)
6. Pimentel, J.F., Freire, J., Murta, L., Braganholo, V.: Fine-grained provenance collection over scripts through program slicing. In: Mattoso, M., Glavic, B. (eds.) IPAW 2016. LNCS, vol. 9672, pp. 199–203. Springer, Cham (2016). https://doi.org/10.1007/978-3-319-40593-3_21
7. Rampin, R., Chirigati, F., Shasha, D., Freire, J., Steeves, V.: ReproZip: the reproducibility packer. J. Open Source Softw. 1(8), 107 (2016)
8. That, D.H.T., Fils, G., Yuan, Z., Malik, T.: Sciunits: Reusable Research Objects. arXiv:1707.05731 [cs], September 2017. arXiv: 1707.05731
9. Willis, C., Stodden, V.: Trust but verify: How to leverage policies, workflows, and infrastructure to ensure computational reproducibility in publication. Harvard Data Sci. Rev. 2(4) (2020)

Correction to: ISO 23494: Biotechnology – Provenance Information Model for Biological Specimen And Data

Rudolf Wittner⑩, Petr Holub ⑩, Heimo Müller ⑩, Joerg Geiger ⑩,
Carole Goble ⑩, Stian Soiland-Reyes ⑩, Luca Pireddu ⑩,
Francesca Frexia ⑩, Cecilia Mascia ⑩, Elliot Fairweather ⑩,
Jason R. Swedlow ⑩, Josh Moore ⑩, Caterina Strambio ⑩,
David Grunwald ⑩, and Hiroki Nakae⑩

Correction to:
Chapter "ISO 23494: Biotechnology – Provenance
Information Model for Biological Specimen And Data"
in: B. Glavic et al. (Eds.): *Provenance and Annotation*
***of Data and Processes*, LNCS 12839,**
https://doi.org/10.1007/978-3-030-80960-7_16

In the originally published version, the DOI in Reference 7 "Wittner, R., et al.: EOSClife common provenance model. EOSC-Life deliverable D6.2 (2021)" on p.225 was missing. The DOI "10.5281/zenodo.4705074" has been added.

The updated version of this chapter can be found at
https://doi.org/10.1007/978-3-030-80960-7_16

Author Index

Printed in the United States
by Baker & Taylor Publisher Services